VON THÜNEN'S
THE ISOLATED STATE

VON THÜNEN'S ISOLATED STATE

AN ENGLISH EDITION OF
DER ISOLIERTE STAAT

BY

JOHANN HEINRICH VON THÜNEN

TRANSLATED BY

CARLA M. WARTENBERG

EDITED

WITH AN INTRODUCTION

BY

PETER HALL

*Reader in Geography (with special reference to Regional Planning),
London School of Economics and Political Science*

PERGAMON PRESS

OXFORD · LONDON · EDINBURGH · NEW YORK
TORONTO · PARIS · FRANKFURT

Pergamon Press Ltd., Headington Hill Hall, Oxford
4 & 5 Fitzroy Square, London W.1

Pergamon Press (Scotland) Ltd., 2 & 3 Teviot Place, Edinburgh 1

Pergamon Press Inc., 44-01 21st Street, Long Island City, New York 11101

Pergamon of Canada, Ltd., 6 Adelaide Street East, Toronto, Ontario

Pergamon Press S.H.R.L., 24 rue des Ecoles, Paris 5e

Pergamon Press GmbH, Kaiserstrasse 75, Frankfurt-am-Main

First edition   1966

Library of Congress Catalog Card No. 65–17953

Printed in Great Britain by
Blackie & Son Ltd., Bishopbriggs, Glasgow

(2322/66)

1358313

CONTENTS

(*Chapters which appear only in summary, or as extracts, are italicised.*)

Part One

The Isolated State in its Relation to Agriculture and National Economy

SECTION ONE

The Formation of the Isolated State

SECTION TWO

Comparison of the Isolated State with Reality

SECTION THREE

The Effect of Taxation on Agriculture

Part Two

The Natural Wage and its Relation to the Rate of Interest and to Land Rent

SECTION ONE

SECTION TWO

Fragments from the Inquiries and from the Plan of this Work
(*Extracts*)

ACKNOWLEDGEMENTS

THIS edition would have been much the poorer but for the untiring and devoted help of two of the most erudite students of Thünen in the English-speaking world, Mr. Michael Chisholm of the Department of Geography at the University of Bristol and Dr. Karl Sinnhuber of the Department of Geography at University College, London. Mr. Chisholm read through the entire manuscript with meticulous care and made countless corrections and suggestions; Dr. Sinnhuber also checked parts of the manuscript and made many valuable comments on the editorial introduction. Together they are chiefly responsible for the bibliography of references in English to Thünen. Our most heartfelt thanks are due to both of them.

A special debt is also due to Mr. Brian Bunting of Birkbeck College (University of London) for his particular help with the translation of many of the agricultural expressions, the meanings of which were often obscure.

Grateful acknowledgement is also made to Birkbeck College for their generosity in making a grant from their Publications Fund towards the cost of indexing.

P.H.
C.M.W.

INTRODUCTION

I HAVE long ago forgotten Cournot; and I may be wrong. But my impression is that I did not derive so much of the substance of my opinions from him as from von Thünen. Cournot was a gymnastic master who directed the form of my thought. Von Thünen was a *bonâ fide* mathematician, but of less power: his blunder as to the natural wage is not of the same order as Cournot's little slips. But, to make up, he was a careful experimenter and student of facts and with a mind as least as fully developed on the inductive as on the deductive side. . . . And I loved von Thünen above all my other masters. Professor Fisher has cared for Cournot. I wish that someone would care for von Thünen. He should not, I think, be translated: but an abstract of his work should be given, with translations of a good deal of his second volume.[1]

Thus wrote Alfred Marshall, of the economist whom he described as "the great unrecognized".[2] Marshall was writing about 1900 (the quotation is undated): Thünen's work first appeared in 1826, and by 1863 it was completed. Yet, since Marshall, unrecognised he has remained in the English-speaking world, though his influence on English economics, chiefly through Marshall, has been incalculable. In Marshall's own statement, he borrowed the concept of the margin from Thünen (and not from Jevons, whose book appeared after Marshall had read Thünen).[3] Marshall's treatment of marginal productivity, his analysis of rent, his careful distinction between partial and total equilibrium, his separation of the short and the long term: all these derive from Thünen, and have passed into the central tradition of English economic thought. Yet Marshall's conclusion, in retrospect, is understandable. His main interest did not lie in location theory; and English economic tradition followed him, to separate sharply from the German. Only in recent decades has Thünen begun to receive his recognition in the English-speaking world, and then in large measure through the work of economic geographers, who have always been centrally concerned with location theory; there now exists one book on agricultural location, that of

[1] A. C. PIGOU (ed.) *Memorials of Alfred Marshall* (1925), 359–60.
[2] *Ibid.*, 412.
[3] A. MARSHALL, *Principles of Economics* (1st edition, 1890), *x* (note); PIGOU, *op. cit.*, 412.

Chisholm,[1] which is firmly based on a close analysis of Thünen theory. Yet with this awakening, the danger will inevitably be the same as that long experienced in Germany, where the original text of Thünen has been readily available for decades. In the words of Thünen's most important interpreter and critic, Asmus Petersen:

> It is an open secret, that though many feel qualified to judge the doctrine of the (Thünen) rings, only a few have read the book in which they are developed.[2]

For this reason no apology is offered for breaking Marshall's injunction. This edition of Thünen's *The Isolated State* has been prepared especially for economists and economic geographers interested in location theory. It concerns itself only in a summary way with the other main concern of Thünen's work, the wage theory, which has been translated and criticised elsewhere.[3]

This introduction to the translation is in four parts. Part I is a brief biography of Thünen, with special reference to the writing of *The Isolated State*. Part II is a guide to the successive German editions of the book and of earlier translations of it, plus an explanation of the basis of this translation. Part III is an attempt to provide a guide to the main lines of the location theory in *The Isolated State* with special reference to some of the commoner misapprehensions about Thünen's thesis. Part IV attempts to set Thünen in the context of his age and of the age which followed him—the era of world trade in agricultural products.

I. THÜNEN: LIFE[4]

Johann Heinrich von Thünen[5] was born on 24th June 1783[6] in the family home of Canarienhausen, parish Waddewarden in the Jeverland district near the North Sea coast in East Friesland, northwest Germany. His father stemmed from a long line of landowners;

[1] M. CHISHOLM, *Rural Settlement and Land Use* (1962). For a bibliography of references in English to Thünen, see pp. xlv–xlvii.

[2] A. PETERSEN, *Thünens Isolierte Staat: Die Landwirtschaft als Glied der Volkswirtschaft* (Berlin 1944), VI.

[3] B. W. DEMPSEY, *The Frontier Wage: The Economic Organization of Free Agents* (Loyola University Press, Chicago 1960). The translation stands at pp. 187–367.

[4] This biographical account is based mainly on H. SCHUMACHER, *Johann Heinrich von Thünen: Ein Forscherleben* (Rostock 1868); O. VON BISMARCK, "Studien zur Geschichte der Familie v. Thünen", in W. SEEDORF and H.-J. SERAPHIM (eds.), *Johann Heinrich von Thünen zum 150. Geburtstage* (Rostock 1933), 9–29; and A. PETERSEN, *op. cit.*, 1–19. Useful short biographies, with appreciations of Thünen's work, published since 1950 include: A. PETERSEN, "Landwirtschaftliche Betriebslehre", in O. KEUNE (ed.), *Männer die Nahrung schufen* (Hannover 1954), 27–51; H. NIEHAUS, "Johann Heinrich von Thünen 1783–1850", in H. HEIMPEL, etc. (ed.), *Die grossen*

his mother was the daughter of a bookseller in the town of Jever. Thünen's father died in 1786 from a fever, and in 1789 his mother remarried a timber merchant, von Buttel, in Hooksiel, a small port on the Bay of Jade. Here Thünen attended the local school, and, with his experience in his stepfather's business, he soon outpaced his teacher in arithmetic. So at the end of his thirteenth year he went to live with his maternal grandfather in Jever, where he attended the celebrated local secondary school and received supplementary instruction in differential and integral calculus. He left the school in 1799, an interest in agriculture already awakened, and went to gain practical experience on a farm at Gerrietshausen, in the Jeverland. The proprietor, H. G. von Tungeln, was a typical farmer of the Germany of his day, hardworking but suspicious of scientific method; and here Thünen gained valuable insight into the average agricultural conditions of the time.

Thünen's career was now decided. In 1802 he went to the Agricultural College run by Lukas Andreas Staudinger at Gross-Flottbeck in Holstein, just north-west of Hamburg, and today a suburb of the city. Here his analytical grasp rapidly developed. He soon noticed the profound influence which the cities of Hamburg and Altona exerted on the agriculture of the surrounding area. In a paper written early in 1803—*Description of Agriculture in the Village of Gross-Flottbeck*—he is already pointing out that only farms relatively near the town could make use of town dung to increase their yields, and is indeed already putting forward the idea which is the germ of *The Isolated State*:

> If one assumed that in a province of 40 miles diameter, a big town lay in the centre, and that this province could only send its products to this town, and that the agriculture in this district had attained the highest level of cultivation, then one could assume that four types of farming systems would exist around this town.[1]

Deutschen, Band V (Berlin 1957), 229–35; S. v. FRAUENDORFER, *Ideengeschichte der Agrarwirtschaft und Agrarpolitik* (München 1957), 285–300; and H. HAUSHOFER, *Die deutsche Landwirtschaft im technischen Zeitalter* (Stuttgart 1963), 138–48.

[5] Although *von* was an integral part of Thünen's name, and not a signification of knighthood, modern German literature invariably omits it; and we shall do so for the sake of brevity.

[6] As given by Thünen himself, and quoted in all biographical sources. But the church register gives 25th June. *Johann Heinrich von Thünen: Ein Wegweiser durch die Ausstellung über das Leben und Wirken* ... (Landesmuseums Oldenburg. Oldenburg 1958), 2.

[1] Quoted in SCHUMACHER, *op. cit.,* 15. The full text of this paper appears in Thünen-Archiv, *Organ für exakte Wirtschaftsforschung,* I (1906), 122 ff.

Here also Thünen first became aware of another of the great influences on his life and work. For here he read the *Introduction to a Knowledge of English Agriculture*,[1] by Albrecht Thaer (1752–1828), the leading German agricultural writer of the time; inspired by what he read, he went to see Thaer at his home in Celle, some 45 miles (70 km) south of Hamburg, in 1803, and spent the summer attending Thaer's seminar at Celle. Thaer had set himself the task of introducing to the Germans the knowledge of the great English eighteenth-century agricultural improvements; he emphasised that the farmer should aim constantly to intensify his system of cultivation, above all through improved crop ratios. Higher levels of investment would as a rule bring higher returns. So Thaer was an enthusiastic pro-selytiser of the most intensive system of cultivation of all: the so-called "crop alternation" system, in which a grain crop and a non-grain crop regularly alternated. The non-grain crop did not exhaust the soil and might enrich it; in any case it supported extra stock, which put manure back on the land. Thünen came to question Thaer's thesis: he believed that no one system was universally right for all times and places; that indeed the attempt to introduce an intensive system on to a wrong soil would result in diminished returns.[2] This belief proved to be one of the most important in-fluences in the birth of *The Isolated State*. But Thaer's influence was more than merely negative. From lectures given in Celle, Thünen came to realise the importance of mathematics to the theoretical study of agriculture. Under Thaer's influence he interested himself in the new science of agricultural statics (the science of establishing a state of equilibrium between yields and exhaustion in the soil). This, he thought, would provide a technique for testing Thaer's hypothesis about crop systems; and from then till 1810, his theor-etical research was almost exclusively concerned with this essential foundation to his life work.

In 1803, though, Thünen's formal education was not quite com-plete. From Celle he went to the University of Göttingen, where for two semesters he studied philosophy, biology, economics and languages. Thence, in the summer of 1804, armed with a letter

---

[1] A. Thaer, *Einleitung zur Kenntnis der englischen Landwirtschaft* (Hannover 1798).
[2] Cf. R. Krzymowski, *Geschichte der deutschen Landwirtschaft* (Stuttgart 1939), 165 (Third edition, 1961); E. Schneider, "Johann Heinrich von Thünen und die Wirtschaftstheorie der Gegenwart", *Schriften des Vereins für Sozialpolitik*, N.F. 14 (Berlin 1959), 24; and E. Woermann, "Johann Heinrich von Thünen und die landwirtschaftliche Betriebslehre der Gegenwart", *ibid.*, 32–3.

of introduction from Thaer, he embarked on an agricultural tour. He travelled via Saxony to Mecklenburg, where he visited Herr von Berlin, the father of a student friend in Göttingen, and proprietor of the Liepen estate. The youngest of von Berlin's nine children, his daughter Helene, immediately won Thünen's heart. They were married two years later, on 14th October 1806.

On marriage Thünen had to consider where he would pursue his life's vocation as a farmer. The family farm of Canarienhausen would pass to his younger brother Friedrich; so Thünen decided to look for an estate in his father-in-law's country, far to the east of Friesland, in the province of Mecklenburg. But he postponed final decision in the then troubled political state of Germany and of Europe. As the Napoleonic and Prussian armies fought their way across central Europe, there were a thousand impositions and uncertainties for the farmer: quartering of troops, the requisitioning of horses and men, forage and cattle, heavy taxes, recurrent animal and human epidemics. In the meantime Thünen took a lease on the Rubkow estate near Anklam in western Pomerania, belonging to his brother-in-law. The farm was in poor condition, and caused Thünen to brood long on problems of agricultural improvement. Finally, after inspecting thirteen farms in Mecklenburg, he bought the 1146-acre Tellow estate from his brother-in-law Heinrich Schröder, on 28th June 1810, four days after his twenty-seventh birthday.

Tellow lies 5 miles (8 km) north-north-west of the small market town of Teterow, and 23 miles (37 km) south-east of Rostock, in the administrative district (*Regierungsbezirk*) of Neubrandenburg in the former *Land* of Mecklenburg. The main road from Neubrandenburg to Rostock passes just east of the estate. It lies at just over 40 m (130 ft) above sea-level, in a country of glacial ground moraine, many small lakes, and alluvial marsh. *The Agricultural Atlas of the German Democratic Republic* officially classed the land, in 1956, as "loamy sand—strongly loamy sand". Out of the 21 grades of soil recognised in the Atlas, the soils of the Tellow region rank in the eighth grade; they are ranked 5·5. The best soils, those on the loess of the Halle-Magdeburg *Börde* country, are graded 2 and 2·5.[1]

Mecklenburg is a remote land, and in the early nineteenth century it was yet more remote. The pace of economic development in

[1] *Agrar Atlas über das Gebiet der Deutschen Demokratischen Republik* (Deutsche Akademie der Landwirtschaftwissenschaften zu Berlin/Institut für Agrarökonomik, Gotha 1956).

Germany had begun to quicken a little in the far west, along the Rhine and in the towns of Westphalia, but here change came slowly. Mecklenburg, when Thünen first made it his adopted home, was a land with no major navigable rivers and without improved highways. Only after his death, in the mid-1860s, did the railway penetrate to Teterow, the town near Tellow; only in the 'eighties did a branch come close to Tellow. The possibilities of commercial agriculture then were poor. And the technical development of Mecklenburg agriculture had been much retarded, first by the Thirty Years' War (1618–48), which had reduced the population of Mecklenburg from 300,000 to 50,000, then by the Northern War (1700–21), then by the Seven Years' War (1756–63). But fundamental change did come, in the late eighteenth century. The age-old medieval three-field system (spring grain, winter grain, fallow) was replaced by the system developed in the province of Holstein to the west, which the Germans call the *Koppelwirtschaft* and which we have translated, throughout this edition, as the improved system. The essential features of the improved system, as with some English improved systems of the eighteenth century, were that it was based on enclosed fields; and that it combined cereal crops and a short grass ley. And a little later, root crops were introduced. One other essential feature of the English improved system was, however, late to develop in Mecklenburg. The grass ley provided pasture; but the lack of transport facilities for dairy products held back the full exploitation of that pasture.[1] These facts are important for our understanding of *The Isolated State*. For though the thesis of the work itself has a general validity unlimited by time or place, the actual working-through of the examples is closely conditioned by the facts of agricultural life as Thünen knew them. It is, as the Germans say, *zeitgebunden*.

We have seen that, in the years up to the purchase of Tellow, Thünen had laid the first foundations of *The Isolated State*, in the study of statics. In this time, too, he had allowed his mind full speculative play, and he had developed many of the basic ideas of *The Isolated State*. But they remained speculations. Thünen realised —and here lay the unique nature of his contribution to economics—

---

[1] This is based on F. HONCAMP, "Die mecklenburgische Landwirtschaft unter besonderer Berücksichtigung der Zeit von Johann Heinrich von Thünen", in W. SEEDORF and H.-J. SERAPHIM, *op. cit.*, 63–78. This account would indicate that Mecklenburg was strictly speaking outside the area of Thünen's Isolated State, where even the most remote ring could produce milk for conversion into butter or cheese.

INTRODUCTION

reality. This research took the form of laborious investigations into
costs and returns on his own estate at Tellow, which took him ten
years; the basic bookkeeping was undertaken from 1810 to 1815,
and the results were checked from then to the end of 1819; and, as
Thünen said in his New Year letter to his brother at the beginning of
1821, the work had proved so colossal that it had precluded almost
all other study. But, as the results emerged, they could be fitted
directly into Thünen's speculative framework. Thünen had now got
what he wanted: an abstract model of an economy, based upon actual
facts. In his middle thirties, he had already produced what was to
make him, in Schumpeter's words, "one of the patron saints of
econometrics".[1] The work itself could now be written fairly quickly.
The first draft of *The Isolated State* was produced in 1818–19, but was
thoroughly revised in 1824. It was published in 1826.

With the appearance of this, which was to become Part I of his
work, Thünen had really completed his major contribution to location theory. Part I reappeared in 1842, revised but not substantially
so; and Thünen did continue to develop and revise his location theory
between 1826 and 1842, as the fragments published posthumously
in 1863 show. But even before 1826 Thünen had turned his attention
to the other major inquiry of his life: the study of wages. He had
indeed discovered the famous formula for the "natural wage",
$A = \sqrt{ap}$, as early as 1830.[2] But it was not until 1850, the year of his
death, that part of the wage theory was published, as Part II, Section
1 of *The Isolated State*.[3]

All through the years from 1810, Thünen was engaged simultaneously in ceaseless agricultural improvement on Tellow. He was
marling, deepening the level of arable soil, improving moor soils,
afforesting parts of the estate, increasing the capital stock, creating
a big park. In 1840–1 he replaced the six-course rotation, which he
had found on the estate when he took it over, by a ten-course
rotation on the inner part of the farm and a five-course rotation on
the outer part—a system described in the 1842 revision of Part I of
The Isolated State.[4] He was an enthusiastic advocate of sheep-rearing,

[1] J. A. SCHUMPETER, *History of Economic Analysis* (1954), 466.
[2] For the meaning of this expression cf. the text at p. 251 below.
[3] Other material appeared in the posthumous fragments published as Part II,
Section 2 in 1863; much remains unpublished in the Thünen archives in Rostock.
[4] O. MIELCK, "Die Wirtschaftsgeschichte von Tellow seit dem Ausgang des Mit-
telalters", in W. SEEDORF and H.-J. SERAPHIM, *op. cit.*, 48–50.

and doubled the number of sheep on Tellow between 1820 and 1839. And on the basis of his experience he was producing a steady flow of papers on practical agricultural matters, which were published in the local Mecklenburg agricultural journal, the *Neue Annalen der Mecklenburgischen Landwirtschaftsgesellschaft.* The University of Rostock recognised the distinction of his work by granting him an honorary doctorate in 1830.

The last years of Thünen's life were years of intense political activity and revolutionary change in Germany. In the year of revolution, on 15th April 1848, he felt able to carry into operation his long-conceived scheme for profit-sharing on the Tellow estate. In 1848 also he was elected a representative to the German National Assembly, the ill-fated "Professors' Parliament", at Frankfurt-am-Main, but could not take his seat.

Thünen died at Tellow on 22nd September 1850, "quickly and in autumn, when the leaves fall", as he had wished. He was buried in the village churchyard of Belitz, the village next to Tellow. Under his name on the gravestone, following his wish, is engraved his formula for the natural wage: $A = \sqrt{ap}$.

II. THE ISOLATED STATE: GUIDE TO EDITIONS AND

TRANSLATIONS: PLAN OF THIS TRANSLATION

Part I of *The Isolated State* contains Thünen's theory of agricultural intensity and of the location of agricultural systems and of crop zones. It was first published in 1826 by Perthes, in Hamburg. A second edition, improved and extended, was published in 1842 by Leopold, in Rostock.

Part II, Section 1 (generally known as II. 1) contains Thünen's wage theory, but starts with a long introduction in which the inquiry of Part I is summarised, and subjects for further inquiry are outlined. It was published in 1850 by Leopold, in Rostock. Thünen himself undertook this edition before his death.

Part II, Section 2 (II. 2) consists of selections of Thünen's posthumous papers dealing mainly with the problems of Part I: taxation, customs duties, settlement policies, the consequences of improved roads and railways. Some of the papers are important because they show the ways in which Thünen wished to develop his inquiry so as to take into account all factors which affect the location of agricultural production. The selection was made by Hermann Schumacher of Rostock, and was published in 1863 by Hinstorff, in Rostock.

Part III consists of a separate selection of posthumous papers on forestry, also made by Schumacher of Rostock, and published by Hinstorff, in Rostock, in 1863.

The first collected edition of *The Isolated State*, and the only complete one, was edited by Schumacher and published by Wiegandt, Hempel and Parey, in Berlin, in 1876.

A collected edition containing only Part I and Part II, Section 1 was edited by Heinrich Waentig, and published by Fischer, in Jena, in 1910. Further, similar editions came from the same editor and publisher in 1921 and 1930.

A selection of passages from Part I and from Part II Section I, was made by Walter Braeuer, and published as *Johann Heinrich von Thünen: Ausgewählte Texte*, by Anton Hain, in Meisenheim, in 1951.

The most important critical guide to *The Isolated State* is Thünens *Isolierte Staat*, by Asmus Petersen, published by Parey, in Berlin, in 1944. It is nothing less than a detailed companion to the work, and it is indispensable to the serious student of Thünen. It forms the basis of the analysis in Part III of this introduction below.

A French translation of Part I of *The Isolated State* was made by Jules Laverrière and published in Paris in 1851.[1] A translation of Part II, Section 1 was made into French by Mathieu Wolkoff and published in Paris in 1857.[2] Wolkoff also translated *The Isolated State* into Russian; this translation was published in Darmstadt in 1857.[3] An Italian translation appeared in Turin in 1860 and was published in a journal in 1875.[4] A Czech translation appeared in Prague in 1926.[5]

Part II, Section 1 was translated into English by Bernard Dempsey and was published as part of his book *The Frontier Wage*, in Chicago in 1960.[6]

[1] J. LAVERRIÈRE, *Recherches sur l'influence que le prix des grains, la richesse du sol et les impôts exertent sur les systèmes de culture*. Paris, 1851.

[2] M. WOLKOFF, *Le Salaire naturel et son rapport au taux de l'intérêt*. Paris, 1857.

[3] M. WOLKOFF, *Uedinennoe Gosudarstvo v otnosenii k obscestvennoj ekonomii*, Karlsruhe, 1857.

[4] *Richerche sull'influenza che il prezzo del grano, la richezza de suolo e le imposte esercitano sui sistemi di coltura*, Turin, 1860. Appeared in *Biblioteca dell' Economista*, 2a serie, Torino, 1875, 819–1046.

[5] *Tschechische Uebersetzung anlässlich eines Kongresses zum 100. Jahrestag des "Isolierten Staates"*. Prag, 1926.

[6] *Op. cit.*

The present translation has been prepared specifically for students of location theory. It presents in full most of Part I, summarising only some of the detailed calculations of yields and costs, and omitting a long discursion into agricultural statics which has little organic connexion with the rest of the work. It presents a new translation of the introduction to Part II, Section 1 (which also appears in Dempsey's translation) but then presents only a bare summary of the rest of II. 1, which is accessible in full in Dempsey's version. But it gives in full most of the important Chapter 19, where Thünen develops his concept of marginal productivity, because this concept is of interest to the student of Part I. Lastly it presents extracts from II. 2, which are important for students of location theory. These extracts are in a sense exhumed for the English edition, because they have not appeared in the German editions since that of 1876.

III. GUIDE TO THE STRUCTURE OF THE ISOLATED STATE

Krzymowski, one of the major figures of German agricultural studies, published his history of German agriculture in 1939, near the end of his career. It is a model of lucid exposition. Yet of Thünen and his book he had to write:

> About this book an enormous amount has been written, and there is still no end to the literature on Thünen. The doctoral dissertations which have appeared in Germany on Thünen's theories alone run into several hundreds. And Thünen's work is in fact an inexhaustible mine. But it is a book that is difficult to read; I myself have found no book on agriculture such heavy going as von Thünen's. The beginner, who wants to study Thünen, would do well first to prepare himself, by reading relevant text and handbooks, for the closer study of von Thünen's work.[1]

Fortunately, five years after Krzymowski published this, there appeared Petersen's commentary. The analysis which follows of the main lines of Thünen's thesis is largely based on this work. But it is necessarily a bald summary. The serious student of Thünen would be well advised to turn first to Petersen.

Petersen first disposes of two common misconceptions in Germany about Thünen. There the book is thought difficult because of the old-fashioned measurements and weights and currencies which Thünen used (the decimal system was introduced in Germany only in the

[1] R. KRZYMOWSKI, *op. cit.*, 172.

second half of the nineteenth century, and there was a proliferation of local measures when Thünen wrote), and because of the mathematical formulae in which the book abounds. Both ideas are unfounded. One soon becomes familiar with the measures used (and, it should be said, modern British readers may at least have less difficulty than modern Germans); and the formulae soon prove to depend on relatively simple mathematics. (A guide to measurements and currencies appears in the alphabetical glossary of terms before the present translation at pp. xlix–liv.) We can then turn to the book itself with less apprehension.

Part I starts with a brilliant, and celebrated, summary picture of *The Isolated State*. It can only be quoted in full.

> Imagine a very large town, at the centre of a fertile plain which is crossed by no navigable river or canal. Throughout the plain the soil is capable of cultivation and of the same fertility. Far from the town, the plain turns into an uncultivated wilderness which cuts off all communication between this State and the outside world.
>
> There are no other towns on the plain. The central town must therefore supply the rural areas with all manufactured products, and in return it will obtain all its provisions from the surrounding countryside.
>
> The mines that provide the State with salt and metals are near the central town which, as it is the only one, we shall in future call simply "the Town".
>
> The problem we want to solve is this: what pattern of cultivation will take shape in these conditions?; and how will the farming system of the various districts be affected by their distance from the Town? We assume throughout that farming is conducted absolutely rationally.
>
> It is on the whole obvious that near the Town will be grown those products which are heavy or bulky in relation to their value and which are consequently so expensive to transport that the remoter districts are unable to supply them. Here also we find the highly perishable products, which must be used very quickly. With increasing distance from the Town, the land will progressively be given up to products cheap to transport in relation to their value.
>
> For this reason alone, fairly sharply differentiated concentric rings or belts will form around the Town, each with its own particular staple product.
>
> From ring to ring the staple product, and with it the entire farming system, will change; and in the various rings we shall find completely different farming systems.

Two things need to be noticed about this opening statement. The first is that Thünen makes immediately clear the nature of his method. It is the method of *idealisation*. In the first draft, it is significant that the title was *The Ideal State*: that is, the *idea* of a State. We are dealing here with the world's first economic model, and one which proves to be extraordinarily completely developed. Thünen himself found it necessary to defend, in the preface to the 1842 edition, this novel method of analysis:

> I hope that the reader who is willing to spend some time and attention on my work will not take exception to the imaginary assumptions I make at the beginning because they do not correspond to conditions in reality, and that he will not reject these assumptions as arbitrary and pointless. They are a necessary part of my argument, allowing me to establish the operation of a certain factor, a factor whose operation we see but dimly in reality, where it is in incessant conflict with others of its kind.
>
> This method of analysis has illuminated—and solved—so many problems in my life, and appears to me to be capable of such widespread application, that I regard it as the most important matter contained in all my work.

The model, then, works by assuming that most of the factors which normally co-determine the location of agricultural production are either uniform or unique, so putting them temporarily at rest: the climate, the quality of the soil, the existence of alternative supplies or alternative markets, the quality of management, the character of the transport network. Thus one can isolate the operation of one factor: transport costs, as an expression of distance. This Thünen does deliberately, with the full intention of later relaxing his assumptions, one by one. The method essentially assumes that one factor can be independently varied without affecting the fixed assumptions; and on that ground it has been criticised for logical inconsistency.[1] But the criticism should not detract from the fact that here is the first use of the method of "fiction", of "As if"; a method which received philosophical recognition only two generations later, in the work of Vaihinger.[2] From the basic concept of fiction Thünen comes

---

[1] Carell has argued as follows (my paraphrase): Thünen assumed constant gross product for any given cultivation system at every distance from the market (expressed in grain); and constant costs, including constant labour costs expressed as money or grain. But a constant gross product is possible only if real (grain) wages are constant, money wages falling with the fall in grain prices. Thünen however assumes constant money wages, which imply a rise in real (grain) wages with increasing distance from market. This is inconsistent with his assumption of a stationary or static state; for it implies that workers are blind to differences in real wages. Carell's solution is to abandon the assumption of a static state, and then to allow the other Thünen assumptions. "Situation rent" then becomes a form of "intensity rent" produced by extra applications of (cheaper) labour near the market. E. CARELL, "Die Lagerente", *Zeitschrift für die gesamte Staatswissenschaft*, **106** (1950), 473–91. Thünen realised this inconsistency (Carell says elsewhere), but thought that partial analysis could be justified on the *ceteris paribus* argument. Cf. E. CARELL, "Johann Heinrich von Thünen und die moderne Wirtschaftstheorie", *Zeitschrift für die gesamte Staatswissenschaft*, **106** (1950), 600–10.

[2] A. JACOBS, "Johann Heinrich von Thünen als Lehrmeister der Statistik", in W. SEEDORF and H.-J. SERAPHIM, *op. cit.*, 161–9; E. GUTENBERG, *Thünen's Isolierter Staat als Fiktion* (Bausteine zu einer Philosphie des "Als-Ob", 4. Bd., Munich 1922).

directly to this technique of isolation. But Thünen's originality does
not end there. He is not content to isolate the force of one factor in
a situation, and to find a mathematical expression for it; he must
then fit to his formulae detailed empirical data, taken from his experience at Tellow. The result is an astonishing pioneer triumph of
econometric model construction. In 1958 Schneider, the German
economist, said of Thünen's achievement:

> . . . here the importance of model construction for the understanding of reality
> is made evident with unsurpassable lucidity and forcefulness . . . And within
> the area of his model, the Isolated State, he now shows with great care the
> importance and fruitfulness of partial analysis, which he handles with masterly
> virtuosity . . . Thünen shows us that neither experience alone, nor theoretical
> speculation, can illuminate the unfathomable sea of reality . . . His work is
> econometrics in the best sense of the word.[1]

The second point concerns the objects of Thünen's inquiries in
Part I. Here he is concerned to analyse the pattern of agricultural
production around the central Town, as affected by distance. But in
the paragraphs of his opening chapter which follow the quotation
above, he writes of the *direction* of agricultural production, the nature
of the main crop produced. Only in the last paragraph of his opening
section does he imply, rather obscurely, that as the main product
changes, so does the whole *system* of agriculture, the *way* crops are
produced. This introductory obscurity has been the source of the
most fundamental confusion about the whole of Thünen's analysis;
indeed one may say that the majority of critics and commentators
have been guilty of it, and that Petersen's work was concerned to
remedy it.

For the most important fact about *The Isolated State*, as Petersen
emphasised, is that it has *two* aspects, *two* main objects of inquiry;
that these are to a large extent separable; that they are indeed
separated in the book, though its formal organisation, in three
sections, obscures the point. The *first* inquiry can be summarised
thus: A given crop, say a grain crop, may be cultivated under different systems, some more intensive than others; that is, some
systems involve higher costs than others, but (in the right circumstances) they bring higher returns. We may find that though the
crop is the same, it is produced by an intensive system in one place,
an extensive system in another. How, Thünen asks, is this variation
related to distance from the sole consuming market?

1 E. Schneider, *op. cit.*, 17, 19. Cf. M. Chisholm, *op. cit.*, passim.

The second subject of inquiry is the one Thünen stresses in this opening quotation. As well as the same crop being grown in different places under different systems of intensity, the crop itself may vary. How is this phenomenon related to distance from the market?

These two subjects must not be confused. There is an intensity theory and a crop theory. But the crop theory is not a theory of intensity. It has indeed something to do with intensity; but the main factor is something other.

Thünen's first major analysis is concerned with the intensity theory. He develops this in Chapters 4 to 18, and then in Chapters 21 to 23 he describes the pattern of "intensity rings" which develop for a given grain crop. In all these chapters he is concerned directly only with one crop, the most important of crops, grain; but the analysis could be applied to any other one crop.

Thünen's intensity theory says that the intensity of production will, other things being equal, depend on the price the farmer gets for his grain, and that this will depend directly on transport costs and thus on distance from the sole market. In Chapter 4 he therefore starts by finding a formula for the farm price of grain. Up to now he has worked in purely hypothetical terms. Now he must introduce reality. He gives transport costs per mile and these are based on actual conditions around Rostock at the time he wrote. But notice that these are empirical facts fitted into a model; the model remains; this is not itself a description of reality.

The formula for the net farm price is based on a market price of 1·5 thalers per bushel. That price is determined conjointly by the size of the town demand and by the costs of the marginal producer (the farmer who just finds it profitable to get his grain on the market). This hypothesis is maintained almost throughout, being relaxed only in a chapter on intensive systems of grain production (Chapter 16) and one on taxation (Chapter 35), as well as in the famous diagrams at the end of the book, which, Thünen was concerned to point out, were not important to the understanding of his thesis. From this fixed market price, transport costs are subtracted. The actual formula produces a complicated sliding scale, in which farm price falls progressively more slowly with increasing distance from the market.

Now Thünen has the farm price he can study the output of the farm and the costs which must be balanced against price. First, in Chapter 5, he studies output and costs under a system of middle intensity: the Improved (Koppel) System. The data are based on the Tellow accounts of 1810–19 but are applied to a poorer soil which Thünen used as standard throughout the Isolated State. (This is theoretically inadmissible and leads to errors, but these are small.) They are also applied throughout to a standard area slightly smaller than Tellow: 100,000 square rods or 217 ha. Thünen's fundamental assumption about costs is that they fall into two groups. One group of costs originates on the farm and can be expressed in grain. Agricultural wages are a good example; they then chiefly represented means of subsistence, and a quantity of grain was the direct measure of that. Seeds, manure and draught animals are other "farm-based" costs. But a smaller proportion represented things that had to be bought for money from the town; for instance, agricultural implements made in town workshops. Thünen determined that at all times and under all systems (not just the improved system, which we are considering at the moment) $\frac{3}{4}$ of costs should be rendered in grain (as "farm-based" costs) and $\frac{1}{4}$ in money (as "town-based" costs). This distinction is important because finally both sets of costs have to be rendered in money, and when this is done the "farm-based" costs will vary directly with grain prices (that is, they will decrease as grain price decreases, away from the town); but "town-based" prices, which are rendered already in money, remain fixed. (Actually, they should rise away from the town, because these products will incur rising transport costs; curiously, though fortunately for the sake of simplicity, Thünen's formula takes no account of this.) The result is that since only a part of costs falls with falling grain price, while the other part remains fixed, *costs fall more slowly than grain prices away from the market*, and thus there must come a point where the surplus of grain, expressed in money, can no longer meet the fixed money costs. A numerical statement for the improved system will make this clear. On a standard unit of 100,000 square rods, in the Isolated State, this system gives a gross product of 3144 bushels of grain. The total costs, expressed $\frac{3}{4}$ in grain and $\frac{1}{4}$ in money, are 1976 bushels and 641 thalers. Subtracting, this means that the farmer has left a surplus for sale of 1168 bushels, but still has to find 641 thalers to cover his "town-based costs". All now depends on the farm price at which the farmer can sell his grain surplus. Let us look at this at the critical margin, between 25 and 30 miles from the market.[1]

---

[1] Cf. PETERSEN, *op. cit.*, 65.

Miles from market	Price of grain on the farm per bushel th	Gross product in money th	"Farm-based costs" in money th	Market surplus for sale in money th	Fixed "town-based costs" in money th	Net product or land rent under improved system in money th
25	0·656	2062	1296	766	641	125
28·6	0·549	1726	1085	641	641	0
30	0·512	1610	1012	598	641	−43

As the price of grain falls away from the market, so do gross product and "farm-based costs", both converted from grain into money. The difference between them, or the "surplus for sale", falls too. But the "town-based costs" remain constant, and there must come a point where the "surplus for sale" can no longer meet this burden. The point at which this will occur is implicit in the nature of the formula: it is the point at which 1168 bushels of grain (the surplus expressed in grain) will fetch exactly 641 thalers in money. The calculation shows that this happens 28·6 miles from the market, and here is the marginal farm under the improved system. At all sites nearer than this, when the fixed costs are subtracted from the residual surplus, there remains a net product, or land rent. This is pure situation rent, arising from the more favourable situation of the site as compared with the marginal site.[1] It is purely a function of the more favourable farm price near the market, costs (in grain and money) remaining constant. In the table above, the situation rent 25 miles from the market, or 3·6 miles nearer the market than the marginal farm, is 125 thalers per 100,000 square rods.

[1] This statement is true for all sites as long as we consider the improved system in isolation, as the only possible system. In comparison with a less intensive system (e.g. the three-field system), we shall shortly see that rent under the improved system may include an element which arises from a factor other than situation. This second type of rent does not however arise on a site 25 miles from the market, so the statement above remains true.

"Situation rent" is similar to the "fertility rent" enjoyed by producers in physically-superior locations (better soil, kinder climate or superior aspect). Strictly speaking this latter type of rent does not exist in the Isolated State, where the soil is of uniform fertility; but Thünen does discuss it in order to understand reality better. For a discussion see I. BRINKMANN, "Die von Thünensche Rentenlehre und die Entwicklung der neuzeitlichen Landwirtschaft", *Zeitschrift für die gesamte Staatswissenschaft*, **107** (1951), 311,

In Chapters 12 and 13 (supplemented by calculations in Chapters
7 to 11) Thünen calculates in a similar way the rent formula for the
less intensive three-field system. It is in the nature of this system that
it gives a lower gross product but that it involves lower costs. The
precise comparison between the two systems is set out below.

Per 100,000 square rods:	Improved system	Three-field system
Gross Product	3144 bushels grain	1720 bushels grain
Costs	1976 bushels and 641 th	1024 bushels and 327 th
Land Rent	1168 bushels minus 641 th	696 bushels minus 327 th

It is important to keep in mind the exact nature of the land rent
formulae shown above. Each formula contains a fixed surplus of
grain, available for sale; but from the proceeds of that sale must be
subtracted a fixed burden of money costs. The improved system
enjoys a bigger grain surplus than the three-field system; but it bears
a bigger burden of money costs. (In fact the *percentage* increase in
costs is greater than that in product: but *absolutely* there is an
increase in the surplus for sale.[1]) It can afford these only if the price
of grain is high; that is, near the market in the Isolated State. As we
move away from the market, the farm price of grain falls, and this
causes the land rent of the improved system to fall faster than that of
the three-field system, because with lower prices the bigger grain
surplus of the improved system is progressively less capable of
meeting the relatively higher money burden associated with the
system. At a distance of 24·7 miles from the market, the formulae
give equal rents for the two systems, expressed wholly in money;
from then on the three-field system yields a higher rent and will
therefore take over from the improved system according to the rules
of a free economy. At 28·6 miles the improved system ceases to yield
any rent and would necessarily disappear anyway; at 31·4 miles the
three-field system ceases to yield rent and will disappear, so that
cultivation stops here.

1 Cf. I. BRINKMANN, *op. cit.*, 315.

Miles from market	Price of grain on the farm	Land rent under improved system	Land rent under three-field system	
20	0·809	304	236	(Improved wins)
24·7	0·665	136	136	(Equal advantage)
25	0·656	125	130	(Three-field wins)
28·6	0·549	0	55	(Improved yields no rent)
30	0·512	−43	29	(Improved yields negative rent)
31·4	0·470	−92	0	(Three-field yields no rent; cultivation ends)

To put the matter in exact numbers: the less intensive three-field system works on a basis of a surplus of 696 bushels minus 327 thalers; it becomes viable where 696 bushels fetch 327 thalers, that is at 0·47 thalers the bushel, which price obtains at 31·4 miles from the market. The more intensive improved system works on a basis of 1168 bushels minus 641 thalers; compared with the three-field system it bears twice the money costs, but it enjoys less than twice the market surplus of grain, reflecting the operation of the law of diminishing returns following intensification. In *absolute* terms however the increase in grain surplus is large. The system produces 472 extra bushels but they have to bear 314 extra thalers; that is each extra bushel costs 0·665 thalers to win. This is only economic when the price of grain reaches the level of 0·665 thalers per bushel, that is at 24·7 miles from the market. From this point inwards towards the market, the extra bushels which the improved system produces continue to cost 0·665 thalers to win, but they are sold at a price which progressively rises higher than this. As compared with the three-field system, the more intensive improved system is here producing an *extra* surplus, which should properly be called *Intensity Rent*. This is additional to the basic *Situation Rent*, which more favourably sited farms cultivated on the three-field system would also enjoy. At the market itself the "intensity rent" of the improved system rises to a maximum of 394 thalers: 1111 thalers minus the 717 thalers of "situation rent" which the three-field system would have produced there anyway.

This then is the Thünen system of intensity. It says essentially that (given a certain level of soil fertility) at higher net farm prices, that is at sites nearer the market, it will pay to choose a more intensive system of cultivation, in which a higher level of cost is associated with a later point of diminishing return. This point is however brought out fully only in Part II, Section 1 of the *Isolated State*, where in Chapter 19 Thünen develops the concept of the marginal productivity of units of labour applied to land.

The concept of marginal productivity does however implicitly underly the first Part of *The Isolated State*; and it may be approached through a simple illustration. Imagine that land, everywhere of equal fertility, may be cultivated for wheat at varying levels of intensity. On each acre of land the farmer may apply one unit of capital, or two, or more; each application will bring forth an additional return, but, because of the law of diminishing returns, each additional return will be smaller than the last. Imagine further that the wheat is worth $1 at market, and that everywhere there are uniform transport costs of 2½c per bushel per mile; so that at a farm 10 miles from market wheat will be worth only 75c a bushel, at 20 miles only 50c, and so on. The following table may now be produced (all figures apply to 1 acre of farm land):

Applications of capital	Cost of each application	Total crop bushels	Extra crop bushels	Value of the extra crop resulting from the extra $1 application of capital at transport costs of 2½c, per bushel per mile				
				at market	10 miles	20 miles	30 miles	35 miles
				where farm price will be:				
				$1	75c	50c	25c	12½c
1	$1	4	4	$4	$3	$2	**$1**	50c
2	$1	6	2	$2	$1·50	**$1**	50c	25c
3	$1	7½	1½	$1·50	**$1·12**	75c	37½c	18¾c
4	$1	8½	1	**$1**	75c	50c	25c	12½c
5	$1	9	½	50c	37½c	25c	12½c	6¼c

The values shown here in heavy type are the marginal values: that is, they are the values where production ceases to be profitable. Below them, the italicised values indicate losses. At the marginal points, the total costs and returns are:

	At market	10 miles	20 miles	30 miles	35 miles
Total costs per acre	$4·00	$3·00	$2·00	$1·00	—
Total crop per acre (bushels)	8½	7½	6	4	—
Total value of crop	$8·50	$5·60	$3·00	$1·00	—
Surplus rent per acre	$4·50	$2·60	$1·00	nil	—

Thus intensification brings a higher rent; but as compared with the less intensive methods, it stops being profitable at smaller distances from the market.

Here the farmer is allowed a very free choice. He may apply successive dollars of cost and consider the profitability of each. In reality it is not usually so easy for the farmer. He has in effect a choice between two or three fully developed agricultural *systems*, with certain levels of costs and returns. This is the choice Thünen gives the farmers in Part I of the Isolated State, although he stresses the importance of transitional forms. It is mainly because of this that the concept of marginal productivity does not appear with any clarity in Part I.

But there is another main subject of study in *The Isolated State*, and it is if anything the central study. That is the general location theory for a number of different agricultural products, which is developed in Chapters 19 to 32.[1] It is important at the outset to emphasise that the pattern of location which Thünen describes in these chapters in no way follows any simple rule of intensity. Thus in the second ring, between 4 and 7·3 miles from the market, there is forestry, a very extensive activity; within this zone, the firewood producing part, which is more extensive, is inside the more intensive structural timber part. And in the sixth or outermost ring we find a whole series of intensive cash crops such as oilseeds, hops, tobacco and flax. Intensity provides no explanation; and that explanation must be sought elsewhere.

It is necessary to stress this point because even in the German literature, which is based on a long tradition of Thünen study, there has been the most fundamental confusion about it. Again and again

[1] Cf. the commentary by PETERSEN, *op. cit.*, Ch. 8.

the statement recurs that "the central feature of the Thünen system is that intensity of cultivation rises towards the market". Weigmann asserts this, in his account of Thünen's location theory published for the 150th anniversary of Thünen's birth;[1] Theodor Brinkmann, perhaps the leading worker on agricultural location theory in twentieth-century Germany, says it at one point of his analysis:

> Districts near the market—that is, districts with favorable economic locations —are therefore districts of intensive methods of farming. Districts far from the market—that is, districts with unfavorable economic locations,—are the areas of extensive methods of farming. In the "isolated state" the optimum degree of farming intensity reaches its maximum in the immediate vicinity of the market, its minimum where communication with the market disappears entirely and agriculture becomes a purely self-sufficing economy. . . . Zones near to the market are locations of specifically intensive types of land use. Zones at a distance from the market are locations of specifically extensive types of land use. Increasing intensity of land cultivation therefore means not only increasing expenditure in cultivating the given crops but at the same time a change to specifically intensive crops.[2]

Brinkmann is led to this conclusion from the observation that the spread between the prices of agricultural products, and those of the production goods necessary (agricultural costs) is greatest near the market; the greater the spread, the greater the number of units of cost that can be applied before, under the operation of the law of diminishing returns, the marginal point is reached. (Cf. the simple arithmetical explanation on p. xxix.) This is perfectly true for any one crop. But in comparing two different crops, we are dealing with two different patterns of costs and returns. In this analysis it is necessary to use the words "intensive" and "extensive" very carefully, in their strict sense: to refer to the number of cost inputs that are applied up to the economic margin. This concept has no necessary connexion with physical yield. One of the two crops may have very low production costs, per unit of weight of product, but nevertheless (because of the relationship to price) experience diminishing returns quickly, so that the margin is soon reached, and the pattern of production remains extensive. Nevertheless, if the yield is relatively high compared with other crops (and it may be, even though cultivation is extensive; recall that there is no necessary connexion) then the

[1] H. WEIGMANN, "Standortstheorie und Raumwirtschaft", in W. SEEDORF and H.-J. SERAPHIM, op. cit., 139.
[2] Theodor Brinkmann's Economics of the Farm Business (English translation of Die Oekonomik des Landwirtschaftlichen Betriebes (Tübingen 1922, being part of Vol. VII of Grundriss der Sozialökonomik)) (Berkeley 1935), 14, 20. But cf. his analysis later on pp. 86–7, where he correctly interprets the relevant passage in Thünen.

product will be produced near the market. Forestry is the example of this in the Thünen system. Or the opposite may occur. In the *Isolated State*, industrial crops, like grain for distilleries and flax, have high production costs, per unit weight of product, but they can bear a considerable number of cost *increments* without showing diminishing returns, i.e. they are intensively cultivated. Yet if such crops also show relatively low weight yields per acre (through being compressed or processed for the market as the commercial crops invariably are) they become highly transportable, and can and will be cultivated far from the market.

It will perhaps be evident from this that the analysis which must be made is a fairly complex one; several factors enter into it. In considering the production of a single crop under a single system, we have seen that only one factor—the farm price—varied. When we came to consider the production of a single crop under alternative systems, the farm price still varied (though for any crop at one place it was the same, whatever the system); but in addition the gross output, and the costs per unit of area, varied under the one system as against the other. When we come now to consider the production of alternative crops, we have to reckon with the fact that all these variations will be repeated for each crop; for every crop cultivated under a given system there will be a certain level of gross output per acre, costs per acre, and a range of farm prices depending on the transportability of the crop. The precise advantage which one crop derives from cultivation near the market may be very different from the advantage derived by another crop. To discover which crop will produce the highest returns at any particular distance from the market, it is then necessary to analyse *all* costs that go into its production.[1] When this is done, the general rule will be that the site nearest the market will be appropriated by that product which experiences the greatest cost reduction nearest the market, or in other words, the greatest cost increase away from the market.[2] When this happens (and only then) will private advantage and social gain both reach their maximum. For the interests of consumers will best be

---

[1] As I. Brinkmann points out, Thünen observed that the choice is invariably more complex even than this; for crops are not usually grown by themselves, but combined with other crops in agricultural systems. Cf. I. BRINKMANN, *op. cit.*, 323–4.

[2] This concept is the same as Th. Brinkmann's "Ground Rent Index": the product with the highest "ground rent index", will preempt the site nearest the market. Cf. TH. BRINKMANN, *op. cit.*, 78–99. Petersen also drew attention to this fact. PETERSEN, *op. cit.*, 97.

served when production is so arranged that for a particular location near the market, that product preempts the area which saves the greatest sum of total costs by location near the market; but in doing so, it will produce the highest ground rent.[1] The rules of advantage from the supply and demand side, for the individual proprietor and the many consumers, for what the Germans call *Privatwirtschaft* and *Volkswirtschaft*, prove to be the same.

This pattern of "cost reduction" is to be found from the patterns of costs per load transported to the market, multiplied by the number of loads lifted from the unit area of land. The product gives us the total costs involved in raising a crop from a given area of land, and then getting that crop to market. But Thünen finds it is simplest to present the sums in terms of costs per load, and to make the variation in other costs accordingly, in terms of the load; we will follow him.

Let us produce a simple case. Imagine that grain is being produced everywhere in the Isolated State, but that farmers are considering whether to grow other crops instead. These are the cost data for grain at varying distances from the market:

Grain	Thalers per load			Total
	production costs	transport costs	land rent	
0 miles	30	0	10	40
5 miles	25	10	5	40
10 miles	20	20	0	40

The total of all three costs is the same for the one crop at every site. That follows from the nature of rent as a residual: it merely expresses the saving in the other two sets of costs, as compared with the least advantageous site (the marginal site) where no land rent is produced; here, the site 10 miles from the market.

Now consider four possible alternative crops. We are going to assume that the transport costs, *per load*, are in all four cases the same as for grain. That would be the case, unless they had some special peculiarity (such as extreme perishability, which required

---

[1] Cf. E. WOERMANN, *op. cit.*, 41. Notice that here the successful product is producing a *third* type of rent, over and above "situation rent" and "intensity rent"; it might be called "displacement rent". Cf. I. BRINKMANN, *op. cit.*, 328 n.

specially rapid transport, or (in a day later than Thünen's) refrigeration plant. But production costs and land rent may vary.

Now the point about the comparison is that the farmer must consider for each crop not merely the production costs, and the transport costs, but also *the land rent which grain would produce on any given site.* The reason is that only in this way can we see the relative advantage of producing the crop in question, as against grain. If the new crop is to displace grain, it does not merely have to produce a land rent, but a land rent bigger than the rent grain would produce; because grain is there, and has to be displaced. (Of course it is all the same if grain is not there, but only potentially there.)

Consider a first alternative crop. It has the same yield per unit of area as grain. That means that we can directly substitute the grain land rent figures above. The production costs of this crop, per load (and per unit of area, since we assume equal yields) are however only half those of grain.

| Crop 1 | Thalers per load | | | Total |
	production costs	transport costs	equivalent grain land rent	
0 miles	15	0	10	25
5 miles	12½	10	5	27½
10 miles	10	20	0	30

Here, production is more profitable near the market than that of grain, and the crop will displace grain.

Consider a second, opposite case. Again the yield, per unit of area, is the same as with grain. But this time the production costs, per load, are double those of grain.

| Crop 2 | Thalers per load | | | Total |
	production costs	transport costs	equivalent grain land rent	
0 miles	60	0	10	70
5 miles	50	10	5	65
10 miles	40	20	0	60

Here production is unprofitable, compared with grain, anywhere within 10 miles of the market. This crop will be produced very far from the market, and grain will not be displaced from its position near the market.

From these two cases, we can conclude that with equal yields per acre, the product with the lower production costs (per load) will be cultivated nearer the market, and vice versa. According to this general rule, production of crops will be distributed round the market according to rising production costs. This is because, in the Thünen system, production costs fall away from the market. A product in which production costs loom especially large will therefore be produced in the area far from the market, where production costs generally are lower

Consider a third, slightly different case. This crop has double the yield, per unit of area, that grain has. Or, to put it in a slightly more convenient way for our purpose, it has only *half the land requirement of grain*.[1] The same amount of land, which would produce two loads of the new crop, would produce only one of grain. The land rent for grain, considered in terms of a load, will only be half that of the new crop. But in this case production costs, per quantity of product, are equal.

Crop 3	Thalers per load			Total
	production costs	transport costs	equivalent grain land rent	
0 miles	30	0	5	35
5 miles	25	10	$2\frac{1}{2}$	$37\frac{1}{2}$
10 miles	20	20	0	40

Here total costs near the market are lower than for grain. The crop will displace grain.

Consider a fourth case, opposite to the third. This crop has only half the yield, per unit of area, of grain. A given load of the crop therefore only bears half the grain land rent; or in other words, per load, the land rent of grain itself is double that of the product. Again production costs, per quantity of product, are equal.

[1] Cf. I. BRINKMANN, *op. cit.*, 325–6.

Crop 4	Thalers per load			Total
	production costs	transport costs	equivalent grain land rent	
0 miles	30	0	20	50
5 miles	25	10	10	45
10 miles	20	20	0	40

This crop can be grown as profitably as grain 10 miles from the market. Outside that range it will begin to displace grain; but nearer the market grain will not be displaced.

From these third and fourth examples we may draw another general conclusion. With equal production costs per load, the product with the higher yields must be produced nearer the market; and vice versa. According to this second general rule, production will be ordered around the market according to a pattern of falling yields. The reason for this lies in transport costs per unit of productive area. A product with high yield per unit of area has to carry high transport costs because it produces more loads to be carried. In the case of Crops 3 and 4 above, this is expressed in terms of the grain land rent, which represents saved transport costs for grain. Crop 3 bears double the transport cost, per unit of area, that grain does; or inverted, in comparison with crop 3 grain bears only half the transport costs, per unit of area; or in other words, it bears only half the land rent per load.

The comparison of four crops made here is a very simple one. I have done this deliberately, for the sake of clear exposition. Thünen's own is more complex; it is made on pp. 114–118 of this edition of *The Isolated State*.[1]

Petersen considers Thünen's calculations, and the resulting laws of location for agricultural products, in great detail. He concludes that the laws suffer from two limitations. One is that the first law is *zeitgebunden*. Thünen makes his production costs decline away from the market, because three-quarters of them consist of grain, which is cheaper away from the market. This answered to reality in Thünen's day. But since then an increasing proportion of agricultural production costs have become costs of industrial, town-based products, which if anything will become more costly away from the market.

---

[1] Cf. Petersen's analysis of it; PETERSEN, *op. cit.*, Ch. 8.

The other limitation is perhaps of greater theoretical importance. Both laws work only for those products for which they are in agreement. That is, they apply for products which show higher yields accompanied by lower production costs and for products which combine lower yields and higher production costs. But for products which show contradictory tendencies—for instance, in the case of one product compared with another which has higher yields *and* higher production costs—the laws will not resolve the location question; they will not tell us which product will be cultivated nearer the market. In that case it is necessary to work from separate formulae for production costs, transport costs, and land rent of the alternative product, for each product. This rather laborious technique is of general application, and its results have a general validity.

But for most products the laws do work, and on their basis it is now possible to understand more clearly why certain products are grown where they are in the Isolated State. Forestry[1] is carried on near the market, because as compared with grain it has both high yield per unit of area (partly because the whole area is in production), and low production costs per load. Given the very poor and expensive transport which Thünen assumed as the basis of the Isolated State, this is correct. But even then, as Thünen himself points out, it was often not correct in reality, because many if not most towns lie on navigable water, which does not exist in the Isolated State. Besides, fertility and topography play a large part in the real world.

Butter[2] is a very interesting extreme case of a product produced far from the market. It has a very low yield per unit of area (or a high "land requirement"). It also has high production costs but they fall very rapidly away from the market, because they consist mainly of grain. Essentially therefore, it is not excluded from the locations near the market by inability to pay the rent; as Petersen says, it seeks distant locations of its own accord.

Wool[3] is an even more extreme case; it has higher production costs and an even lower yield (high land requirement). Therefore it should occupy the outermost place of all within the cultivated area of the Isolated State. Much of Thünen's description of sheep farming, in Chapter 30, is devoted to explaining why this was not the case at the time he wrote, due solely to short-term inelasticities

[1] Cf. PETERSEN, *op. cit.*, Ch. 9.
[2] Cf. PETERSEN, *op. cit.*, Ch. 10.   [3] *Ibid.*

in the supply of certain types of wool. The position righted itself shortly after Thünen's death, and wool-production occupied the place he had assigned it.

Perhaps the most interesting locational case of all is presented by the industrial crops,[1] which Thünen discusses in Chapter 31. These provide the most direct contradiction of the common misapprehension that intensive crops are grown near the market, because they are intensively cultivated in the outermost ring of all. They tend to have low yields compared with grain, and very high production costs per load. Chicory[2] is the sole exception: it had higher yields and lower production costs. In the same class as the majority of commercial crops are crops grown specially for industrial production; for instance, grain grown for distilleries, which is found in locations where grain for flour would not bear the land rent. Because such crops are reduced in weight, the effective yield, per unit of area, is very low. Because the reduction in weight involves manufacturing costs on top of purely farm costs, the costs of production are very high. Such products will positively seek the farthest locations.

Is there, then, any relation at all between intensity and the crop pattern in the Isolated State? Petersen attempts an analysis of this difficult question.[3] His answer is that there is, but not a simple one. The common idea that intensive crops are grown near the market depends on a vague assumption that there is some necessary connexion between *yield* and *intensity*; that crops with a high yield per acre involve high basic costs per acre, and vice versa. But this is only partly true. Admitted, there are few products with a high yield per acre and low basic costs. (Forestry is the obvious example in the Isolated State.) But there are many cases of the opposite: products with low yield per acre and high basic costs. The commercial and industrial crops of the sixth ring mainly fall into this class. Nevertheless, when one has said all this, the predominant impression is one of rising intensity towards the town. Wool, meat and butter production all have a low intensity and are produced far from the town; vegetables, milk and potato production have a high intensity and are produced near; grain has intermediate characteristics and occupies the intermediate positions. The two conspicuous exceptions are forestry in the second ring and industrial crops in the sixth.

[1] *Ibid.*, Ch. 11.
[2] For processing, not for use as a vegetable.   [3] *Ibid.*, Ch. 12.

INTRODUCTION   xxxix

Petersen drew repeated attention[1] to the misleading quality of the famous graphical illustrations in *The Isolated State*, if considered apart from the analysis. These easily give the impression that the rings are intensity rings, because in ring 2 the distinction between firewood and constructional timber, and in ring 6 all mention of the commercial crops, are omitted. In addition the diagrams include a crop system for grain cultivation—the so-called crop alternation system—which has no actual place in the Isolated State, and which Thünen considered only as a theoretical possibility in the event of higher soil fertility.

This brings us to the end of Part I of *The Isolated State*; and with it, we abandon the particular assumptions which have governed the partial equilibrium analysis made there. In the introduction to Part II, Thünen is already posing the questions that arise when the assumptions are relaxed. Suppose we allow differences in soil quality and in climate, the effect of navigable rivers and of railways? Suppose we no longer regard the presence of the town and its industries as given, but seek to ask why they are there? These questions he poses; but he admits straightaway that a complete solution to the problem is not to be found within the covers of a single work, but in that of a generation. In fact many generations have gone by since Thünen wrote this; but we are still little nearer the final resolution that he sought.

The analysis Thünen actually proceeds to make in the rest of Part II, Section 1 of *The Isolated State* is actually rather surprising after the sweeping nature of the introduction. Having there posed seventeen questions for further inquiry, he concentrates on the first of them: "What is the wage which Nature has determined for the labourer; and what governs the interest rate?" This inquiry, Thünen stresses when he first poses it, is only very indirectly concerned with the Isolated State itself. The connexion is a wholly methodological one, for Thünen finds that his method of isolation allows him to produce an answer to the question; he discovers a formula for the "natural wage" by asking "What is the wage on the frontier of the Isolated State, where no land rent occurs, and where any agricultural labourer can have land, free for the asking?" Thünen's method, and his resulting formula for the natural wage, have proved to be the

---

[1] First in *Die fundamentale Standortslehre Joh. Heinrich von Thünens, wie sie bisher als Intensitätslehre missverstanden wurde and was sie wirklich besagt* (Jena 1936) and then in PETERSEN (1944), *op. cit.*, 142–5.

most fiercely debated, and the most fiercely criticised, of all his writings. This is not the place to summarise the controversy or enter into it; it is most fully discussed by Dempsey.[1] But it must be said that even if the formula for the natural wage proves based on a misapprehension, this must not divert attention from the fact that before arriving at it Thünen has already made a discovery of the most fundamental significance. He turns to apply the principle of diminishing returns, no longer to land, but to labour and capital. In the Introduction he develops the idea that the increased yield, due to the additional cost of capital and labour, will eventually decline, so that a point is reached where the value of the increased yield is equal to the value of the increased cost. Later, in Chapter 19 of Part II, Section 1, he says more specifically that extra labour will be employed to that point where the extra product of the worker last employed is just absorbed by the wage he is paid. Here Thünen introduces the notion of the margin (*Grenze*) which Marshall took from him. He has discovered, in fact, the concept of marginal revenue productivity.[2] And he has already suggested the parallel notion of the marginal efficiency of capital: that continued investment in any particular direction will pay until the marginal rate of interest in the marginal investment equals the market rate of interest.

Thünen saw that he could not hope to complete the work he had started. But had he lived longer, we cannot doubt that his mind would have engaged with some of the other topics he had put forward for inquiry. As it is, the posthumous fragments published in Part II, Section 2 offer extraordinary glimpses of the range and quality of his perceptions. Perhaps the most astonishing of all is the section on industrial location, where he clearly anticipates Alfred Weber's concept of agglomeration. Hardly less fascinating is the section on highway construction, where he begins to grapple with the problem of the rate of return on public investments—a subject which has begun to receive serious attention in Britain and North America only in our own day. These fragments, unformed and speculative as they are, offer an amazing picture of the free-ranging quality of Thünen's imagination.

[1] *Op. cit.*
[2] The American economist John Bates Clark, who is usually credited with the discovery of marginal productivity, acknowledged his debt, though he claimed that Thünen had failed to develop the implications. Cf. J. B. CLARK, *The Distribution of Wealth: A Theory of Wages, Interest and Profits* (New York 1899), 322–4.

IV. THÜNEN AND HIS AGE

It would be wrong to say that Thünen wrote his book in a pre-commercial economy, one with ill-defined or rudimentary markets. The specific feature of the Thünen system as it is described in *The Isolated State* is that it is a highly specialised economy, but one conducted on a small scale; even stock farming ends 50 German miles (or 230 English miles) from the central town. This is characteristic of a rather remarkable transitional economy within which Thünen wrote. The complete self-sufficiency of the medieval economy was broken down, if indeed it had ever existed. The work of Heinrich Backe[1] shows that the ancient world had possessed an advanced and large-scale system of Thünen rings; that though the Middle Ages had seen some regression, there were nevertheless considerable long-distance movements of foodstuffs, especially grain. And to some extent *The Isolated State*, because of its very simplification, is not a true picture of the Mecklenburg of the period; for Thünen does not allow it in the first place to contain any navigable water, the chief means of transport of his day.

Even while Thünen was revising Part I for the second (1842) edition, though, the European economy was changing rapidly. In 1840, Britain had become a great grain importer, but 65·4 per cent of her imports came from western and central Europe, and Germany alone accounted for 46·3 per cent. Only thirty years later, in 1870, Germany's share had dropped to 8·7 per cent; the steppes of east and south-east Europe were then supplying about half Britain's imports. By 1913 *all* Europe's share of Britain's grain imports was down to 13 per cent; Argentina then accounted for 28·5 per cent and Canada for 15·4 per cent.[2] Sheep production, which was important in Mecklenburg when Thünen wrote, moved out even more rapidly. The total number of sheep in Germany fifteen years after Thünen's death—in 1865—was 30 million; by 1913 it was down to 5·5 million.[3] Sheep rearing on a large scale was by then relegated to those countries and areas—Central Asia, Australia and New Zealand, South Africa, southern South America—most remote from the great population centre of north-west Europe; and this had constituted by 1913, as

---

[1] H. BACKE, *Um die Nahrungsfreiheit Europas: Weltwirtschaft oder Grossraum* (Leipzig 1942).
[2] *Ibid.*, 45–8.   [3] *Ibid.*, 42; KRZYMOWSKI, *op. cit.*, 148.

Backe says, a great "World Thünen Town", whose demands for foodstuffs and industrial raw materials embraced the whole world. By then Mecklenburg, and indeed all Germany, were well within an inner Thünen ring, which finds no precise place in the Thünen scheme but which Thünen himself realised would come to spread across Europe: the system of crop alternation, which combines intensive production of grain with that of certain specialised crops.

In this dramatic geographical change, which was complete in less than a century, three factors were at work. They were changes in agricultural techniques; changes in transport techniques; and, most fundamental of all, the rapid rise of population during the nineteenth century, which increased demand and made improvements profitable. In Germany alone the density of population rose from 17–20 per square kilometre in 1300 to only 26–28 in 1700, but then to 40–45 in 1800, 104 in 1900, and to 133 in 1925.[1] For German agriculture Krzymowski concluded:

> It was not Albrecht Thaer who overturned the old three-field system and put intensive crop alternation in its place, as is often claimed; the whole course of history has done it, and Thaer himself was only the tool of this historical process.[2]

The growth in demand could be met, as already suggested, in two ways. Yields could be increased on the existing agricultural areas, by improvements; or more could be fetched from new land, which could be brought within the margin of cultivation by transport improvements. Both types of change came about in the nineteenth century, and they were to some extent contradictory. For a transport improvement will (assuming for the moment that demand remains constant) cause a reduction of farm prices near the market and an increase away from the market; thus the incentive to intensify near the market will be reduced. This contradiction led Theodor Brinkmann to inquire how much world agriculture had benefited, since 1870, from improved yields on "old" land and from taking in "new" land, respectively. He concluded that grain production had risen between 1870 and about 1930 by about 200 million tons, of which one-third had come from the "old" land and two-thirds from the "new".[3] The United States provides a particularly dramatic illustration of the contribution of the "new" land. Its agricultural

---

[1] *Ibid.*, 142. [2] *Ibid.* [3] Quoted in I. BRINKMANN, *op. cit.*, 346.

settled area in 1860 was 148 million acres, in 1880 284 million acres, in 1900 415 million acres; wheat exports in 1851–60 averaged 5·5 million bushels per annum, in 1860–70 22 million bushels, in 1875 55 million bushels, and in 1880 150·5 million bushels, their maximum.[1] At that time no less than 58 per cent of the total grain imports into England came from the United States;[2] and the agricultural economy of the wheatlands of North America was disproportionately geared to the needs of the "West European Thünen Town". To some extent, the story after that is of the growth of other, independent Thünen towns, in North America itself, in eastern Asia. The pattern has therefore been complicated, though in a way that Thünen allowed for in *The Isolated State*; for even in Part I he does relax the assumption of a single consuming centre.

The size and the form of *The Isolated State*, if not the principles underlying them, are thus powerfully conditioned by the time when and the place where Thünen wrote his original manuscript. And the very subject-matter, of course, is similarly influenced. Thünen's main concern is firmly with the dominant form of economic activity of his age and his region. Agriculture is seen as the central economic activity; the manufacturing industry of the town, which produces the things to exchange with the products of the countryside, is relatively unsophisticated in character, and the very location of the town does not centrally excite Thünen's attention. It took in fact over half a century after Thünen's death before the first satisfactory theory of location for manufacturing industry, that of Alfred Weber, appeared in 1909.[3] The gap is understandable; for when we move from agricultural to industrial location, we face a new set of problems. Thünen deals with immobile soil; there is no choice of location other than the source of raw material; the only questions open to the farmer are first, shall he cultivate at all?; secondly, what shall he cultivate? With industrial production, the question is different, as Chisholm[4] and Engländer[5] have pointed out: the type of production is postulated, and the place of production is sought; the new choice arises

1 *Ibid.*, 349.   2 BACKE, *op. cit.*, 47.
3 A. WEBER, *Über den Standort der Industrien*, Teil I: *Reine Theorie des Standorts* (Tübingen 1909). English translation, edited by C. J. FRIEDRICH: *Alfred Weber's Theory of the Location of Industry* (Chicago 1929). For the link between Thünen and Weber, cf. C. PONSARD, *Histoire des Théories économiques spatiales* (Paris 1958).
4 CHISHOLM, *op. cit.*, 41.
5 O. ENGLÄNDER, "Kritisches und Positives zu einer allgemeinen reinen Lehre vom Standort", *Zeitschrift für Volkswirtschaft und Sozialpolitik*, 5 (1927), 475–6. Cf. also H. WEIGMANN, *op. cit.*, 144–5.

because the factors of production tend to be mobile, so mobile indeed that one of the chief problems is to set one or more of them at rest for analytic purposes. This was a more complex problem for a more complex age. Fifty years after Weber, it is still not satisfactorily resolved. In justice to Thünen, though, it is right to record two things here. The first is that, just before his death, he was already reaching out into general location theory, and groping towards concepts which were properly developed by others decades later. The second is that the most important later development of general location theory was done by Germans, in full knowledge of the foundation which Thünen had laid. Without this magnificent foundation, indeed, it is difficult to believe that location theory would have developed quite as it did. All in all, we can but echo the verdict of the German economist, Schneider, before the conference held to honour Thünen's name on the 175th anniversary of his birth in 1958:

> Wherever economic theory is studied today, his ideas, his working methods, the problems he posed, have proved seminal right up to the present day— even there, where his name seems to have been forgotten, Thünen *has* worked. His work shines brighter than ever today. Much, which seems self-evident to us, goes back to him. And still not all the riches which are buried in his work are brought to light. To find them, you must without doubt read *The Isolated State* carefully and often.[1]

London, December 1963.   PETER HALL

---

[1] SCHNEIDER, *op. cit.*, 27–8.

A BIBLIOGRAPHY OF REFERENCES TO THÜNEN IN ENGLISH

THIS bibliography deals only with Thünen's location theory. For references to the wage theory readers should consult the bibliography in DEMPSEY, B. W. below.

ARTLE, R. (1959) *Studies in the structure of the Stockholm economy*, The Business Research Institute at the Stockholm School of Economics, Stockholm, pp. 115–16.

BECKMANN, M. and MARSCHAK, T. (1955) "An activity analysis approach to location theory", *Kyklos*, **8**, Basel, pp. 125–43.

BENEDICT, E. T., see BRINKMANN, T.

BEST, R. H. and GASSON R. (1965) *The location of intensive crops in Kent*, Wye, Kent.

BRINKMANN, T. (1935) *Theodor Brinkmann's Economics of the Farm Business.* Translated from *Die Oekonomik des Landwirtschaftlichen Betriebes* (Tübingen 1922, being part of Vol. VII of *Grundriss der Sozialökonomik*) by E. T. Benedict. Berkeley, California. *Passim.*

CHISHOLM, M. (1961) "Agricultural production, location and rent", *Oxford Economic Papers*, **13**, Oxford, pp. 342–59.

CHISHOLM, M. (1962) *Rural Settlement and Land Use: an essay in location*, London. Especially Chapter 2.

COHEN, R. L. (1954) *The economics of agriculture*, Cambridge, Chapter 3.

COSSA, L. (1893) *Introduction to the study of political economy.* Translated by L. DYER, London, pp. 404–6.

DAGGETT, S. (1955) *Principles of inland transportation*, New York, Chapter 8 *passim.*

DEMPSEY, B. W. (1960) *The frontier wage: the economic organization of free agents*, Chicago. With bibliography.

DICKINSON, R. E. (1964) *City and region*, London, pp. 246–9.

DUNN, E. S. (1954) *The location of agricultural production.* Gainesville, Fla. *Passim.*

DYER, L. see COSSA, L.

ELY, R. T. and WEHRWEIN, G. S. (1940) *Land economics*, New York. *Passim.*

FRIEDRICH, C. J. see WEBER, A.

GARRISON, W. L. (1959) "Spatial structure of the economy". *Annals of the Association of American Geographers*, 49, Lawrence, Kan. pp. 232–9.

GREENHUT, M. L. (1956) *Plant location in theory and in practice.* Chapel Hill, N. C. pp. 5–8 and *passim.*

GREENHUT, M. L. (1957) "Games, capitalism and general location theory," *The Manchester School of Economic and Social Studies*, **25**, Manchester, pp. 61–88.

GROTEWOLD, A. (1959) "Von Thünen in retrospect", *Economic Geography*, **35**, Worcester, Mass. pp. 346–55.

HARTSHORNE, R. (1939) *The nature of geography.* Lancaster, Pa. p. 421.

HEIMANN, E. (1945) *History of economic doctrines: an introduction to economic theory.* London. Chapter 4 *passim.*
HIGGS, H., ed. (1926) *Palgrave's Dictionary of Political Economy,* London. Vol. III, p. 540.
HINRICHS, A. F. see WIESER, F. VON.
HOOVER, E. M. (1937) *Location theory and the shoe and leather industries,* (Harvard Economic Studies, 55), Cambridge, Mass., Chapter 2 *passim.*
HOOVER, E. M. (1948) *The location of economic activity,* New York, Chapter 6.
HURWITZ, N. (1957) *Agriculture in Natal 1860–1950,* (Natal Regional Survey, Vol. 12), Cape Town, Chapter 9 *passim.*
ISARD, W. (1956) *Location and space-economy,* New York and London, Chapters 1 and 2.
JOHNSON, H. B. (1962) "A note on Thünen's circles", *Annals of the Association of American Geographers,* 52, Lawrence, Kan. pp. 213–20.
JONASSON, O. (1925) "Agricultural regions of Europe", *Economic Geography,* 1, Worcester, Mass., p. 277–314. (Especially pp. 284–6.)
KAPP, K. W. and KAPP, L. L. (1949) *Readings in economics,* New York, pp. 299–309.
KLAGES, K. H. W. (1942) *Ecological crop geography,* New York, Chapter 5 *passim.*
KRZYMOWSKI, R. (1928) "Graphical Presentation of Thünen's theory of intensity". Translated by P. G. Minneman. *Journal of Farm Economics,* 10, Menasha, Wis., pp. 461–82.
LALOR, J. J. see ROSCHER, W.
LEIGH, A. H. (1949). "Von Thünen's theory of distribution and the advent of marginal analysis". *Journal of Political Economy,* 54, Chicago, pp. 481–502.
LÖSCH, A. (1954) *The economics of location.* Translated by W. H. WOGLOM, New Haven. *Passim.*
MARSHALL, A. (1890) *Principles of economics,* London, Introduction, p. x.
MELAMID, A. (1955) "Some applications of Thünen's model in regional analysis of economic growth", *Papers and Proceedings of the Regional Science Association,* 1, Pennsylvania, pp. L1–L5.
NEWMAN, P. C. (1952) *The Development of economic thought,* New York, Chapter 13 *passim.*
OHLIN, B. (1933) *Interregional and international trade,* Harvard. Especially pp. 183–4.
OHLIN, B. (1935) "Some aspects of the theory of rent: von Thünen vs. Ricardo", in N. E. HIMES (ed.), *Economics, Sociology and the modern world: Essays in honor of T. N. Carver,* Cambridge, Mass., pp. 171–83.
PIGOU, A. C., ed. (1925) *Memorials of Alfred Marshall,* London, pp. 359–60.
PREDÖHL, A. (1928) "The theory of location in its relation to general economics". *Journal of Political Economy,* 36, Chicago, pp. 371–90.
ROSCHER, W. (1878) *Principles of political economy.* Translated by J. J. LALOR, New York, Book III, Chapters 2 and 3 *passim.*
SALIN, E. (1934) "Thünen, J. H. v.", *Encyclopaedia of the Social Sciences,* 14, New York, pp. 627–8.
SCHLEBECKER, J. T. (1960) "The world metropolis and the history of American Agriculture", *Journal of Economic History,* 20, New York, pp. 187–208.
SCHNEIDER, E. (1934) "Johann Heinrich von Thünen", *Econometrica,* 2, London, pp. 1–12. Reprinted in H. W. SPIEGEL (ed.), *The development of economic thought: Great economists in perspective,* New York and London, 1952, pp. 445–57.
SCHUMPETER, J. A. (1955) *History of economic analysis,* New York, pp. 465–8.

SPANN, O. (1930) *Types of economic theory*, London, Chapter 8.
VITANOV, M. P. (1936) 'A Study of the Labour to the Distance of Fields from Farmsteads'. *Bulletin of the Department of Agriculture Economics, Faculty of Agriculture and Forestry, University of Sofia.*
VON BÖVENTER, E. (1963) "Towards a united theory of spatial economic structure". *Papers of the Regional Science Association*, 10, Philadelphia, pp. 163–87.
WARNTZ, W. (1959) *Toward a geography of price*, Philadelphia, p. 18.
WAUGH, F. V., ed. (1954) *Readings on agricultural marketing*, Ames, Iowa, pp. 114–42.
WEBER, A. (1929) *Theory of the location of industries*. Translated by C. J. FRIEDRICH, Chicago, Introduction.
WEHRWEIN, G. S. (1942) "The rural–urban fringe", *Economic Geography*, 18, Worcester, Mass., pp. 217–28.
WIESER, F. VON (1928) *Social economics*. Translated by A. F. HINRICHS, London, pp. 315–16, 336.
WOGLOM, W. H. see LÖSCH, A.
YAGI, Y. (1934) "Horizontal and vertical differentiations in the agricultural production of Japan", *Kyoto University Economic Review*, 9, Kyoto, pp. 33–60.
YOKENO, N. (1956) "Thünen's structure in the agriculture of Japan", *Sophia Economic Review*, 3, No. 1 Tokyo, pp. 14–22.
YOUNGBLOOD, B., and COX, A. B. (1922) "An economic study of a typical ranching area on the Edwards Plateau of Texas", *Texas Agricultural Experiment Station*, Bulletin 297, Brazos County, Texas. Chapter 5 *passim*.

GLOSSARY OF TERMS USED IN
THE ISOLATED STATE

Acre. See *Prussian Acre.*

Belgian System. See *Crop Alternation System.*

Bushel. (*Scheffel.*) Thünen uses the Berlin bushel (*Berliner Scheffel*) of his day. 1 Berlin bushel equalled 1·542 English bushels, or 54·4 l.

Bushel-crops. (*Körner.*) In *The Isolated State* Thünen adapts to his own use a colloquial measure from the agriculture of his day, which roughly conveyed the same sense as the old English "six-fold", "ten-fold" measure. Here it is translated throughout as "six (etc.) bushel-crops", which better conveys Thünen's own very precise meaning of "a crop of six (etc.) bushels from 100 square rods". The expression "*x* bushel-crops" also can be rendered approximately by the formula "a crop of *x* centners (100*x* Hamburg lb) per Prussian acre". 1 bushel-crop is equal to a yield of 2·88 English bushels per acre (2·51 hl per hectare). 8 bushel-crops, the standard measure of soil fertility in *The Isolated State*, is therefore equal to a yield of 23·04 English bushels per English acre (20·08 hl per hectare); 10 bushel-crops to 28·80 English bushels per acre (25·1 hl per hectare).

Capital, Return to. (*Kapitalgewinn.*) Thünen uses this in the strict classical economic sense, as that share of the product which is due to the contributor of capital. It is expressed as rate of interest (*Zinsfuss*).

Centner. (*Zentner.*) Throughout Thünen uses this to mean a unit of 100 Hamburg lb (106·79 English lb or 48·42 kg) and *not* the prevailing unit in Mecklenburg at the time, which was 112 English lb.

Cord. (*Faden.*) A unit of timber measurement of 224 ft³ in Mecklenburg measure, or 194·7 English ft³ (18·1 cubic metres).

Crop Alternation System, Enterprise. (*Fruchtwechselwirtschaft.*) The most intensive system of grain cultivation described in *The Isolated State*, though it had no actual place in the ideal State which Thünen postulated. Its two essential features were that it (1) had no fallow and (2) alternated grain and non-grain crops. The Belgian

xlix

crop alternation system, which Thünen describes in Chapter 17, had the following rotation: 1. potatoes, 2. rye and stubble beet, 3. oats, 4. clover, 5. wheat and stubble beet. Another variation, to which Thünen makes frequent reference, was the *six-course crop alternation system* (*sechsslägigen Fruchtwechselwirtschaft*): 1. potatoes, 2. barley, 3. mown clover, 4. rye, 5. tares for fodder, after manuring, 6. rye.

Degrees. (*Grad*.) See under *Fertility*.

Dreeschbrache. See *Ley Fallow*.

Dreifelderwirtschaft. See *Three-field System*.

Einkünfte. See *Revenue*.

Estate. See *Farm*.

Faden. See *Cord*.

Farm. (*Gut*.) The German word *Gut* has been translated as "estate" where it refers to Tellow or a similar large farm, but as "farm" elsewhere.

Fertility. (*Reichtum*.) The level of fertility which a soil has currently attained under cultivation. It is to be distinguished from "Inherent Quality of the Soil" (*physische Beschaffenheit*), which refers to a quality or ease of working, independent of good or bad cultivation. Thünen measures fertility in degrees (Grad): strictly the degree is a measure of the *exhaustion* of the soil by a crop, because it represents the amount of fertility taken from the soil by a harvest of one Berlin bushel (1·542 English bushels or 54·4 l.) of rye, but Thünen then applies the measure to the amount of fertility contained in the soil at a given time. The fertility in degrees can be equated with the amount of manure necessary to replace the lost fertility: for top grade barley soil Thünen put one load of manure (2000 Hamburg lb) at 3·2°. There is a relation between fertility (in degrees) and yield (in bushel crops), and in certain calculations in *The Isolated State* Thünen assumes that it is a simple direct one: an increase of one-fifth in fertility will produce a one-fifth increase in yield, and so on. Thünen's later findings showed that this assumption was incorrect; see Chapter 7b.

Foot. (*Fuss*.) Thünen worked with the Lübeck foot, which was one-sixteenth of the (Mecklenburg) rod (q.v.) 1 Lübeck ft equalled 0·9544 English ft.

Free Cash Cropping. (*Freie Wirtschaft*.) The system of cultivation in the innermost ring of *The Isolated State*. Its central feature was that there was no fixed rotation: at any time, the farmer would grow that crop which he thought would yield the greatest net revenue. This was possible because the fertility of the soil was raised, and then maintained, by manure brought from the central Town.

Freie Wirtschaft. See *Free Cash Cropping.*

Fruchtwechselwirtschaft. See *Crop Alternation System.*

Fuss. See *Foot.*

Geldertrag. See *Revenue.*

Gold Thaler. See *Thaler.*

Grad. See *Fertility.*

Groschen. (*Silbergroschen.*) A unit used only rarely in *The Isolated State.* It equalled 1/30 of the current Prussian thaler (*Preussische Courant*) which was worth marginally less than the gold or new thaler (see *Thaler*).

Gross Product. (*Roher Ertrag, Rohertrag.*) The product of a farm, before deduction of costs. In *The Isolated State* it is usually expressed in bushels of grain, but these may be converted into money by use of the farm price of grain.

Gut. See *Farm.*

Improved System. (*Koppelsystem, Koppelwirtschaft.*) Also known as the *Mecklenburg system.* A system still in use in Schleswig-Holstein, Mecklenburg and as far east as East Prussia, in which arable rotates with intensively-used ley grass; a typical rotation was: 1. Fallow, 2. Rye, 3. Barley, 4. Oats, 5. Ley, 6. Ley, 7. Ley. The fallow, which came after the grass ley, was known as a ley fallow (*Dreeschbrache*) (q.v.) The German name *Koppel* referred to the small enclosed plots into which the farm area was divided. *Koppelsystem* or *Koppelwirtschaft* is translated throughout as "improved system" because of its affinities with the "improved rotations" introduced under enclosure in eighteenth-century English farming.

Inherent Quality of the Soil. See *Fertility.*

Kapitalgewinn. See *Capital, Return to.*

Kavel. See *Stand.*

Konsequenz, mit höchster. See *Rationally.*

Koppelsystem, Koppelwirtschaft. See *Improved System.*

Körner. See *Bushel-Crops.*

Kreis. See *Ring.*

Land Rent. (*Landrente.*) That part of the total (gross) product of land which remains as a surplus after deduction of all costs, including interest on invested capital. Equivalent to "economic rent" in English classical economics.

Landrente. See *Land Rent.*

Lb. See *Pound Weight.*

Ley Fallow. (*Dreesch, Dreeschbrache.*) The so-called *Dreesch-system,* or *Feldgrassystem,* formerly common in Germany, consisted of a year's fallow, followed by 2–4 years of grain, followed by a 3–4 year grass ley (*Dreesch*). This is equivalent to the improved or *Koppel* system described in *The Isolated State.*

Mecklenburg System. See *Improved System.*

Meilen. See *Miles.*

Miles. (*Meilen.*) Thünen uses the old German miles. One German mile was equal to 7·42 km or to 4·61 English miles. Tellow was 5 German miles, or 23·05 English miles (37·1 km.), from Rostock; in the Isolated State, grain cultivation stretched for 31·5 German miles or 145·2 English miles (233·7 km) from the central Town, and the Isolated State itself had a radius of 50 German miles or 230·5 English miles (371·0 km).

Morgen. See *Prussian Acre.*

Mürbebrache. See *Soft Fallow.*

Net Product. (*Reiner Ertrag* (*des Bodens*).) The total (gross) product of land minus all production costs. At the first appearance of this term Thünen equates it directly with land rent (q.v.).

Net Revenue. (*Reiner Geldertrag.*) See *Revenue.*

New Thaler. (*Taler N 2/3.*) See *Thaler.*

Physische Beschaffenheit. See *Fertility.*

Pound Weight. Thünen uses Hamburg lb. 100 Hamburg lb equalled 106·79 English lb or 48·42 kg.

Preussischer Morgen. See *Prussian Acre.*

Prussian Acre. (*Preussischer Morgen.*) An area equal to 117·86 Mecklenburg square rods, and thus to 0·63 of an English acre or 0·256 ha.

Rationally, Rationality. (*Mit höchster Konsequenz.*) Thünen uses the term in the traditional sense of the English classical economists: an enterprise is conducted rationally when the entrepreneur pursues maximum profit and when he is possessed of all necessary knowledge to that end.

Reichtum. See *Fertility.*

Reine Ertrag, Reinertrag. See *Net Product.*

Reiner Geldertrag. See *Revenue.*

Revenue; Net Revenue. (*Geldertrag, Einkünfte; Reiner Geldertrag.*) Thünen uses these terms in the strict economic sense, to mean the equivalent, in money terms and from the viewpoint of return to the producer, of the *product*. (See *Gross Product, Net Product*.)

Ring. The translation used here for *Kreis*; a ring is one of the zones of cultivation in the Isolated State.

Rod. (Rute.) The Mecklenburg rod equalled 15·27 English ft or 4·65 m.

Roher Ertrag, Rohertrag. See *Gross Product*.

Rute. See *Rod.*

Scheffel. See *Bushel*.

Schilling. See *Shilling*.

Shilling. (Schilling.) 1/48 of a new thaler (see *Thaler*).

Silbergroschen. See *Groschen*.

Silver Groschen. See *Groschen*.

Soft Fallow. (Mürbebrache). The fallow which follows a grain crop under the three-field system. The literal translation is "granular" fallow: the ground was intensively harrowed to pulverise the soil.

Soil, rich (good) or poor (bad). When Thünen uses these terms he invariably refers to the fertility *(Reichtum)* of the soil as measured in degrees. (See *Fertility*.)

Square Rod. (□ *Rute.*) The unit of area used throughout. 100 Mecklenburg square rods equalled 0·535 English acres, or 0·217 hectares. 100,000 Mecklenburg square rods, a unit used frequently, thus equalled 535 English acres or 217 hectares. See also *Prussian Acre*.

Stand. (Kavel.) *Kavel* was a north German word meaning a "lot"; Thünen used it to mean an area of standing timber. In the particular case discussed it is 1/100 part of an area of 100,000 square rods, or 1000 square rods (5·35 English acres or 2·17 hectares.)

Statics. (Statik des Landbaues). The study of the relation between manure application and crop yields. It was based on the notion (then current) that yields were related to the humus content of the soil.

Statik des Landbaues. See *Statics*.

Taler. See *Thaler*.

Thaler. (Taler.) The thaler or dollar was the basic unit of Prussian (and therefore of Mecklenburg) currency when Thünen wrote. When he writes of thalers without further qualification, he means gold thalers. In 1850 one gold thaler was worth about 3*s* or 75c. It was divided into 30 silver groschen *(Silbergroschen)*. Often, though, Thünen works with an alternative unit, the *new thaler (Taler N 2/3)*. This was based on a unit of silver, not of gold. 14

new thalers equalled 15 gold thalers, i.e. 1 new thaler equalled 1·071 gold thaler. Thünen sometimes works with decimal fractions of thalers; sometimes with thalers and shillings, one shilling being 1/48 of a new thaler.

Three-field System, Enterprise. (*Dreifelderwirtschaft.*) The historic system combining spring corn, winter corn and fallow. The example Thünen used had the rotation: 1. rye, 2. oats, 3. fallow.

Zentner. See *Centner.*

CONVENTIONS USED
IN THIS TRANSLATION

1. *Pagination.* The numbers in the outer margin refer to the 1842 Rostock edition (in the case of Part I); to the 1850 Rostock edition (in the case of Part II Section 1); and to the 1863 Rostock edition (in the case of Part II Section 2). In each case this is the original definitive edition. The Jena editions of 1910, 1921 and 1930 also have references back to these editions (except for II.2 which is not reproduced there), so that cross-reference is possible.

2. *Breaks.* A line (————) indicates that a line occurs in the original. Asterisks (* * *) indicate an editorial break in this translation; material from the original has been omitted.

3. *Summaries.* Editorial summaries of material not translated in full are in italics. To indicate breaks in the original, asterisks are placed both at beginning and end of italicised passages.

4. *Footnotes.* Footnotes indicated by conventional symbols (*, †) are Thünen's originals. Footnotes indicated by numbers are editorial explanations. Where these are explanations of technical terms used in the text, the explanation is also to be found in the alphabetical glossary (pp. lix–liv).

The Isolated State in its Relation to Agriculture and National Economy

Part One

THE EFFECT OF GRAIN PRICES, FERTILITY AND TAXATION ON AGRICULTURE

BY

JOHANN HEINRICH VON THÜNEN
OF TELLOW IN MECKLENBURG

PREFACE TO THE SECOND EDITION

THE first edition of this work, which has been out of print now for seven years, appeared in 1826.

In this second edition I have considerably enlarged the chapters on land rent, agricultural statics,[1] stock farming, and rape production. The entire work has been revised carefully; several points are defined with greater precision, and others, where long experience has modified my former ideas, have been altered.

Above all I have endeavoured to give long and detailed explanations of points which—in part through fault of my own—were misunderstood when this work was first published, in the hope that all these changes will make the present edition easier to understand.

Enough material being left related to my theme to fill a further volume, I am calling the present work Part One.

In Part Two I mean to consider the Isolated State under different assumptions, in order to establish the operation of factors not considered in the present work; to present some calculations (which form the basis of Part One) on cultivation costs and the net product; to extend the discussion of forestry; to add some essays on the mean distance, highway construction, and other topics.

Part Two will therefore deal with topics which it is possible to study by themselves; and as it is not certain that I shall have the time to finish the entire work, it may appear in pamphlet form.

I hope that the reader who is willing to spend some time and attention on my work will not take exception to the imaginary assumptions I make at the beginning because they do not correspond to conditions in reality, and that he will not reject these assumptions as arbitrary and pointless. They are a necessary part of my argument, allowing me to establish the operation of a certain factor, a

vi

---

[1] Statics. The study of the relation between manure application and crop yields. It was based on the notion (then current) that yields were related to the humus content of the soil.

[2] These actually appear in Part II Section 2. Not all of them are fully translated here.

factor whose operation we see but dimly in reality, where it is in incessant conflict with others of its kind.

This method of analysis has illuminated—and solved—so many problems in my life, and appears to me to be capable of such widespread application, that I regard it as the most important matter contained in all my work.

Tellow, March 1842   J. H. V. THÜNEN

SECTION ONE

THE FORMATION OF
THE ISOLATED STATE

CHAPTER 1

HYPOTHESES

IMAGINE a very large town, at the centre of a fertile plain which is crossed by no navigable river or canal. Throughout the plain the soil is capable of cultivation and of the same fertility. Far from the town, the plain turns into an uncultivated wilderness which cuts off all communication between this State and the outside world.

There are no other towns on the plain. The central town must therefore supply the rural areas with all manufactured products, and in return it will obtain all its provisions from the surrounding countryside.

The mines that provide the State with salt and metals are near the central town which, as it is the only one, we shall in future call simply "the Town".

CHAPTER 2

THE PROBLEM

THE problem we want to solve is this: What pattern of cultivation will take shape in these conditions?; and how will the farming system of the different districts be affected by their distance from the Town? We assume throughout that farming is conducted absolutely rationally.[1]

It is on the whole obvious that near the Town will be grown those products which are heavy or bulky in relation to their value and hence so expensive to transport that the remoter districts are unable to supply them. Here too we shall find the highly perishable products, which must be used very quickly. With increasing distance from the Town, the land will progressively be given up to products cheap to transport in relation to their value.

For this reason alone, fairly sharply differentiated concentric rings[2] or belts will form around the Town, each with its own particular staple product.

From ring to ring the staple product, and with it the entire farming system, will change; and in the various rings we shall find completely different farming systems.

---

[1] *Absolute rationality, rationally* (mit höchster Konsequenz). Thünen uses the term in the traditional sense of the English classical economists: an enterprise is conducted rationally when the entrepreneur pursues the maximum profit and when he is possessed of all necessary knowledge to that end.

[2] *Rings, belts. Kreise.*

CHAPTER 3

FIRST RING:
FREE CASH CROPPING[1]

DELICATE horticultural products such as cauliflower, strawberries,   3
lettuce, etc., would not survive long journeys by wagon. They can,
moreover, be sold only in small quantities, while still quite fresh.
All these products will be grown near the Town.
Gardens will therefore occupy the land immediately around the
Town.

Next to fruit and vegetables, milk is a prime necessity for the
Town; and as this is a difficult and costly product to transport and
is, besides, highly perishable, particularly in warm weather when it
quickly becomes unpalatable, milk too will be produced in the first
ring.

The price of milk will rise to the point where the land used to
produce it cannot be more profitably devoted to any other product.
Since the rental of land is extremely high in this first ring, the larger
quantity of labour which may be required is here of little account.
The aim is to obtain the largest possible amount of feed from the
smallest area of land; and since a given area is capable of supporting
many more animals when these are stall-fed and not put out to
pasture (on pasture the animals inevitably do much damage to the
growing plants, by treading on them and ripping them off—a
system of stall-feeding allows the farmer to cut his clover at the
optimum moment), the local farmer will endeavour to grow a lot of
clover and stall-feed his animals. But even where—owing to its
greater cleanliness—a grazing system is adopted, the pastures will
only be small, and the animals will in the main continue to be fed
on cut green clover and on the left-overs from the potatoes, cabbage,
roots, and the like.

---

[1] *Freie Wirtschaft.*

The distinctive feature of this ring is that it buys most of the manure it uses from the Town, unlike the remoter areas, which produce their own.

4   It is this which puts the first ring so far ahead of all the rest, enabling it to sell crops the other regions have to raise merely to keep their soil fertile.[1]

The sale of hay and straw is next to milk of paramount importance to this ring. Since the remoter districts cannot compete in this, the price of these commodities will rise to the point where their production constitutes the most profitable use of land inside this ring. Grain production is here only a sideline, for the outlying rings, where wages as well as land rent are lower, can produce this far more cheaply. Grain will be grown only for the sake of its by-product of straw; and by close sowing, the local farmers will deliberately sacrifice a portion of their potential grain crop so as to obtain a greater quantity of straw.

This ring will also provide the Town with all the products which become too costly if they are brought in from farther districts: potatoes, cabbages, roots, green clover, and so on.

Here again milch-cows will make the highest use of the smaller and unmarketable potatoes and of the inferior sort of cabbages, roots, etc.

No land in this ring will ever lie in bare fallow. In the first place, the land rent[2] here is far too high to allow any portion of the arable land to remain uncultivated, and secondly, the fertility of the soil may, by the purchase of Town manure, be raised to the point where it yields its maximum output, so that in contrast to the farther rings the need does not arise here to nurse the soil by means of a bare fallow.

5   Crops will be grown in such sequence that each prepares the soil for its successor; but none that fetch low prices need be cultivated merely to afford the soil a change. This then is the system of free cash cropping, where the crops do not have to rotate according to a fixed order.

Buying Town manure is most profitable for the district of the first ring immediately adjacent to the Town. With growing distance the advantage falls rapidly, since the cost both of fetching the manure and of taking the product to the Town increases. At a certain

[1] See p. 25 for a definition of *fertility*.
[2] See p. 18 for Thünen's definition of *land rent*.

distance from the Town the advantage of buying Town manure begins to look doubtful, and a little farther out it will decidedly be more profitable for a farm to produce its own manure than buy this from the Town. This point marks the boundary of the first and the beginning of the second ring.

HOW IS THE PRICE OF GRAIN DETERMINED IN THE VARIOUS DISTRICTS OF THE ISOLATED STATE?

BEFORE we pass on to look at the farming systems of the second and the following rings, we must try to discover how the grain price varies with distance from the Town.
We are supposing:

1. That the Town is the only market for grain.
2. That there is no navigable river or canal in the entire State, so that all grain has to be taken to the Town by horse and wagon.

In these conditions the Town grain price will be the norm for the entire country. But grain cannot be as valuable in the rural areas as in the Town, because, in order to fetch its market price, it must first be taken to the Town. It follows that in the country districts grain is less valuable than in the Town by the cost of its transport.

To give a numerical expression to this decline in the value of grain we have to apply to the Isolated State an illustration taken from the real world.

At Tellow, an estate[1] five miles[2] from the market town of Rostock, the average cost (over five years) of taking a wagon-load of grain to Rostock comes to 3·60 Rostock bushels of rye plus 1·52 new thalers. Or, converting the units, to 2·75 Berlin bushels of rye plus 1·63 gold thalers.*

---

* The Rostock bushel is equivalent to five-sevenths of the Berlin bushel; [3]in this and all subsequent calculations 14 new thalers are reckoned as equal to 15 gold thalers.[4] Whenever thalers or bushels are mentioned below without further explanation, they should be taken to mean gold thalers and Berlin bushels.

[1] *Gut*. This word will be translated as "estate" wherever it refers to Tellow or to a similar actual large-scale capitalist farm, but as "farm", "property" or "holding" elsewhere.

[2] *Meilen*. Thünen refers to the old German mile, which was equal to 7·42 km, or

The normal load for a four-horse team is 2400 lb.[1] But on a two-day journey the horses consume about 150 lb of feed; so that only 2400 minus 150 lb, or 2250 lb arrive in the Town. This is the same as 37·5 Rostock bushels, or 26·78 Berlin bushels.

Assume now that the average rye price in the central Town of the Isolated State is 1·5 gold thalers the Berlin bushel, and that transport costs are calculated from the Tellow findings.

7

What, in these conditions, will grain fetch in the Isolated State on a farm five miles from the Town?

In the Town one load of 26·78 Berlin bushels of rye will fetch 26·78 × 1·5, or 40·17 gold thalers. From this sum must be subtracted the transport costs (which have already been calculated at 1·63 gold thalers plus 2·57 bushels of rye), leaving 38·54 thalers minus 2·57 bushels. In other words, the revenue realised on the 26·78 bushels of rye delivered in the Town and on the 2·57 bushels that have to be taken along as feed—a total of 29·35 bushels—comes to 38·54 thalers, or 1·313 thalers the bushel.

At a distance of ten miles the journey to and from the Town takes four days.

For this distance, 300 lb of feed must be taken, and the grain load which is sold is therefore 2400 minus 300 = 2100 lb.

Transport costs come to $2 \times 2·57 = 5·14$ bushels of rye, plus $2 \times 1·63 = 3·26$ thalers.

A calculation similar to the above will show that on the farm ten miles from the Town the bushel of rye is worth only 1·136 thalers.

Applying the calculation to greater distances, we obtain the table on the following page:

In these conditions grain cannot be brought from a distance of 50 miles, because the horses and their drivers would consume the entire load, or its equivalent value, on the journey.

4·61 English miles. The distance from Tellow to Rostock was thus 23·05 English miles or 37·1 km.

[3] *Bushels.* 1 Berlin bushel equalled 1·542 English bushels or 54·4 l.

[4] *Thalers.* The *thaler or Taler* was the basic unit of Prussian (and therefore of Mecklenburg) currency when Thünen wrote. When he writes of "thalers" without further qualification, he means gold thalers. More commonly though, he works with the new thaler (*Taler N 2/3*). This was based on a unit of silver, not of gold. 14 new thalers equalled 15 gold thalers, i.e. 1 new thaler equalled 1·071 gold thalers. Thünen sometimes, as here, works with fractions of thalers; sometimes he works with thalers and shillings (Schillings), one shilling being equal to 1/48 of a new thaler.

---

[1] *lb.* 100 Hamburg lb equalled 106·79 English lb, so that this load equalled 2563 English lb.

8
1000 Berlin bushels of rye are worth:	gold thalers
in the Town itself	1500
on the farm 5 miles from the Town	1313
10 miles from the Town	1136
15 miles from the Town	968
20 miles from the Town	809
25 miles from the Town	656
30 miles from the Town	512
35 miles from the Town	374
40 miles from the Town	242
45 miles from the Town	116
49·95 miles from the Town	0

Hence even if it were possible to produce grain free of cost, tillage would have to cease at 50 miles from the Town. But since the production of grain costs money as well as labour, it will cease yielding a net product[1] already very much nearer to the Town; and with the net product, cultivation also will cease.

It may strike some readers as wrong that in calculating transport costs for long journeys we assume that the wagon sets out with the feed for both journeys, since it is, after all, cheaper to buy feed on the return journey than to reduce the grain load by carrying this along right from the outset.

9   Feed that is bought on the way can never be as cheap as at the place of its production, because the price has to cover the profit made by the innkeeper or middleman. Even so, this extra outlay cannot be as costly as taking the feed along over great distances.

But in considering great distances we have to remember the following:

The transport costs in my calculations are worked out on the basis of feeding the horses over a distance of five miles (Tellow to Rostock). At this small distance, horses used in field-work in summer can take the grain to the Town in winter[2] and there is no need to keep a special team of horses. The only additions to the cost of transporting grain are those due to the greater exertion of the horses: shoeing, wear and tear on the wagon, the greater quantity of feed consumed; but neither the interest on the capital value of the horses nor the feed necessary to keep them through the winter enters into the calculation.

---

[1] *Reinertrag.* Translated throughout as "net product".
[2] i.e. when there is no other work for them to do.

But where the distance is great, special teams have to be kept to carry the grain; hence transport costs (expressed in bushels of rye) rise greatly with distance.

The extra expense of keeping special teams comes to probably quite as much as is saved on the purchase of feed on the journey; at any rate the two errors, consciously made, will help to cancel each other out. Although I have tried several times to discover a better way of calculating transport costs, I have always found this method the most apt.

We shall often want to know the value of rye at the various distances from the Town listed in the table on p. 14. This, however, requires a generally valid formula, and before we can proceed, we have to solve the following problem:

What is rye worth on the farm x miles from the market?

One wagon carries a total load of 2400 lb, or, as we are assuming the bushel of rye to weigh 84 lb, 2400/84 bushels of rye. From this we still have to subtract the feed that has to be taken along for the horses: 150 lb for a distance of 5 miles, or $30x$ lb for x miles.

Hence only $2400-30x$ lb, or $(2400-30x)/84$ bushels of rye, arrive in the Town. The revenue for this, taking the bushel of rye at 1·5 thalers, comes to $\{(2400-30x)/84\} \times 1·5 = (3600-45x)/84$ thalers.

For a distance of 5 miles, transport costs come to 2·57 bushels of rye plus 1·63 thalers; for x miles this makes

$$\frac{2·57x \text{ bushels} + 1·63x \text{ thalers}}{5}$$

From the receipts of $(3600-45x)/84$ thalers we have to subtract the $(1·63x \text{ thalers} + 2·57 \text{ bushels})/5$ transport costs, which comes to

$$\frac{3600-45x \text{ thalers}}{84} - \frac{1·63x \text{ thalers}}{5} - \frac{2·57x \text{ bushels}}{5}$$

or

$$\frac{18{,}000-361·92x \text{ thalers}}{420} - \frac{2·57x \text{ bushels}}{5}$$

This is the net revenue for one load of $(2400-30x)/84$ bushels of
11   rye delivered to the Town. $(2400-30x)/84$ bushels of rye are therefore worth $(18,000-361\cdot92x)/420$ thalers $-2\cdot57x/5$ bushels of rye, or
$(2400-30x)/84$ bushels of rye $+(2\cdot57x)/5$ bushels of rye

$$= \frac{(18,000-361\cdot92x)}{420} \text{ thalers}$$

Thus $(12,000+65\cdot88x)/420$ bushels of rye $= (18,000-361\cdot92x)/420$
thalers, or $12,000+65\cdot88x$ bushels of rye $= 18,000-361\cdot92x$ thalers.
It follows that one bushel of rye is worth $(18,000-361\cdot92x)/$
$(12,000+65\cdot88x)$ thalers.

Which, with only a trifling deviation, may be reduced to the
following formula:

$$1 \text{ bushel of rye} = \frac{273-5\cdot5x}{182+x} \text{ thalers}$$

A calculation of the freight costs of taking one full load of 2400 *lb
to the Town*

If the full load is to arrive in the Town, other wagons carrying the
feed for the animals must accompany those with the produce.

For a distance of 5 miles from the Town the normal load per
wagon is 2250 lb of grain or produce and 150 lb of feed; so that here
it will take one wagon with feed to get 15 full loads of 2400 lb each
delivered to the Town.

Sixteen teams of horses, whose labour costs $16(2\cdot57$ bushels of
12   rye $+1\cdot63$ thalers), deliver only 15 loads to the Town. In freight
charges this makes $(16/15)(2\cdot57$ bushels of rye $+1\cdot63$ thalers) for
each full load.

For a distance of 10 miles, a wagon must normally take 300 lb
of feed, so that the load itself will only be 2100 lb. Seven full loads
will need 1 wagon with feed; so that here one full load delivered to
the Town costs in transport $(8/7)(2\cdot57$ bushels of rye $+1\cdot63$ thalers).

At a distance of x miles, the feed to be taken along for each full
load is $30x$ lb, so that the load itself is $2400-30x$ lb. For each wagon
that is to arrive in the Town with a full grain load, $30x$ lb of feed have
to be taken along on another separate wagon. One wagon can thus

carry the feed for $(2400-30x)/30x$ others, or one wagon carrying feed has to accompany every $(2400-30x)/30x$ full loads.

$\{(2400-30x)/30x\}+1$ wagon $= 2400/30x$ wagons, each of which costs $(2\cdot57x$ bushels of rye $+1\cdot63x$ thalers$)/5$, and together they therefore cost $(2400/30x)(2\cdot57x$ bushels of rye $+1\cdot63x$ thalers$)/5$ bringing to the Town $(2400-30x)/30x$ full loads.

The freight per load therefore comes to

$$\frac{(2\cdot57x \text{ bushels of rye}+1\cdot63x \text{ thalers})}{5} \times \frac{2400}{2400-30x}$$

$$= (2\cdot57x \text{ bushels of rye}+1\cdot63x \text{ thalers}) \times \frac{16}{80-x} \qquad 13$$

$$= \frac{41x \text{ bushels}+26x \text{ thalers}}{80-x}$$

But in the district x miles from the Town, the price of rye (per bushel) $= (273-5\cdot5x)/(182+x)$.

When we set this price for rye in the formula given above, we find that

$$\frac{11,193x-225x^2}{(182+x)(80-x)} + \frac{26x}{80-x} = \frac{15,925x-199\cdot5x^2}{(182+x)(80-x)}$$

An insignificant difference apart, this formula coincides with the following: $199\cdot5x/(182+x)$.

In all subsequent calculations I therefore assume that transport costs per load of 2400 lb are $199\cdot5x/(182+x)$ thalers.

When x (the distance from the Town) is	Transport costs (per load) are
1 mile	1·09 thalers
5 miles	5·33 thalers
10 miles	10·4 thalers
20 miles	19·8 thalers
30 miles	28·2 thalers

CHAPTER 5A

THE CONCEPT OF LAND RENT

WE MUST distinguish carefully between the farm revenue[1] and the pure product[2] of the soil as such.[3]

Every farm is endowed with buildings, fences, timber and other objects of value which may be separated from the land. It follows that the income of the farm does not entirely derive from land but is in part the interest on the capital invested in these objects.

That portion of the farm revenue that is left after deduction of the interest on the value of the buildings, timber, fences and all other valuable objects *separable from the land*, that portion which pertains to the land itself, I shall call *land rent*.[4]

Someone who thinks of buying a farm on which every building, tree and fence has burned down will, when estimating its value, first calculate the net product which may be yielded by this property when everything upon it has been rebuilt; but he will not decide on the price he is prepared to pay until he has worked out how much land rent will remain when all the interest on the capital that is invested in the reconstruction has been repaid.

A problem so simple in practice has, however, proved difficult to express in scientific terms and has led several economists into conceptual error.

Adam Smith,* who on this matter has been followed by most economists even in most recent times, asserts that *"land rent"*[5] is

* See his discussion in Chapter XI of the *Enquiries into the Wealth of Nations*.[6]

1 *Einkünfte:* translated throughout as revenue, or income.
2 *Ertrag:* here translated as product, in other contexts as yield, and occasionally as output.　　　3 *"an sich"*.
4 *Landrente*. It will later be seen that this term is equivalent to "economic rent" in English classical economics, and Dempsey so translated it in Part II of *Der Isolierte Staat* (cf. *The Frontier Wage*, 193, and subsequently).
5 Smith's own term is "the rent of land".
6 The relevant passage stands at the beginning of the chapter: "Rent, considered as the price paid for the use of land, is naturally the highest which the tenant can

that which remains of the product of a farm or its equivalent value in money after the tenant farmer has paid his labourers, borne all the other costs of management, and drawn the current rate of return[1] from the capital he has invested.

From this, and from Smith's use of the term "land rent", it follows that what he calls land rent is the income which a landowner who has rented out his property draws from it.

But this rent, which henceforth I shall call "estate rent"[2] is composed of the pure rent of land and of the interest on the value of the buildings and other equipment.

Between the amount of capital thus invested in a farm and the pure rent of land there is no fixed relation; and depending on variations in the price of the product and in the physical quality of the soil, etc., any relation between the two is possible. Adam Smith's "land rent" (estate rent) therefore supplies us with no measure of the actual land rent, or pure rent of land.[3] By dividing the price of products into (1) wage, (2) return on capital, and (3) land rent, and allowing land rent—in Adam Smith's use of the term—to contain an indeterminate amount of return on capital, we are losing all possibility of clear and accurate thinking.

If we accept Smith's definition, and want to show how a change in the return on capital—wage and land rent remaining constant— affects the price of the product, we would be leaving out of the calculation that portion of return on capital which is contained in the land rent (estate rent). If, on the other hand, we want to show how a rise in land rent—wage and return on capital remaining constant— changes the price of the product, we would, in raising land rent, simultaneously be raising that portion of the return on capital which

afford to pay in the actual circumstances of the land. In adjusting the terms of the lease, the landlord endeavours to leave him no greater share of the produce than what is sufficient to keep up the stock from which he furnishes the seed, pays the labour, and purchases and maintains the cattle and other instruments of husbandry, together with the ordinary profits of farming stock in the neighbourhood". A. SMITH, *An Inquiry into the Nature and Causes of the Wealth of Nations*, ed. E. CANNAN London (1950), I. 145.

[1] *Kapitalgewinn*. Thünen uses the term in the strict classical economic sense, as that share of the product which is due to the contributor of the capital. The translation seems preferable to "interest", since Thünen himself uses *"Zinsfuss"* and *"Zins"* in Part Two.
[2] *Gutsrente*. The translation "estate rent" conveys the sense of "real estate" better than "farm rent" would do.
[3] *Rente des Bodens, Bodenrente:* equivalent to "rent" in the English classical sense, and to "land rent" as Thünen uses the term. Subsequently translated as pure rent, or rent.

is contained in the land rent and ought to remain constant. In both cases the findings would be wrong.

---

16   Adam Smith's concept of land rent appears to be based on the following considerations.

Capital that is invested in the buildings of a farm cannot be removed and put into another property; it has become part of the land, yielding interest only where this is farmed. Now if, as a result of a fall in the price of agricultural products, the estate rent falls until it is less than the interest payable on the capital invested in the buildings, the pure rent will not merely sink to zero, but will become negative. This however ought not to stop the owner from continuing to farm his land, for if he were to do so, he would derive no revenue whatever from his invested capital. However, if the estate rent remains constant, while the local rate of interest rises, the pure rent will sink by precisely as much as the rent from the invested capital will rise. There is thus an inverse relation between the two types of rent, and since cultivation still continues when the pure rent has become negative, it appears that the division of estate rent into pure rent and capital rent is not only inadmissible, but pointless, since estate rent (land rent according to Adam Smith) is the actual regulator.

This is how the problem appears when regarded in terms of isolated instances and short-term periods; it looks quite different from a more general point of view, when our sights are fixed on the ultimate objectives.

Suppose that there is a sum of capital, newly formed by work and thrift, which cannot be invested in existing enterprises at the *ruling interest rate*. Its owner therefore decides to cultivate a hitherto
17   worthless piece of wasteland and to construct buildings on it, and as a result he is able to draw from his farm the rate of interest obtaining elsewhere in the country. If we ignore the cost of reclaiming the land —which we must do to avoid confusing the general picture by studying two independent factors simultaneously—we shall find that the entire estate rent of this new holding consists of return on capital, and that the pure rent equals zero.

Suppose now that the interest rate rises from 4 to 5 per cent, while the farm revenue remains unchanged. The pure rent would become negative, though cultivation would continue because the capital invested in the buildings is immobile.

But if all the buildings are burnt down, no fresh capital will be spent on their reconstruction, and the land will revert to wilderness.

Fire destroys at once. Time too destroys buildings, though more slowly; and once they begin to crumble they will, in the given situation, not be rebuilt, and here too the land will revert to wilderness.

If in the course of a century a hundred such farms are founded in succession, and the life of their buildings is estimated at one hundred years, each year one farm will be abandoned, and after a hundred years the entire complex will have disappeared.

Thus it is not the size of the estate rent which determines whether land continues in cultivation, but the size of the pure rent.

Several errors in Adam Smith's system derive from his theory of land rent, which treats the interest on the capital used to construct the buildings as the product of the land as such. These are:

1. That wherever land is farmed it must yield rent.
2. That labour employed in agriculture is more profitable and productive than that employed in industry.
3. That Nature helps the farmer while doing nothing for the manufacturer.

Let us briefly deal with these points.

1. Where the interest payable on the value of the buildings used in an industry is not deducted, this industry too will yield rent.
2. Where the interest is not deducted, far more remains of the labour product of the workers[1] after the entrepreneur has drawn the normal current return for his efforts and for the capital he has invested in the machinery and equipment (not including the buildings) than the workers can consume. Here again labour will be very productive.
3. Industrial production depends as much on natural forces as does farming.

That so profound a thinker as Adam Smith, whose study of national wealth lays bare the workings of an inquiring and inventive mind and provides, in my opinion, an inexhaustible source of

---

[1] *Arbeitsprodukt der Arbeiter.*

enlightenment and knowledge, that such a man remained baffled by the nature of land rent, though he unravelled so many problems in political economy, is perhaps explicable in the following way.

19   Smith's system appears to have been based on the physiocratic school; and though he qualifies and amends their—mistaken—doctrine that "*labour employed in agriculture is the only productive form of labour*", he himself knew too little of the practical side of farming to free his mind wholly from the physiocratic error by means of personal experience and observation.

Ricardo, in his work on Political Economy (which I had not read when I wrote the first draft of this work), attacks Smith's theory of land rent and puts up the following thesis: "*Rent is that portion of the produce of the earth, which is paid to the landlord for the use of the original and indestructible powers of the soil.*" [1]

According to this definition, Ricardo distinguishes between interest on the capital invested in the buildings and the product of the soil as such.

It is interesting, and instructive, to see how Say, in his notes on Ricardo's Work and in his *Traité d'Economie Politique*, endeavours to attack Ricardo and to defend his own, mistaken, theory.

If this may happen to a man as intelligent as Say, it ought to warn each and everyone of us to be alert to the dangers of a closed mind.

We must have the flexibility of mind to abandon theories and beliefs which have grown obsolete; so that we may be able to comprehend and assimilate truths that contradict our own cherished ideas.

———————

    Adam Smith's theory of land rent still has many followers; and since all I shall be saying on the theme of land rent would become

20 hopelessly confused if his concept were applied to what I describe as land rent, I have thought it necessary to explain both views.

———————

[1] *The Works and Correspondence of David Ricardo*, ed. P. SRAFFA, Vol. I: *On the Principles of Political Economy and Taxation* (Cambridge 1951), 67.

THE EFFECT OF THE GRAIN PRICE ON LAND RENT

WE HAVE now reached the point whence the present author set out on his inquiries.

A deep urge compelled him to obtain a clear picture of the influence of grain prices on farming and of the laws governing these prices. This problem could be solved only by means of precise and detailed calculations on the costs of every branch of farming, based on data taken from reality; and with this end in view the author kept (and is still keeping) extremely detailed accounts on his estate at Tellow.

Every single task which is undertaken at Tellow is noted in the work-book; and at the end of each year the entries are summarised to show how many people were required for mowing or harrowing, how much work one labourer or one team of horses could perform, and so on. In the same way the Tellow finance- and grain-books, when edited in association with the work-books, supply the data for working out the "energy costs",[1] e.g. the cost of a day labourer's family, a team of horses, or a hoeing machine.

The amount and expense of the labour taken to till a field and harvest a crop gives us the production costs of this crop, and the gross product,[2] minus the production costs, gives us the net surplus obtained from its cultivation.

For the five years from 1810 to 1815, I worked out the net product[3] of each crop, of dairying, sheep-farming, and of every branch of my estate at Tellow, and, but for 29·8 thalers annually, my findings coincided with the total net product.

The findings of this calculation form the basis for all the calculations and findings in this work.

[1] *arbeitende Kräfte:* i.e. all energy, whether human (labour costs), animal or mechanical.
[2] *Rohertrag*, translated throughout as "gross product".
[3] *Reinertrag*, translated throughout as "net product".

But because we are setting out from the experience of one particular estate, gathered over a very short period of time, the following problem immediately arises, namely: How will the land rent and farming system change at Tellow if we assume a gradual fall in the grain price?

In the discussion of this problem (which is based entirely on real conditions (Tellow)), the Isolated State is only a graphic representation, a model to help us see the problem as a whole; but it is a model which we cannot abandon, because it is, as we shall see, so rich in consequences.[1]

22

* * *

On the farm itself the value of grain falls with increasing distance from the Town. By working out how gradually declining grain prices affect the Tellow farming system, we shall be able to locate the precise point in the Isolated State which corresponds to each stage in the declining price of grain. We may, then, imagine Tellow in the Isolated State, obtaining by this means a graphic illustration, a diagram, of the adjustments this estate would have to undergo in answer to reductions in the grain price.

23

The various types of labour required in grain production fall into two groups:

1. Those related to the size of the arable acreage.
2. Those related to the size of the harvest.

The first group includes: ploughing, hoeing, harrowing, sowing, clearing ditches, etc.,—whether the harvest is good or poor the amount of work to be performed remains the same for any given area of land, depending on the quality of the soil, not on its yield. All these types of work are included in the term "work of cultivation", and their costs I shall call "cultivation costs".

The second group includes: manuring, bringing in the harvest, threshing, and so forth. Threshing and bringing in the harvest quite evidently depend on the size of the harvest. So, however, does manuring, because the degree to which soil fertility is exhausted depends on the size of the harvest; and the greater the exhaustion, the larger the amount of manure required to restore the lost fertility. The costs of the labours in this group are covered by the term "harvesting costs".

[1] Here the original contains a long footnote on the philosophical nature of Thünen's analysis.

For any given soil, variations in the yield per unit area—assuming
farming system and all other factors of relevance remain stationary 24
—will be determined by the amount of plant food in the soil.*
Since cultivation costs per unit area do not change, whereas
harvesting costs vary directly with yield per unit area, it is possible,
by differentiating precisely between the two types of cost, to work out
the revenue of a farm for every level of soil fertility.

Applying the observations made at Tellow to top-grade barley
land and to the Mecklenburg improved seven-course rotation[1] with 25
the following sequence:

1. Fallow
2. Rye
3. Barley

* I refer always to soil of the same original quality, but at different levels of
fertility.[2] There is no doubt that an exhausting farming system may reduce to a
mere 4 bushel-crops the output of a soil with a yield of 10 bushel-crops;[3] and
though this lower yield reduces harvesting costs, cultivation costs are the same
as for a higher yield.
   Soils differing in physical quality may, *given the same content of manure and
humus*, yet produce widely differing yields; loam perhaps 10 bushel-crops, a
sandy soil only 6, and for loam the cultivation costs will be far higher than for a
sandy soil. But the effect on the yield and on cultivation costs of soils differing in
quality is nowhere the object of my inquiry. I ought to mention at this point that
the figures I use and the resulting numerical proportions stem from a single point
of my experience, and thus are valid only for that particular standpoint; so that
similar calculations made for different conditions will have to be based on different figures, and will produce different numerical results. My method, however,
is universally applicable; and that which has been studied from every angle will
invariably lead to the same general conclusions.

   [1] *Mecklenburgische siebenschlägige Koppelwirtschaft:* a system still common in
Schleswig-Holstein and East Prussia as well as Mecklenburg, in which arable land
rotates with intensively-used ley grass. Cf. E. OTREMBA, *Die Deutsche Agrarland-
schaft* (Wiesbaden 1956), p. 51. The Koppel was the small enclosed plot into which
the farm was divided; cf. *Brockhaus ABC der Landwirtschaft*, I. (Leipzig 1957) p. 772.
Koppelwirtschaft is translated throughout by "improved system", since it has simi-
larities to the "improved rotations" introduced in eighteenth-century English mixed
farming.
   [2] *Reichtum:* translated in this edition as "fertility", "level of fertility" or "the amount
of plant food in the soil". This is the first introduction to the important distinction
Thünen draws between the *physische Beschaffenheit des Bodens*, translated as the
"inherent quality of the soil", or "basic fertility", and *Reichtum*, the level of fertility the
soil has currently attained under cultivation. At this point Thünen is equating *Reichtum* with the *yield*, measured in bushel–crops (see p. 26); later, in Chapter 7a, he will
begin to measure *Reichtum* in degrees, but in various places he will assume a direct
and simple relationship between fertility (in degrees) and yield (in bushel-crops).
But his later researches, recorded in Chapter 7b (here summarised), led to the
conclusion that the relationship was more complex.
   [3] *Bushel-Crops.* (*Körner.*) Thünen introduces this important term here without
defining it. See his definition on p. 26.

4. Oats
5. Pasture
6. Pasture
7. Pasture

we obtain the following results.

If on 100 square rods the yield in bushel-crops* is 10 Berlin bushels of rye, and on the farm itself (i.e. after subtraction of the transport costs) rye is worth 1·291 gold thalers the Berlin bushel, then a plot of 100,000 Mecklenburg square rods yields:

	Gold thalers	Gold thalers
a gross product of		5074

The costs are as follows:

1. Sowing costs—the seed value of the three grain crops and of the clover	626	
2. Cultivation costs	873	
3. Harvesting costs	765	

4A. General farming costs, which cannot be ascribed to any single branch of the enterprise, i.e.:

(a) Administration.
(b) Maintenance of the buildings.
(c) Insurance (hail and fire).
(d) Church and school rate.
(e) Interest on the working capital (the interest on the value of the tools and equipment being distributed among the various branches).
(f) Support of the needy on the estate.
(g) The night-watchman's wage.
(h) Maintenance of paths, bridges, streams and ditches.
(i) Various costs related to the enterprise as a whole.

* The expression "the soil yields a crop of so and so many Berlin bushels of rye on 100 square rods", is so tortuous, but would nevertheless have to recur so frequently, that I have decided to give the yield in bushel-crops (*Körner*)[1] in future. Whenever I mention yield in bushel-crops, I am referring to the product from an area of 100 Mecklenburg square rods, expressed in Berlin bushels of rye; this avoids any misunderstanding that might otherwise arise from this expression.

[1] Here Thünen adapts to his own definition a colloquial measure from the agriculture of his day. The term conveys the rough sense of "ten-fold", "six-fold", etc., in English. Here it is translated throughout as "bushel-crops", which better conveys Thünen's own special meaning of "a crop of *x* bushels from 100 square rods".

4B. Interest on the value of the buildings and
fences. At a 5 per cent interest rate, the
general farming costs* together with the
interest on the value of the buildings and
so on come to   1350
or 26·6 per cent of the gross product, to
which these expenses[1] are closely related,
though the ratio is not an exact one.

Together, these four kinds of costs come to 3614 thalers, and
subtracting this from the gross product, or 5074 thalers, we find that
the net product of the soil,[2] or land rent, is 1460 thalers.

Here I must draw attention to the fact that the costs I list as
connected with farming do not include, either directly or indirectly,   27
taxes paid to the state. The object of our inquiry demands that
initially we consider the Isolated State and its system of farming
under the assumption that no taxes are paid to the state.[3] What
we mean by land rent is therefore the net revenue of soil before
deduction of taxes.

The propositions given above make it possible also to work out
the land rent produced by the same soil where it contains less plant
food and is consequently at a lower level of fertility.

Let the rye yield be 8 bushel-crops. The rye yield is also the
measure of the productivity of the two succeeding grain crops and of
the pasture; bearing thus a direct relation to the total gross product.

	thalers	thalers
		5074
At a yield of 10 bushel-crops the gross product was		
For 8 bushel-crops it will therefore be $\frac{8}{10}$ × 5074 or	4059	
Sowing costs remain	626	
Cultivation costs remain	873	
Harvesting costs vary with yield, and come to $\frac{8}{10}$ × 765, or	612	
General farming costs (which include the interest on the value of the buildings) are related to the gross yield and come to $\frac{8}{10}$ × 1350 or	1080	
Total costs	3191	

Therefore land rent is   868 thalers

* Subsequently, the costs listed under 4B are included in the term "general
farming costs".

[1] i.e. Items 4A and 4B.
[2] der reine Ertrag des Bodens. Thünen equates net product of the soil—that is after
deduction of interest on the farm capital—directly with land rent.
[3] In Section 3, Chapters 34-8, Thünen relaxes this assumption.

28 But these calculations, where money is the measure, can refer only to one set of conditions and one particular price of grain (here 1·291 thalers the bushel); with the slightest variation in the grain price the results too will change. And since rye fetches such very different prices in the different rings of the Isolated State we must, to obtain a general formula, take rye as our measure, because costs and revenue are related to, and can be measured in, rye.

The gross product of a holding farmed in the pure seven-course improved system (as we have just depicted it) is made up in part of rye and in part of animal products. The other grain types, oats and barley, may be expressed in rye in terms of their relative nutritive value; so that it is possible to express the entire grain harvest by its rye equivalent.

Two possible price-relations may exist between rye and animal products such as meat and butter.

1. To the extent that meat is of greater nutritive value and replaces a larger quantity of bread, a fixed price-relation exists between the two.
2. To the extent that animal products cost either more or less to produce than does grain, their market price will vary with the ruling grain price.

29 This inquiry will be based on the first assumption: That the price-relation between grain and animal products is constant throughout the Isolated State.

Where this condition obtains, animal products can be expressed in their equivalent in rye, and it is possible to give the gross product of cultivation entirely in rye.

The results of the discussion will show whether or not this assumption holds for the Isolated State.

Of the various farming costs, sowing costs consist almost entirely of grain and need only be converted to rye.

A portion of the cultivation, harvesting and general farming costs consist likewise directly of grain: the thresher's wage for instance, the cost of feeding the men and horses, and others. Another portion is paid partly in money and partly in grain. Thus the day labourer's wage and the artisan's fee do not depend entirely on the grain price; but they are higher where the average price of grain is high and lower where it is low. These costs must therefore be given in rye as well as in money, in the proportion each represents in the total labour cost.

The third and last part of these costs, the cost of salt and metals, is not connected with the grain price, for although the price of these products has some connexion with the ruling grain price in the district where they are mined and processed, their value cannot be measured by the rye price obtaining in the district where they are used. If they have to be brought over long distances these minerals may be most costly in areas where grain is very cheap. This part of costs will have to be expressed in money.

The portion of costs to be expressed in grain and money respectively will differ for each country and each province. The more a nation produces its own necessities, the more evenly mines and factories are spread throughout the countryside, reducing transport costs on the exchange of goods, the more rye will be the measure of value, and the greater will be the portion of farming costs which may be expressed in rye. The fewer factories there are in a region, the more it depends on trade with distant places (i.e. the greater the distance between consumer and producer), the larger will be the portion of farming costs which has to be expressed in money.

But however much this numerical price-relation differs for different conditions, it is certain that such a relation exists everywhere, that there is not a single country where these costs may be given wholly in money or wholly in grain. For each different set of circumstances the calculations will be based on different figures, but the method of obtaining the results will remain the same.

* * *

Thünen then uses the empirical results obtained earlier, to consider the case where costs must be expressed one-quarter in money, and three-quarters in grain. In the case above, the gross product of the harvest was 5074 thalers, or 3930 bushels of rye. He finds that the total costs were 2220 bushels of rye and 747 thalers. Subtracting the costs from the product, we have 3930 minus 2220, or 1710 bushels; from this 747 thalers are still to be subtracted. This inconsistency in the units can be resolved by finding the money value of the output at various prices of grain. Doing this Thünen discovers that the net land rent (i.e. the remaining surplus) varies very greatly in relation to the price of grain; at the price of 2 thalers the bushel, rent on the 10,000 square rods is 2673 thalers; at 1½ thalers it is 1818 thalers, at 1 thaler it is 963 thalers, at ½ thaler only 108 thalers, and at the price of 0·437 thalers the bushel, rent disappears altogether.

30

30–35

Thünen proceeds to calculate the pure rent for soils of varying fertility. With falling fertility, the gross output decreases, and while sowing and cultivation costs remain constant, harvesting and general farming costs decline. The total costs therefore decrease, but not as fast as gross output decreases, so that relative to output costs rise, and land rent eventually disappears. Thus:

Soil fertility	Gross product bushels	Costs bushels thalers	Land rent bushels thalers	Price (in thalers) per bushel at which land rent vanishes
10 bushel-crop land	3930	2220 plus 747	1710 minus 747	0·437
9 bushel-crop land	3537	2098 plus 694	1439 minus 694	0·482
8 bushel-crop land	3144	1976 plus 641	1168 minus 641	0·549
7 bushel-crop land	2751	1854 plus 588	897 minus 588	0·656
6 bushel-crop land	2358	1732 plus 535	626 minus 535	0·855
5 bushel-crop land	1965	1610 plus 482	355 minus 482	1·358
4 bushel-crop land	1769	1549 plus 455	220 minus 455	2·068

* * *

35   This table demonstrates the following law:

The lower the fertility of soil, the more expensive the crop is to produce—and soil of low fertility can be cultivated only when the price of grain is high.

───────────

Before we may continue, we have to take a look at the method we have been using, and ask whether generally-valid laws can be developed from observations made for one particular set of circumstances.

36   The following point might—and doubtless will—be made:

"These calculations of the labour costs and the relation between gross and net product may well be taken from observed experience with the utmost faithfulness: nevertheless they apply only to one set of conditions, one particular estate. On the very next holding conditions are already different; the soil is different, so are the labourers. The soil may be easier or more difficult to farm, the workmen more or less industrious; the soil will consequently require more or less labour for its cultivation, and labour itself, depending on the varying capacities of the workmen, will be cheaper or more costly. Calculations based on data taken from the first estate cannot be wholly valid for any other place, they hold true only of the place where they were made. And from something that is valid for one place, and one place only, no generally-valid laws can be constructed."

My answer is this:

"True, my calculations do not entirely apply to the farm next-door, and even less to distant ones in other regions of the world, where the national characteristics of the workers may differ totally. But surely we are not prepared to say that all the detailed knowledge of net product and production costs a farmer gains in years of observation on one holding becomes useless when he moves to another farm? If this were so, a farmer would have to start his apprenticeship anew with every change of habitat, and no-one could learn husbandry but in the place where he will pass his life. This argument is clearly inadmissable, and knowledge gained in one particular spot must therefore have some general validity which is not limited to time or place. It is this generally-valid knowledge, which it is my object to discover."

I have already given three propositions which I hold to be of general validity, whose accuracy determines that of my entire inquiry. I shall, therefore, repeat them.

First. On the farm itself the value of grain falls with increasing distance from the market.

The greater the distance between farm and market, the more expensive grain is to transport, and the lower, consequently, its value on the farm.

Grain, like every other commodity, is valueless if there is no demand for it. In the Isolated State, the only consumers for the grain that is produced over and above the needs of the farm are the Townsmen. If grain is brought to the Town from districts so remote that the draught animals consume half the load (or its equivalent value) on the journey, and only half a load reaches the Town, it is easy to see why the farmer will not be able to obtain more money for two bushels of rye in the provinces than for one bushel in the Town.

This proposition probably requires neither proof nor explanation.

37

38   Second. Not all the prices of the articles the farmer has to buy are related to the grain price. In other words, the same amount of grain will not pay the farming costs in the different parts of the State. This proposition derives from the first one, since a product which fetche as much as one bushel of rye in the Town, must necessarily fetch as much as two bushels in a remote province, where rye is worth only half its Town value—assuming of course that this product is obtainable only from the Town.

To this class as we have seen belong salt and metals, so does cloth, and indeed every article which only the Town can supply.

The salaries of professional people are likewise included in this class. The doctor, the civil servant, and many others, can obtain their training only in the Town. The amount of capital they spend on their training depends, therefore, on the prices in the Town; and if these people are to obtain an adequate return on their outlay, their salary cannot be governed by the rye price in the district where they settle down to practice.

Third. One portion of the costs of grain production depends on the area in cultivation, another on the size of the harvest.

I have included in the former the sowing and cultivation costs, and in the latter the harvesting and general farming costs.

People may question this distinction. They may argue that a change in output from any given area of land will affect sowing and 39   cultivation costs; that harvesting costs will not be the same for a small as for a larger plot. But no-one will seriously maintain that a ploughman's labour depends on the size of the harvest, or that the cost of bringing in the harvest is entirely governed by the size of the plot. However much my distinction is modified, it will still be true that some labours depend on the area under plough, others on the size of the harvest.

Suppose now that someone takes as the starting point for his inquiry another property, quite unlike Tellow. Suppose that he calculates the labour costs, the production costs of grain, the land rent, etc., from the data taken from this property; that he continues the calculation on the basis of the propositions and methods I have described; and that he finally draws conclusions from his calculation. Despite the fact that the two inquiries are based on wholly different figures, a comparison would show many of the final findings and conclusions, when expressed in words, to be identical.

And if the same method, applied to a third and a fourth farm, were to produce findings in common, we would have to accept that we had discovered a generally-valid law, for that which remains constant in all conditions must have a general validity not limited by time or place.

Were it permissible to prove this point by anticipating future   40
chapters, we might cite several findings which are considered later; but we may at any rate adduce the law already stated: with declining soil fertility, grain production becomes progressively more costly.

These laws, being universal, are valid for each farming system and each property. The size of the harvest, of the net revenue, etc., are the visible expression of these laws, modified by local circumstances.

If for a given set of circumstances we do not assume arbitrary quantities, but take these from reality, drawing the logical conclusions from these quantities and from the general principles, we may be certain that even these conclusions, based as they are on one particular set of circumstances only, will contain some general laws; though it is also certain that not every result which is obtained in this way will be a general law; many will be only locally-valid rules.

No human being can study a subject from several points of view, let alone every point of view (which as we have shown distinguishes the generally-valid from the merely local); it follows therefore that it is extremely important to discover ways whereby the individual may learn to distinguish general laws from laws of only local validity.

Algebra provides us with the necessary tool; for if the nature of the subject allows letters to be substituted for numbers, and if the calculations made with the letters reach the same result as those made with figures, then this result will be generally valid, not merely a local rule.

To demonstrate this procedure, we shall use a general formula to   41
express land rent and the price of rye at which land rent becomes equal to zero.

Let the yield, in bushel-crops, be[1,2] y
The gross product ay thalers
Sowing costs b
Cultivation costs c

[1] y has been substituted here for x in the original, because Thünen usually uses x to express distance from the Town.
[2] Thünen evidently means all the items here to refer to a *unit of area*.

Between the gross product and the costs related to the size of the harvest—that is the harvesting costs together with the general farming costs—let the ratio be $1 : q$, where q must be a fraction, because these costs can consume only a portion of, but never the total, harvest.

And since $1 : q = ay : aqy$, the costs related to the gross product $= aqy$ thalers.

Let the portion of the labour and general farming costs that has to be expressed in money be p; then the portion to be expressed in grain will be $1-p$, where p is a fraction. Let the value of rye on the farm itself be equal to h thalers.

If the costs are expressed in both grain and money, in the proportion that each constitutes in the costs, we obtain the following sum:

The gross product equals ay/h bushels of rye

Sowing costs b/h bushels of rye

Cultivation costs $c(1-p)/h$ bushels of rye $+ pc$ thalers

Harvesting and general farming costs $aqy(1-p)/h$ bushels $+ apqy$ thalers

Land rent therefore equals

$$\frac{ay}{h} - \left(\frac{b+c(1-p)+aqy(1-p)}{h}\right) \text{ bushels} - p(aqy+c) \text{ thalers.}$$

If the land rent becomes equal to zero, then

$$\frac{ay}{h} - \left(\frac{b+c(1-p)+aqy(1-p)}{h}\right) \text{ bushels} = p(aqy+c) \text{ thalers;}$$

therefore $(ay-b-(1-p)(aqy+c))$ bushels $= hp(aqy+c)$ thalers;

therefore   1 bushel $= \dfrac{hp(aqy+c)}{ay-b-(1-p)(aqy+c)}$ thalers

The object of this calculation was to discover the effect of increases or reductions in the yield per unit area on the price at which land rent becomes equal to zero.

But the formula we have found does not yet tell us whether the price of rye rises or falls when y (the volume of output in bushel-crops) rises, since y is present in both numerator and denominator.

We must therefore rearrange the equation in order to discover the effect of y on the price of rye.

The price of one bushel is $= \dfrac{hp(aqy+c)}{ay-b-(1-p)(aqy+c)}$ thalers

Therefore it also $= \dfrac{hp}{\dfrac{ay-b}{aqy+c}-(1-p)}$ thalers

1358313

Let us suppose that $aqy+c=z$, where z increases with increasing values of y, and vice versa. Therefore $y=(z-c)/aq$. When this value for y is substituted for y in the above formula, we obtain

$$\frac{hp}{\dfrac{az-ac-baq}{aqz}-(1-p)} = \frac{hp}{a-\left(\dfrac{ac+baq}{z}\right)-(1-p)}$$

Now unquestionably $(ac+baq)/z$ decreases with increasing values of z; but the smaller the negative part of the denominator, the greater the whole denominator. y increases with any increase in z, and the denominator continues to grow with an increasing y while the numerator remains constant: hence the size of the fraction that expresses the rye price will fall with rising y and conversely, the smaller the value of y, the higher the price of rye.

43

With this, the proposition, "the greater the fall in soil fertility the more expensive is production per bushel-crop", has been proved a generally-valid law.

But such a simple and familiar proposition is equally well proved by direct reasoning; and had it not been our aim to demonstrate the method of obtaining proof, and to establish, once and for all, the standpoint from which all subsequent discussions are to be regarded, such a careful calculation would scarcely have been worth the bother.

———————

Problem. To discover the land rent of a farm with a yield of 8 bushel-crops at x miles from the Town.

At 8 bushel-crops, the land rent on 100,000 square rods is equal to 1168 bushels of rye less 641 thalers.

In Chapter 4 we saw that on the farm x miles from the Town, rye is worth $(273 - 5 \cdot 5x)/(182 + x)$ thalers the bushel. It follows that the land rent equals

$$\left(\frac{1168(273 - 5 \cdot 5x)}{182 + x} \right) - 641 \text{ thalers}$$

$$= \frac{202,202 - 7065x}{182 + x} \text{ thalers}$$

44

When x, the distance from the market, is	The land rent on 100,000 square rods with a yield of 8 bushel-crops is
1 mile	1066 thalers
5 miles	892 thalers
10 miles	685 thalers
15 miles	488 thalers
20 miles	301 thalers
25 miles	124 thalers
28·6 miles	0 thalers

CHAPTER 6

GRAIN PRICE AND FARMING SYSTEM

LET US assume that in all parts of the Isolated State, with the exception only of the first ring, the soil has the level of fertility to produce a yield, after the fallow, of 8 bushel-crops of rye in a seven-course improved rotation (which is 8 bushels per 100 square rods, or 9·44 bushels the Magdeburg Morgen).[1] The soil of the surrounding wilderness is of the same physical quality and contains the same amount of plant food as that of the cultivated plain and therefore has the same productive potential.

In Chapter 5 we saw that a plot of 100,000 square rods with this yield per unit area produces a land rent of 1168 bushels of rye minus 641 thalers.[2]

Land rent disappears or becomes equal to zero when 1168 bushels of rye have the same value as 641 thalers, i.e. when the bushel of rye costs 0·549 thalers, or 26·4 shillings.

We must see now where in the Isolated State rye is worth 0·549 thalers.

In Chapter 4 we saw that rye fetches $(273 - 5·5x)/(182 + x)$ thalers the bushel on the farm x miles from the Town. By equating 0·549 with $(273 - 5·5x)/(182 + x)$ we find that $x = 28·6$. Rye therefore fetches 0·549 thalers the bushel in the district 28·6 miles from the Town.

In the conditions we have postulated, the farm 28·6 miles from the Town yields no land rent.

Farther than 28·6 miles, land rent becomes negative, that is, cultivation is associated with losses, and the soil cannot continue to be farmed as in the districts nearer the Town.

But this point, though it marks the limit of farming in the improved system, does not necessarily mark the absolute limit of arable

[1] Here Thünen repeats his own definition of *Körner*, or "bushel-crops". The *Magdeburg Morgen*, which is nowhere else referred to, is evidently the *Prussian Morgen* or acre of 117·86 Mecklenburg square rods. (Magdeburg was part of Prussia when Thünen wrote.) This would however give 9·43 bushels per Morgen, not 9·44.

[2] *Supra*, Table on p. 30.

45

farming; for if there were a system which required less labour (and hence lower costs) than the improved system, soil could still produce a surplus and a land rent at a rye price of 0·549 thalers the bushel. In such a situation, cultivation would remain profitable at a still greater distance from the Town.

Now we must consider how the value of the different plots belonging to one holding will vary with their distance from the farmyard, given that these plots are identical in size and in the quality and condition of their soil. The costs of manuring and bringing in the harvest are directly related to distance between plot and farmyard. On all other types of work performed out in the field, the time the men and horses spend on the journey to and from their work is lost; and this loss rises with distance from the farmstead. It follows that labour costs are lower for plots near the farmstead than for those at a distance, and with the same fertility the former must produce a larger net product than the latter.

If the total product of a holding farmed in the improved system is equal to zero at the point where rye fetches 0·549 thalers the bushel, and the nearer plots yield a higher net product than the distant ones, it follows *that on the one section of the land the net product is positive and on the other negative, and that the losses on the distant plots wipe out the gains of cultivating the nearer ones, so that for the holding as a whole the net product will sink to zero.*

An improved system with a total net product of zero will again produce a positive net product when the distant plots are left untilled and only those near the farmstead remain in cultivation. In these conditions tillage need not cease at 28·6 miles from the Town.

At even greater distance from the market or a still lower price for grain even this version of the improved system, where tillage is restricted to land near the farmstead, will cease to give a positive net product. If some form of cultivation is to continue further labour economies are called for.

In the improved system, the break-up of the ley[1] and its preparation for the winter seed are of vital importance. With a soft fallow,[2]

[1] *Dreesch.* The so-called *Dreesch system,* or *Feldgrasssystem,* formerly common in Germany, consisted of a year's fallow, followed by 2–4 years of grain, followed by a 3–4 year grass ley (Dreesch). Cf. W. MÜLLER-WILLE, *Westfalen* (Münster 1952), 205, quoting J. N. VON SCHWERZ, *Beschreibung der Landwirtschaft in Westfalen und Rheinpreussen* (Stuttgart 1836), I. 174.
[2] *Mürbebrache.* Literally a "brittle" fallow, sometimes known as "granular" fallow: one on which the soil lay loose. In fact this is the ordinary open fallow, following a cereal crop, of the old three-field system.

that is, a fallow which is preceded not by a ley but by a cultivated crop, there is no need to hoe the ley furrow, and the harrowing is roughly half that required for the ley fallow. A system which adopts the soft fallow can therefore still pay in conditions where the improved system ceases to yield a net product—assuming that the yield per unit area remains constant. And this can be achieved by maintaining the correct ratio of tillage to pasture.

But a system incorporating the soft fallow is possible only where the arable section is not laid down to pasture in alternate years but is tilled year-in year-out, and where the remoter plots are in permanent pasture. This gives rise to yet another economy: it is no longer necessary to sow clover.

With these adaptations to changed conditions, we find that in its most significant points our farming system has become identical with the three-field system. Let us now look more closely at this widespread system of cultivation.

In any comparison between improved and three-field farming, the following four questions have to be answered:

1. How much cheaper is the tillage of the soft as compared with the ley fallow?
2. How are the labour costs of cultivation related to the distance between plot and farmstead?
3. What ratio of tillage to pasture will ensure that in the three-field system the soil is kept at a constant level of fertility without supplementary manure from outside the system (as it is in the improved system)?
4. Where there are two plots containing the same quantity of plant food, the one farmed in the improved, the other in the three-field system, how will the rye yield of the first, per unit area, be related to that of the second?

Questions 3 and 4 require for their solution some knowledge of agricultural statics, without which it is impossible to explain or to understand these questions.

We will therefore have to set down one or two basic propositions from agricultural statics. But since a detailed exposition of the subject would occupy far too much space, I shall merely state the proposition without entering into the arguments and proofs. Readers with some knowledge of this relatively new branch of our science, who wish to go more deeply into it, are referred to the writings of Thaer, v. Wulffen, v. Riese, Bürger, v. Voght, and Seidl,* and to my own paper, printed in the 8th Annual Edition of the Mecklenburg Annals.[2]

---

* I received Professor Hlubeck's *The Nutrition of Plants and Agricultural Statics*[1] only after I had finished this manuscript, and was therefore, to my regret, unable either to use or even to consider his ideas.

[1] F. X. W. HLUBEK (*sic*), *Die Ernährung der Pflanzen und die Statik des Landbaues* (Prag, 1841).

[2] "Über die quantitative Wirkung des Dungs und Über die Aussaugungskraft der Gewächse". *Neue Annalen der Mecklenburglschen Landwirtschaftsgese llschaft*, 8 (1821), 166-221.

SOME PROPOSITIONS FROM
AGRICULTURAL STATICS

THE production of a grain harvest reduces the amount of plant food in the soil. A plot that has produced 100 bushels of rye is poorer in plant food by the amount consumed in producing this harvest.

No crop can *in the course of one year* extract all the plant food   49
from any given plot.

The relation between the amount of plant food extracted from the plot by one year's harvest and the total amount present in the plot I shall call the rate of relative exhaustion. This emerges from the diminishing yields of successive harvests; if the first harvest produced a rye yield of 100 bushels, and the second harvest one of only 80 bushels (assuming identical tillage, climate, etc.), we would say that the relative exhaustion of rye is one-fifth.

The rate of relative exhaustion tells us the total wealth of plant food present in the plot: if the first rye harvest produced 100 bushels, and the rate of relative exhaustion was one-fifth, then the plot contained plant food for 500 bushels of rye before the harvest, and for 400 afterwards.

The amount of plant food extracted from the plot by the harvest of one Berlin bushel of rye is called a degree, and is expressed by "$1°$".

The relative exhaustion caused by the other varieties of grain is determined by their cash and nutritive value measured against rye. I assume that the exhaustion caused by a harvest of:

1 bushel of wheat is	$1\frac{1}{3}°$
1 bushel of two-row barley is	$\frac{3}{4}°$
1 level bushel of oats is	$\frac{1}{2}°$

Going by my experience at Tellow, I assume that top-grade barley   50 soil will in the seven-course improved system produce the following comparative yields:

If on 1000 square rods the first course produces 100 bushels of rye, the second course will produce 100 bushels of barley, and the third course will produce 120 bushels of oats.

On average, the fourth, fifth, and sixth courses will supply (from 270 square rods) the pasture needs of one cow, assuming that this cow daily consumes a quantity of grass equivalent to 17 lb of hay and is fed for 140 days of the year entirely on the ley (i.e. there is no need to conserve the stubble or the meadows).

Put down to ley fallow, the seventh course produces only one-fifth as much grass as the same land yields in pasture.

In 1811 and 1816 I conducted some experiments at Tellow in order to discover the comparative straw yield of the various grain crops, and I compared my findings with those of similar experiments made on several other Mecklenburg estates. These are the average figures:

1 bushel of rye produces	190	lb of straw
1 bushel of wheat (not lodged)	190	lb of straw
1 bushel of wheat (one-third lodged)	200	lb of straw
1 bushel of two-row barley	93	lb of straw
1 bushel of oats	64·5	lb of straw

With the same yield per unit area, wheat produces less straw than does rye. Wheat straw is however heavier than rye straw; and whenever I compared the two types subsequently, I always found that the straw from one bushel of wheat weighed as much as that from one bushel of rye, though of course, the proportions might be different for weak wheat with short straw.

In the five years between 1810 and 1815 a careful calculation was made at Tellow of the straw consumed for feed and litter and of the hay and grain feed used, and the findings were compared with the number of manure loads carted to the plots. It was found that 878 lb of dry feed (feed and litter) produce one load of manure. If we assume that a four-horse cart carries 2000 lb of manure (the normal load), we find that one pound of dry feed has produced 2·28 lb of manure. This agrees very closely with the findings of Thaer, who many years ago put the coefficient for the increase of manure at 2·3.

At this coefficient (on which I base my calculations) one load of manure of 2000 lb requires 870 lb of dry feed (2000/2·3) to produce. Whenever I refer to one load of manure I am therefore referring to the manure from 870 lb of dry feed (litter and feed), two-fifths of which is hay, and three-fifths straw.

This enables us to calculate the amount of manure the grain crop returns by way of its straw.

100 bushels of rye produce 19,000 lb of straw (100 × 190), which yield 21·8 loads of manure (19,000/870).

100 bushels of barley produce 9300 lb of straw (93 × 100), which yield 10·7 loads of manure (9300/870); 120 bushels of oats produce 7740 lb of straw (120 × 64·5) and 8·9 loads of manure (7740/870).*

52

It is common knowledge that soil is enriched in ley or pasture.

After many years of observation I have come to the conclusion that it is very likely that the plant food extracted from the soil by the grasses and clovers growing on the pasture is restored when the ley is broken up and the roots of these plants are ploughed in and left to decay, and that the manure dropped on the ley in pasture adds to the stock of manure in the soil—provided, however, that the ley is not more than three years old.

From the number of cows fed on the pasture we can work out the grass production of the ley. A cow weighing 500 to 550 lb and daily eating grass equivalent to 17 lb of hay will eat 2380 lb in 140 days, requiring 270 square rods of land to produce. 1000 square rods will therefore yield 8815 lb of hay (2380 × 1000/270). Thus a barley course which has produced a rye harvest of 10 bushel-crops will annually produce 10·1 loads of manure (8815/870) when it is laid down to pasture.

The effect of the fallow is twofold: (1) it increases the activity of the plant food present in the soil, and (2) because the weeds and grasses growing on the fallow are ploughed in to turn to humus or are eaten by the animals and converted into manure, it also raises the level of fertility.

53

In this increase in fertility I am assuming that the ley fallow is one-fifth, and the soft fallow in the three-field system—providing it is broken up only in midsummer—one-third, as effective as the ley pasture.

---

* This calculation is based also on the assumption that 100 lb of straw, used as feed and litter, yield more manure than 100 lb of hay feed, and that the inferior quality of straw manure as compared with hay manure is offset by its greater quantity.

In an equilibrium situation, where yield and fertility remain constant, the amount of manure that is replaced must balance the amount of fertility the crop has extracted from the plot. If we express the output of the soil-depleting grain crops in bushels of rye, and the nutrient replacement the plot receives from manure and pasture in loads of manure, the fact that exhaustion equals replacement tells us how many bushels of rye are nourished by one load of manure; or, conversely, how many bushels of rye it takes to drain the soil of one load of manure.

Applying this calculation to different types of soil, we found that the ratio varies with the quality of the soil: for equivalent yields a good soil requires less manure than does a bad one.

The following calculations are based on a type of soil which manages to maintain a constant level of fertility in the seven-course improved rotation without any supplement from outside. On such a soil, which is probably identical with top-grade barley soil, the production of 3·2 bushels of rye costs the plot one load of manure; or in other words, one load of manure equals 3·2° fertility.

54

FERTILITY OF A SEVEN-COURSE IMPROVED SYSTEM, EACH COURSE AT 1000 SQUARE RODS

	Yield (bushels)	Degree of exhaustion	Degree of fertility	Replacement (in cartloads of manure)
Fertility at the beginning of the rotation	—	—	500°	—
1st Course. Rye	100	100°	400°	21·8
2nd Course. Barley	100	75°	325°	10·7
3rd Course. Oats	120	60°	265°	8·9
4th Course. Pasture ⎫				
5th Course. Pasture ⎬	—	—	—	30·3
6th Course. Pasture ⎭				
7th Course. Fallow	—	—	—	2·0
Total output of manure				73·7
Fertility remaining in the course after the oat harvest			265°	
73·7 loads of manure at 3·2° each equal			235·8°	
Fertility at the beginning of the second rotation			500·8°	

FERTILITY OF A THREE-FIELD SYSTEM,
EACH FIELD AT 1000 SQUARE RODS

	Yield (bushels)	Degree of exhaustion	Degree of fertility	Replacement (loads of manure)
Fertility at the beginning of the rotation	—	—	500°	—
1st plot. Rye	100	100°	400°	21·8
2nd plot. Barley	100	75°	325°	10·7
3rd plot. Fallow	—	—	—	4·1
Total manure output	—	—	—	36·6
The barley crop left in the field	—	—	325°	—
36·6 loads of manure at 3·2° equal	—	—	117·2°	—
Fertility at the start of the second rotation	—	—	442·2°	—

In the improved system, one pasture course of a fertility of 265°   55
produced 10·1 loads of manure. At a fertility of 325° (as after the
barley harvest) soil laid down to pasture would produce

$$(325/265) \times 10\cdot1$$

or 12·4, loads of manure. And as the soft fallow has been assumed to
yield one-third as much manure as the pasture course, 12·4/3, or
4·1, loads have been taken into account for it.

CHAPTER 7B

FURTHER EXPOSITION OF SOME POINTS FROM AGRICULTURAL STATICS[1]

Here Thünen defines some of the terms he uses elsewhere. The fertility of the soil is the product of two qualities: (1) humus content and (2) soil quality, or the crop-producing capacity given a certain application of plant nutrient in the form of manure. The size of the harvest is in turn the product of (1) the fertility of the soil and (2) the soil activity, or the tendency to lose plant nutrient as a result of one harvest. Soil quality and soil activity both reflect the physical composition of the soil, which gives it its "ultimate capacity". Harvest is therefore a product of ultimate capacity, or physical quality, and of humus content.

In a general theory of statics, fertility, or capacity to produce, is not the same thing as humus content, which is a material quantity. Nevertheless for one soil the two are proportional. Since only one soil is assumed for the Isolated State, the term "fertility" can be used indifferently for either concept.

All earlier systems of statics, Thünen says, were based on a simple and direct relationship between yield and fertility—and, for any given soil, between yield and humus content: thus a soil with double the humus content would give double the yield. But observation has modified this: even on one soil, increments of humus, through extra doses of manure, yield diminishing returns. So the relationship is more complex: on two fields with the same soil, but unequal humus content, given the same cultivation, then the yields will vary as the square roots of the humus content (expressed in figures) of the two fields. If field A contains the humus equivalent of 36 loads of manure, and yields 10 bushel-crops; then if field B contains only the equivalent of 25 loads of manure, its yield will be $(\sqrt{25}/\sqrt{36}) \times 10$ bushel-crops, or 8·33 bushel-crops.

---

[1] This chapter was added for the 1842 edition. Of all chapters in Part I of *The Isolated State*, it stands most apart from the rest. This is a very bare summary.

Nevertheless Thünen has not modified his basic calculations as a result. Most of the relations in statics are not relevant to the Isolated State, where the soil is assumed to be of one and the same fertility throughout. The only tables that would be affected are those showing the fertility of soils under various crop systems, measured in degrees: the calculations for 10 bushel-crop soils, compared with 8 bushel-crop soils, would be s·ightly altered. But because they are only there for comparative purposes and because a large number of corrections would be necessary, Thünen has made no change.

CHAPTER 8

WHAT IN THE THREE-FIELD SYSTEM IS THE RATIO OF TILLAGE TO PASTURE, IF THE TILLAGE IS TO BE KEPT AT A CONSTANT LEVEL OF FERTILITY WITHOUT THE ADDITION OF MANURE FROM OUTSIDE THE SYSTEM?

83

A THREE-FIELD system[1] with a fertility of 500° at the beginning of the rotation had only 442·2° left by its end; it had lost 57·8°.

One load of manure is equal to 3·2° fertility: 57·8° require therefore 57·8/3·2 or 18 loads of manure—which is the annual[2] addition necessary to keep the three-field system at a constant level of fertility.

84

If the additional manure is to be produced on the pasture associated with the cropland, the question arises: How many square rods of pasture does it take to produce 18 loads of manure for the arable section?

As the pasture in the three-field system is never ploughed in or rejuvenated, it is inferior to the pasture of the improved system, and compared with the latter its productive ratio is roughly as 2 : 3. This explains why one single cow requires 405 square rods of land in the three-field system, instead of 270 as in the improved system. In the latter, 1000 square rods of pasture produce 10·1 loads of manure; in three-field farming however, where manure production is related to grass production, the given area yields only two-thirds as much manure, or 6¾ loads ($\frac{2}{3} \times 10\cdot1$).

If this pasture is employed as a sheep run, half the manure it produces is available for the arable section; provided that the sheep

---

[1] Of 3000 square rods; cf. p. 45.
[2] Because the loss of 57·8° must be replaced over three years on each of three fields.

are folded on the fallow overnight. 1000 square rods of pasture will in these conditions produce $3\frac{3}{8}$ loads of manure ($6\frac{3}{4} \times \frac{1}{2}$) for the arable section.

The arable section requires 18 loads of manure; it takes 5333 square rods of pasture ($(18/3\frac{3}{8}) \times 1000$) to produce this amount. Hence if a three-field system is to remain at a constant level of fertility without supplementary manure from outside, 3000 square rods of tillage must be associated with 5333 of pasture, and on a property of 8333 square rods, 3000 will be cropped, and 5333 in pasture.

At this ratio, an area of 100,000 square rods will have 36,000   85
in tillage and 64,000 in grass.

Without meadows, the pure improved system has no more chance of survival than has the pure three-field system in the same situation, for unless the farmer is prepared to replace hay with grain feed, which is extremely costly, hay will be indispensible for keeping the livestock through winter.

But it is necessary, for our ends, to study the manure and money yield of the arable land separately, i.e. not in association with the meadows. It follows that we must discover how much money and manure is yielded by the tillage and the meadows respectively on a farm embracing both kinds of land.

Hay is valuable in two ways: (1) as feed, and (2) as the raw material from which, by way of feeding, manure is produced.

Its feed value may be determined from the pure use value[1] produced by the sheep and dairy cattle.

Its value as manure I have determined according to the following principle:

Suppose that the arable land of a farm is divided into two sections, of the same basic and developed fertility. Suppose that the first section gets all the manure produced from the meadows and that it is farmed in the improved system with such an intensive seeding of grain that it is only just able to maintain a constant level of fertility by means of this supplementary manure. Suppose that the other section is likewise farmed in the improved system, but with such an   86
infrequent cropping of grain in relation to the ley pasture that the land is kept at the same level of fertility without additional manure. In these conditions the higher net revenue of the first section is due only to the extra input of manure. By comparing this extra input

[1] *reine Nutzung.*

with the extra revenue obtained we shall discover the money value of one load of manure.

Statics provide the data for the calculation.

The following example may illustrate how the ratio of tillage to pasture will alter in the three-field system, when the tillage obtains a portion of its manure from the meadows.

Suppose that meadows with an annual output of 100 loads of hay (1800 lb a load) are associated with 100,000 square rods of tillage and pasture.

One load of hay yields 1800/870, or 2·07, loads of manure; 100 loads of hay therefore add 207 loads of manure to the tillage.

A plot of 3000 square rods of cropland requires annually 18 loads of manure; 207 loads will consequently supply the needs of (207/18) × 3000, or 34,500, square rods of tillage. Subtracting these 34,500 square rods from the total area of 100,000 we are left with an area of 65,500 square rods which cannot obtain any additional manure and must therefore maintain its fertility without external aid. But in these conditions, as we have seen, the arable land amounts to 36 per cent of the total acreage, and the pasture to 64 per cent. Hence of the residual area of 65,500 square rods which has to maintain its own fertility, 23,580 square rods will be in tillage and 41,920 in pasture (65,500 × 36/100 = 23,580; 65,500 × 64/100 = 41,920).

87

It follows

	square rods
1. That the section of the tillage which maintains its fertility by means of additional manure from the meadows comes to	34,500
2. That the section of the tillage receiving its requirements in manure from the pasture comes to	23,580
Total	58,080
3. The pasture is	41,920

On arable land of a lower yield per unit area, the same amount of extra manure will suffice for a larger area of land.[1]

---

[1] A passage illustrating this assertion is given in the 1842 edition.

CHAPTER 9

HOW DOES THE RYE YIELD PER UNIT AREA OF THE IMPROVED SYSTEM RELATE TO THAT OF THE THREE-FIELD SYSTEM, IF IN BOTH THE SOIL CONTAINS THE SAME QUANTITY OF PLANT FOOD?

IF A seven-course improved system is introduced on a holding farmed hitherto in the three-field system, one-seventh of the land will use all the manure from the farmyard, which, in the previous system, was spread over one-third the total area.

For this reason rye will already be yielding a higher output in the first year of the new system than it did previously under the three-field system. This however does not mean that the land has as a whole become more fertile—for in one year no such change can occur; it merely illustrates the natural outcome of a greater concentration of manure on a smaller stretch of land.

We must therefore be careful not to compare three-field and improved systems with the same rye yield per unit area. Instead, we must endeavour to discover the comparative yields (per unit area) of both the systems, assuming that the level of fertility is the same in both the plots to be compared.

We discover the fertility of all the land belonging to any given farm by adding the fertility of the different courses into which the land is divided. In summer, the amount of plant food in the soil undergoes continuous change; for whereas plant-growth extracts fertility from the plots where grain is growing, this same growth will on the pastures provide a continuous supply of manure. We have therefore chosen to study this problem in the spring, before the crops begin to germinate, when all the courses still have that degree of fertility which is the norm for their yield.

If we want to compare the different farming systems in respect of the fertility they maintain, our calculations must include not merely the existing level of soil fertility, but the manure from last year's harvest which is still in the farmyard—or has still to be produced. For if in one farming system the manure is taken to the plots in spring, whereas in the other this happens only when the sowing is completed, and our calculation takes into account only the plant food present in the plot, we would not obtain a general and comprehensive survey of the fertility it takes to produce a given harvest—for without the manure accumulating in the farmyard, the latter system would not be able to produce the yield we have assumed for it.

FERTILITY OF A SEVEN-COURSE IMPROVED SYSTEM AT A YIELD
OF 10 BUSHEL-CROPS

	Degrees
Course 1. Rye contains	500°
Course 2. Barley	400°
Course 3. Oats	325°
Course 4. Pasture	265°
Course 5. Pasture	297·3°
Course 6. Pasture	329·6°
Course 7. Fallow	361·9°
Manure from the straw, 41·4 loads at 3·2°	132·5°
7000 square rods contain	2611·3°
On 1000 square rods this is	373°

FERTILITY OF A THREE-FIELD SYSTEM AT A YIELD OF 10
BUSHEL-CROPS

	Degrees
First field. Rye	500°
Second field. Barley	400°
Third field. Fallow	325°
Manure produced from straw, 32·5 loads at 3·2°	104°
3000 square rods contain	1329°
On 1000 square rods this is	443°

We have taken the data for this calculation from the Fertility Tables of the improved and three-field systems given in Chapter 7A.
89   First, however, we ought to mention that since we regard grazing as one of the conditions of improved farming, the manure that is

produced on the pastures will remain there and not be taken to the farmyard, so that the fertility of the total pasture will annually rise by 32·3° (the manure from one pasture course, 10·1 loads, multiplied by 3·2°).

To produce 10 bushel-crops of rye on a plot of 1000 square rods, the three-field system requires therefore a fertility of 443°; in the improved system, 373° will produce the same yield. In the three-field system, 373° would yield only 8·4 bushel-crops, because:

90

$$443° : 373° = 10 : (373/443) \times 10 = 10 : 8·4$$

A plot which yielded 8·4 bushel-crops in the three-field system will therefore yield 10 bushel-crops in the improved system, even though the fertility of the land as a whole has not risen. In other words, the improved system at a yield of 10 bushel-crops, and the three-field system at 8·4 bushel-crops, are at the same level of fertility.

THE FERTILITY DEGREE OF A SIX-COURSE CROP ALTERNATION SYSTEM[1] WHERE RYE AND POTATO COURSE BOTH CONTAIN 500° AFTER TARES

		Degrees
First Course.	Potatoes	500°
Second Course.	Barley	400°
Third Course.	Clover (for cutting)	325°
Fourth Course.	Rye	299°
Fifth Course.	Tares (for green feed) after manuring	525°
Sixth Course.	Rye	500°
6000 square rods contain		2549°
Which on 1000 square rods is		425°

In spring the crop alternation system uses nearly all the manure produced from last year's harvest on potatoes and tares. This is why we have not taken into account any manure still left in the farmyard.[2]

---

[1] *Crop alternation system.* (*Fruchtwechselwirtschaft.*) The most intensive cultivation system described in *The Isolated State*, though it had no place in Thünen's imaginary State (see p. 141). Its two essential features were that it (1) had no fallow, and (2) alternated grain and non-grain crops. The Belgian crop alternation system, which Thünen describes in Chapter 17 of *The Isolated State*, was a five-course rotation: 1. potatoes, 2. rye and stubble beet, 3. oats, 4. clover, 5. wheat and stubble beet.
[2] This paragraph was added in 1842.

91   If in comparing the revenue produced by a crop alternation system with that of an improved system we assume the same yield per unit area for both, we would be comparing the yield of a plot with a mean fertility of 425° with that of a plot with a mean fertility of 373°.

This difference should be borne in mind, or grave errors will undoubtedly ensue.

It is only possible to compare any two farming systems if soil at the same level of fertility is assumed for both. In the improved system the relation of the mean fertility to the fertility of the rye course is as 373° to 500°; in crop alternation, this is as 425° to 400°. Where the soil has a mean fertility of 373°, the rye course will maintain a fertility of only 439° in the crop alternation system, since

$$425 : 500 = 373 : 439.$$

In other words, if crop alternation is introduced into a holding hitherto farmed on the improved system, the rye course will come into soil with a fertility of only 439° instead of 500°; and if only for this reason, the yield per unit area will sink from 10 to 8·8 bushel-crops.

CHAPTER 10

LABOUR SAVING IN THE THREE-FIELD AS COMPARED WITH THE IMPROVED SYSTEM

MY CALCULATIONS of the labour costs of a ley fallow are based on accounts kept over a great number of years for one and the same plot. I possess no such detailed accounts of the labour costs of a soft fallow. However, at the beginning of my career as a farmer I collected some notes on the relation between the labour costs of a soft and a ley fallow, based on personal observations and accounts (kept largely by myself) of two estates on which I was working at the time. Subsequently I was able to make some further comparisons on this matter. The following calculations are based on these notes and the comparisons made subsequently.[1]

	new thalers	new thalers
In the improved system, the cultivation of 10,000 square rods of ley fallow costs		274·5
The cultivation of the soft fallow costs less by:		
1. Hoeing the ley	43	
2. Harrowing the ley furrow	17·6	
3. Harrowing the fallow costs, instead of 24·3 thalers, only 6·5, or less by	17·8	
4. Harrowing the turning-furrow[2] costs 16 instead of 21·4 thalers, or less by	5·4	
5. Clearing the ditches costs 4·6 instead of 9·3 thalers, or less by	4·7	
The total saving therefore is	88·5	
The cultivation of a 10,000 square-rod soft fallow therefore costs		186·0

92

[1] This paragraph was re-written for the 1842 edition.
[2] The deep furrow marking the place where the plough began a new circuit.

CHAPTER 11

HOW DOES THE DISTANCE BETWEEN PLOT AND FARMSTEAD AFFECT LABOUR COSTS?

FOR the purpose of the present investigation labour may be divided into the following four classes:

1. Labour whose amount depends entirely on distance; such as manure carting or bringing in the harvest.

2. That which requires a two-fold daily journey and is frequently interrupted by rain: cutting, binding, and other harvest work. I am assuming that there is one such interruption daily; our account must therefore include a three-fold loss of time on the way to and from the fields.

3. Labour also requiring a two-fold journey, but which is less easily—or at any rate less often—cut short by rain than is harvesting. In this group I include harrowing, hoeing, sowing, digging ditches, and so on.

    Hoeing with a team of oxen may at first sight not appear to belong in this last group, since the hoers, who leave for the field in the morning, returning only at night, cover the distance only once a day. But the oxen are changed three times a day and have to make a four-fold journey; where the field lies far from the farmyard this takes a lot out of them. Hoeing is therefore included in this group.

4. Labour which is performed on the farmyard itself—threshing, loading the manure on to the carts, unloading the grain, and so on. Here the amount of work to be done remains the same however far the plot.

The costs of manuring the plot and of bringing in the harvest are distributed among the various classes.

93

56

In manuring, the labour of the animals belongs to class 1, spreading the manure on the plots to class 3, and loading it on to the carts at the farmyard to class 4.

A detailed calculation shows that of the total costs of manuring:

70 per cent belong to class 1;
10 per cent to class 3;
and 20 per cent to class 4.

In bringing in the harvest, the labour of the oxen belongs to the   94
first, loading the sheaves on to the wagons out in the fields to the
second, and unloading them at the farmyard to the fourth
class.

Of the various kinds of labour listed under "loading and unloading" the work that is done out in the field amounts to nearly one-third, and that which is done on the farmyard to two-thirds, of the total costs.

At Tellow, an estate of 160,000 square rods of irregular lay-out, the mean distance between the farmstead and the various plots is about 210 rods.

How will labour costs change with a change in this distance; and what portion of these costs will remain where the distance between plot and farmstead is equal to zero?

Between March 24th and October 24th, the time of year when most of the field work is done, the average working day at Tellow is $10\frac{2}{3}$ hours.

In my experience, labourers take about 32 minutes to make a return journey of 210 rods.

Of the labours in the second class, which require a three-fold daily journey, 96 minutes (3 × 32), or three-twentieths of the total working day, are daily lost to actual work.

For the other labours in the second class, the time spent on getting to and from the place of work is 64 minutes (2 × 32), or one-tenth of the working day.

I[1] take the mean distance to be the length of the straight line from the centre of the farmyard to the point representing the average distance. However, because fields, meadows or deep ditches lie between these points, the labourers and animals cannot follow the

---

[1] The section starting here was added in the 1842 edition. The "mean distance" is analysed and discussed in the Supplementary Notes, p. 61.

95   direct line but have to make a more or less appreciable detour to get
       from one point to the other. It is scarcely possible to state with any
       precision the relation of the length of this straight line to that of the
       average detour for all the plots taken together; but as, unless I give
       some information on this subject, only those of my readers who are
       familiar with the Tellow layout will be able to apply my calculations
       to other places, I shall make a rough guess and assume that at
       Tellow the relation of the straight line representing the mean distance
       to the distance actually covered by the labourers and animals is as
       100 to 115.

       Labourers take 32 minutes to cover a return distance of 210 rods
       (taken as a straight line); it follows that the distance actually covered
       each way in 32 minutes is 241·5 rods (210 × 115/100).

       For similar geometrical figures of unequal size the distance
       actually covered is directly related to the mean distance of both
       the figures.

       On any given farm the relation of the length of the straight line
       to that of the detour depends on, and is directly related to, the layout
       of the land and the location of the various plots. If these do not face
       in the direction of the farmstead but meet a path cutting straight
       through the land at right angles, then, for a section of each plot at
       least, the relation of the straight line to the detour is like the relation
       of the length of the hypotenuse of a right-angled triangle to the sum
       of the other two sides, and for an equilateral triangle it is therefore as

96     $\sqrt{2} : 2 = 1 : \sqrt{2}$, therefore as 100 : 141.

       This finding ought seriously to be considered in deciding the layout
       of the various courses.[1]

The Tellow calculations show that on 70,000 square rods of tillage
with a yield of 10 bushel-crops and a mean distance of 210 rods:

	new thalers
cultivation costs are	569·8
harvesting costs are	499·5

One specific calculation—which would take up too much space
at this point—showed that labour costs are distributed as follows:

[1] End of the section added in 1842.

	First class	Second class	Third class	Fourth class
(a) *cultivation* costs attributable to distance i.e.			568·3 (thalers) 1/10 56·8 (thalers)	1·5 (thalers) 0
(b) *harvesting* costs attributable to distance i.e.	160·1 (thalers) 1 160·1 (thalers)	96·8 (thalers) 3/20 14·5 (thalers)	13·8 (thalers) 1/10 1·4 (thalers)	228·8 (thalers) 0

At 210 rods from the farmstead, the costs of farming a plot of 70,000 square rods at a yield of 10 bushel-crops are divided as follows:

(a) *cultivation costs:* 570 new thalers.
  (i) attributable to distance from the farmstead: 57 new thalers or 10 per cent of the total;
  (ii) incurred irrespective of distance: 513 new thalers.

(b) *harvesting costs:* 500 new thalers.
  (i) attributable to distance from the farmstead: 176 new thalers or 35·2 per cent of the total;
  (ii) incurred irrespective of distance: 324 new thalers.

The harvest from the given area of land yields, after deduction of the labour and general farming costs, a land rent of 954 new thalers.

If for the moment we ignore the costs of distance, or (which comes to the same thing) assume that the distance equals zero, we shall save, out of the 570 thalers cultivation costs, 57 new thalers, and out of the 500 thalers harvesting costs, 176 new thalers.

At a distance equalling zero, land rent will therefore come to 1187 new thalers.

With every 210 rods, the land rent changes by 233 new thalers, therefore, at the distance of

    0 the land rent is 1187 new thalers
  210 rods the land rent is 954 new thalers
  420 rods the land rent is 721 new thalers
  630 rods the land rent is 488 new thalers
  840 rods the land rent is 255 new thalers

1050 rods the land rent is   22 new thalers
1070 rods the land rent is   0 new thalers

For a soil with a lower yield per unit area cultivation costs remain
98   constant, whereas harvesting costs fall with the size of the product.
The same is true of costs due to distance between plot and farmstead.
At a yield of 9 bushel-crops[1] the costs of distance are as follows:

		new thalers
(a) of cultivation costs		57
(b) of harvesting costs (176 × 9/10)		158
		215

Thus with every change in the distance of 210 rods the land rent
falls or rises by 215 thalers.

With a fall in yield of one bushel-crop the costs of distance fall by
18 thalers (17·6 to be precise). At 8 bushel-crops they therefore come
to 215 minus 18 thalers, or 197 thalers.

The following table is based on these calculations.

ON 70,000 SQUARE RODS OF TILLAGE, LAND RENT COMES TO:

If the distance between field and farmstead is	at a yield of:				
	10 bushel-crops (new thalers)	9 bushel-crops (new (thalers)	8 bushel-crops (new thalers)	7 bushel-crops (new thalers)	6 bushel-crops (new thalers)
0	1187	975	763	551	339
with every increase in the distance of 210 rods, the land rent changes by	(233)	(215)	(197)	(179)	(161)
at 210 rods	954	760	566	372	178
420 rods	721	545	369	193	17
443 rods	—	—	—	—	0
630 rods	488	330	172	14	
646 rods	—	—	—	0	
813 rods	—	—	0		
840 rods	255	115			
952 rods	—	0			
1050 rods	22				
1070 rods	0				

*   *   *

And an average distance of 210 rods.

A. The mean distance between field and farmstead

   Thünen explains that he is not using the term "mean distance" in an ordinary sense. If we take a field of regular shape (e.g. an equilateral triangle), and we measure and add the distances covered by the horses in manuring the whole field, dividing the sum by the number of cartloads taken, that is the "mean distance" as used here. We can then take a point on the straight line which, running from the farmstead to the farm boundary, divides the field into two equal parts, and find the point on it corresponding to the mean distance. In the first edition (1826) Thünen could find no mathematical formula to express the distance. In 1829 Seidl found an expression: in a right-angled triangle ABC, whose base $AB = r$ and whose height $= x$, the mean distance of all parts of the triangle from point A is $2/3\sqrt{(r^2 + x^2/3)}$. But, Thünen asserts, this was not fully proven, for Seidl had summated, by means of integration, a series of which each member stood within a square root sign—which is not permissible. So Thünen produces a more complex formula, which can be proved (though he does not prove it here):

$$\text{the mean distance equals } 1/3\sqrt{(r^2 + x^2)} + \frac{r^2}{3x} \log\left(\frac{x + \sqrt{(r^2 + x^2)}}{r}\right)$$

   Comparison between the two shows a difference which is negligible for triangles whose height does not exceed their base, but becomes very considerable for a triangle whose height is several times its base. For $x = \frac{1}{2}$ the deviation is 0·06 per cent, and for $x = 1$ it is 0·6 per cent, but for $x = 20$ it is 14·7 per cent. Because of its simplicity, Seidl's formula is very useful for triangles whose height does not exceed their base.

*   *   *

B. The Location of Farmsteads in Mecklenburg   102

   When we look at the farm buildings on most Mecklenburg and West Pomeranian properties, the unsatisfactory nature of their location must amaze us.

Visibly they bear the traces of their original foundation and are to be regarded, above all, as monuments and relics of the first settlements. Where there is a lake, a river or a stream, the buildings back on to it and the fields lie to one side of the farmstead, stretching often farther than the eye can see. The first settler on wild and virgin land was right to build his home on a lake, stream or river; he secured in the cheapest way his very first necessity, water; and as he was incapable of tilling a great deal of land, its distance from his hut mattered little. But in later years, when the population increased and became more wealthy, when progressively more land was taken into cultivation and the livestock multiplied, the owner in his search for fresh pastures drove his animals out farther, until he came up against a natural obstacle, a marsh or river, or met with a more powerful neighbour. More recently still, increasingly large sections of these outlying pastures have been taken into cultivation; although the practical consequence of the distance from the farmstead is all too often a negative net product from these new plots.

103

This is how our great properties came into being and changed in time; but their farmsteads still stand where long ago the first settler put up his hut.

Matters are not quite as bad in districts without lakes and rivers.[1] Yet here too the boundaries of farms are haphazard and irregular; and on many adjoining properties the fields belonging to the one stretch nearly to the farmstead of its neighbour which, in its turn, owns plots near the buildings of yet another property.

Calculations made previously enable us to give numerical expression to the losses due to such inefficient layout; and the matter is sufficiently important for us to linger on it for a brief moment.

Suppose that farm A owns a plot of 70,000 square rods with a yield of 8 bushel-crops, which is 400 rods from its farmstead but only a hundred from that of B, the farm next-door. Suppose, further, that B in turn owns a plot of the same size and quality, 400 rods from its own farmstead but only a hundred from that of C.

104

By how much will the land rent of B rise if it hands to C the plot 400 rods from its farmstead and in return receives from A the plot only a hundred rods distant?

From a plot of 70,000 square rods with a yield of 8 bushel-crops B obtains:

[1] Tellow lay on the edge of the so-called "Lake Plateau" of Mecklenburg.

1. where the plot is 100 rods distant, a land rent
   of $763 - 197 \times 100/210 =$ 669 thalers
2. where the plot is 400 rods away, a land rent of
   $763 - 197 \times 400/210 =$ 388 thalers

By this exchange this, *B* obtains	281 thalers
By means of this exchange *B* has gained in land rent and in capital value (at an interest rate of 5 per cent	5620 thalers
C, by acquiring 70,000 square rods only 100 rods from its farmstead, has gained in land rent	669 thalers
and in capital value	13,380 thalers

B has thus increased its capital value by 5620, and *C* its own by 13,380, thalers; and together, the total value of these two properties has risen by 19,000 thalers. *A*, however, which has ceded 70,000 square rods of land, has lost in value by 7760 thalers. When this loss is subtracted from the gain made by the other two holdings, we find that these three properties, by merely adjusting their boundaries, have raised their aggregate capital value by 11,240 thalers.

It is worth bearing in mind that the gains made on such property adjustments are not at all like the profits of normal, so-called sound, business transactions, where one side profits from the other one's loss; for here the increase in value is pure gain for national wealth and income.

Scarcely a single holding has its farm buildings right at the centre of its land and almost all of them would gain from an adjustment of their boundaries; it is surprising, therefore, and depressing, to contemplate the vast amount of capital lost to the nation here—and without benefit to anyone. For Mecklenburg alone this loss must come to several million thalers, at the very least.

But why are the boundaries of farms so rigid, more so indeed than those of states?

The most immediate obstacle to property exchanges is the owner's fondness for a piece of land long-held. The value of a strip that has been in the family for years and generations is readily exaggerated, especially where care and money have been spent on it. This sentiment however, at permanent odds with rational self-interest, would scarcely have prevailed for centuries against the sensible adjustment

105

of farm boundaries, were there not other, and more serious, obstacles.
These are:

1. The fact that in Mecklenburg all property adjustments are
   subject to double taxation, since the high tax that is levied on
   the sale of any strip of land is payable on both the plots involved in an exchange.
2. The cost of surveying the land that is changing hands, of its
   re-registration in the tax-roll, and similar expenses.
3. The legal position of encumbered properties, for it is illegal,
   in Mecklenburg, to sell or exchange any portion of such a
   property without the consent of every single creditor.

Since it prevents frivolous transfers the very high duty payable
on the sale of entire properties is of no disadvantage whatsoever to
agriculture; but the tax that is levied on the exchange of single bits
of land inflicts considerable damage on the country's welfare.

And as this tax, in association with all the other obstacles, is so
prohibitively high that virtually no property adjustments ever take
place, the state has nothing to lose by abolishing it. The very worst
consequence—a trifling decline in the revenue—could easily be made
good, and without injury to farming, by a small addition to the tax
payable on the transfer of entire properties.

I do not presume to say whether and in what manner the third
obstacle, arising from indebtedness, is removable. I can foresee
though that unless we, the people of this old part of the world,
manage to break the bonds that time and custom have imposed upon
us, we shall, in our agriculture and in our national prosperity, fall
far behind the developing countries of the New World.

In villages where the farmers live together and hold their land not
in one large continuous piece but in scattered strips, stretching from
the village to the parish boundary, the loss of land rent is very much
greater than on large holdings, because, however irregular the layout
of the latter, their land lies at any rate in continuous tracts. These
villages suffer all the drawbacks of the great properties—without
enjoying the advantages. A state whose land is scattered among such
villages will have a trifling revenue, and poor defences against an
outside enemy.

In such a country men and horses waste their energies on constant,
tiring journeys to and from the field, and a labourer's family, which

in normal conditions can produce enough on fertile soil to support two others, will here consume nearly all it wins from the land and will have little extra left to sell to the towns.

To remedy this situation is however difficult, since the outlying fields belonging to such a village are usually too poor to support a family, or the cost of new farm buildings. This, however, is not part of my inquiry.

CHAPTER 12

THE DETERMINATION OF LAND
RENT IN THE THREE-FIELD SYSTEM

108   THE determination of the land rent rests wholly on the calculations which I made on the basis of my experiences of the improved system at Tellow, so I think I ought first to state the results of these calculations.

SEVEN-COURSE IMPROVED SYSTEM ON A FARM OF 70,000 SQUARE RODS, AT THE OUTPUT OF 10 BUSHEL-CROPS

Each course of 10,000 square rods	Sowing costs	Culti-vation costs	Costs of harvest-ing	General costs of culti-vation	Gross product	Land rent
	new thalers	new thalers	new thalers	new thalers	new thalers	new thalers
1st course Fallow	—	274·5	—	—	21·8	—
2nd course Rye	143·5	2·2	217·6	—	1274·0	—
3rd course Barley	122·3	165·0	158·5	—	932·8	—
4th course Oats	125·0	125·3	123·4	—	757·8	—
5th course Pasture	18·5	2·8	—	—	109·4	—
6th course Pasture	—	—	—	—	109·4	—
7th course Pasture	—	—	—	—	109·4	—
Total	409·3	569·8	499·5	882·0	3314·6	954·0
Charge per 1 bushel-crop	—	—	50·0	88·2	331·5	193·3
On 100,000 square rods this makes (in gold thalers)	626·4	872·2	764·6	1350	5073·4	1460·2

The same calculation served as basis for determining the land rent of the improved system in Chapter 5.

The cultivation of a ley fallow costs (per
   10,000 square rods)   274·5 new thalers
The soft fallow saves in costs (Chapter 10)   88·5 new thalers

109

A soft fallow therefore costs (per 10,000
   square rods)   186   new thalers
Hence, for 12,000 square rods   223·2 new thalers

At a given yield per unit area, the cultivation costs of barley, as also the harvesting costs of rye and barley, are the same in the three-field as in the improved system.

THREE-FIELD SYSTEM ON 100,000 SQUARE RODS, OF WHICH 12,000 SQUARE RODS ARE FALLOW, 12,000 SQUARE RODS IN RYE, 12,000 IN BARLEY, AND 64,000 PASTURE, AT THE OUTPUT OF 10 BUSHEL-CROPS

	Sowing costs new thalers	Culti-vation costs new thalers	Costs of harvest-ing new thalers	General costs of culti-vation new thalers	Gross product new thalers	Land rent new thalers
1st plot Fallow	—	223·2	—	—	43·8	—
2nd plot Rye	172·2	2·2	261·1	—	1528·8	—
3rd plot Barley	146·8	198·0	190·2	—	1119·4	—
Pasture—64,000 square rods	—	—	—	—	391·0	—
Total	319·0	423·4	451·3	820·0	3083·0	1069·3
Expressed in gold thalers this is	341·8	453·6	483·5	878·6	3303·2	1145·7

* In the improved system, on 10,000 square rods
   1. the utilisation of the pasture is   91·7 thalers
   2. the manure dropped on the pasture saves in manure carting 17·7 thalers

10,000 square rods of ley yield a product of   109·4 thalers

The three-field system makes no savings on manure carting, and on a given area the utilisation from the pasture is as 2 to 3 in comparison with the improved system. On 10,000 square rods this utilisation comes therefore to 61·1 thalers (91·7 × 2/3), which, on 64,000 square rods, is 391 thalers.

*   *   *

CHAPTER 13

THE EFFECT OF DISTANCE BETWEEN FIELD AND FARMSTEAD ON LABOUR COSTS IN THE THREE-FIELD SYSTEM

Thünen calculates the effect on labour costs of the distance of the arable field from the farmstead under the three-field system. Using the same example as in Chapter 12 (2) above, he finds that the three-field system leads to a saving in labour costs, because its more limited arable area (only 36 per cent of the total against 100 per cent under the Mecklenburg improved system) is on average nearer the farmstead: if the "mean distance" for the improved system is 210, that for the three-field system is only 126. In this example (with 10-bushel-crop land) the saving would be 80·9 new thalers (of which 16·8 thalers are cultivation costs and 64·1 thalers are harvesting costs). He corrects the calculations for the three-field system to take account of this. Expressed in gold thalers, the corrected results are:

ALL VALUES IN GOLD THALERS

	Sowing costs	Cultivation costs	Harvesting costs	General farming costs	Gross output	Land rent
For 10 bushel-crops	341·8	435·6	414·8	878·6	3303·2	1232·4
For every 1 bushel-crop change	—	—	41·5	87·8	330·3	201·0

On this basis he presents a re-worked table for the gross output, costs and land rent for a three-field enterprise at various levels of yield; labour, costs (except sowing costs) and rent expressed three-quarters in rye and one-quarter money:

THREE-FIELD SYSTEM ON 100,000 SQUARE RODS

Yield in bushel-crops	Sowing costs (bushels of rye)	Cultivation costs (bushels of rye and gold thalers)	Harvesting costs (bushels of rye and gold thalers)	General farming costs (bushels of rye and gold thalers)	Gross product (bushels of rye)	Land rent (bushels of rye and gold thalers)
10	265	254 bushels 109 thalers	241 bushels 103 thalers	510 bushels 220 thalers	2560 bushels	1290 bushels −432 thalers
change with 1 bushel-crop	—	—	(24 bushels 10 thalers)	(51 bushels 22 thalers)	(256 bushels)	(−181 bushels + 32 thalers)
9	265	254 bushels 109 thalers	217 bushels 93 thalers	459 bushels 198 thalers	2304 bushels	1109 bushels −400 thalers
8	—	—	—	—	—	928 bushels −368 thalers
7	—	—	—	—	—	747 bushels −336 thalers
6	—	—	—	—	—	566 bushels −304 thalers
5	—	—	—	—	—	385 bushels −272 thalers
4	—	—	—	—	—	204 bushels −240 thalers
3½	—	—	—	—	—	113 bushels −224 thalers

COMPARISON OF THE LAND RENT OF THE IMPROVED AND THE THREE-FIELD SYSTEMS

IF WE wish to compare the land rent produced by these two systems, we have to postulate for both not merely plots of the same size and soil of the same basic quality, but also soil that has reached the same level of mean fertility.

In Chapter 9 we saw that at a given level of fertility, a plot which in the improved system yields 10 bushel-crops, yields only 8·4 in the three-field system.

In order to discover which is the more profitable farming system in any given set of circumstances it is therefore necessary to compare the land rent of a holding in the improved system which yields 10 bushel-crops with that of a holding in the three-field system with a yield of 8·4 bushel-crops.

From Chapter 5 we know that at a yield of 10 bushel-crops, 100,000 square rods farmed in the improved system produce a land rent of 1710 bushels of rye minus 747 thalers. Chapter 13 shows that under a three-field-system on land with a yield of 8 bushel-crops the land rent is 928 bushels of rye minus 368 thalers, and that with every change in yield of one bushel-crop the land rent falls or rises by 181 bushels of rye minus 32 thalers. A change of yield of 0·4 bushel-crops therefore will produce a change in land rent of 0·4 (181 bushels minus 32 thalers), or 72 bushels minus 13 thalers.

At a yield of 8·4 bushel-crops, the land rent therefore is 1000 bushels of rye minus 381 thalers.

It follows that when rye costs 1·5 thalers the bushel, the improved system yields a land rent of 1818 thalers (1710 × 1·5 − 747), and the three-field system one of 1119 thalers (1000 × 1·5 − 381). At this price, the improved system yields thus 699 thalers more land rent.

At the price of 1 thaler the bushel of rye, the improved system yields a land rent of 963 thalers (1710 × 1 − 747), and the three-field system one of 619 thalers (1000 × 1 − 381). Therefore at this price, the improved system produces 344 thalers more land rent than does the three-field system.

At half a thaler the bushel, the land rent of the improved system is 108 thalers (1710 × 0·5 − 747), and that of the three-field system is 119 thalers (1000 × 0·5 − 381). At this price the improved system yields therefore 11 thalers less land rent than the three-field system.

We conclude from this that improved farming enjoys no absolute advantage over three-field farming. The price of grain determines which of the two is the best in any given situation; with very low prices, the three-field system is more profitable, with higher ones, the improved system.

At a rye price of 0·437 thalers the bushel, the improved system yields a land rent of 0 thalers (1710 × 0·437 − 747), whereas the land rent of the three-field system is still 56 thalers (1000 × 0·437 − 381). Where the grain price is so low that the improved system ceases to cover its costs, land may therefore still be farmed to advantage in the three-field system.

It follows that there must be a certain price for grain at which a given plot is as profitably farmed in the improved as in the three-field system. This price we shall discover by equating the land rent of the two. At a yield of 10 bushel-crops for instance:

116

1710 bushels of rye − 747 thalers	=	1000 bushels of rye − 381 thalers
minus 1000 bushels of rye + 747 thalers	=	1000 bushels of rye + 747 thalers
710 bushels of rye	=	366 thalers
thus 1 bushel of rye	=	0·516 thalers

Where rye fetches more than 0·516 thalers the bushel, the improved system is the more profitable on land with a 10-bushel-crop yield; where less, the three-field system will yield a larger net product.

In Chapter 4 we saw that when its average Town price is 1·5 thalers, rye will cost 0·516 thalers on the farm 29·9 miles from the Town.

If then the soil in the Isolated State were so fertile that it could produce 10, instead of the 8, bushel-crops we have assumed for it, the improved system would stretch up to 29·9 miles from the Town, giving way there to the three-field system.

As the grain price falls with rising distance from the Town, the land rent of the three-field system will progressively decline until it becomes equal to zero. This will happen when the value of

> 1000 bushels of rye minus 381 thalers is equal to zero

or when   1000 bushels of rye have the same value as 381 thalers

i.e. when   1 bushel of rye is worth 0·381 thalers.

This is what rye fetches on the farm 34·7 miles from the Town.

It follows that if soil were sufficiently fertile to yield 10 bushel-crops, the three-field system would pay up to 34·7 miles from the Town, and would occupy a concentric ring of 4·8 (34·7 minus 29·9) miles.

117   The following tables summarise the calculations which here are given for soil with a yield of 10 bushel-crops, when these calculations are applied to less fertile soil.

The degree of fertility which		The three-field system yields a land rent of	The land rent becomes equal to zero	
in the improved system yields (bushel-crops)	in the three-field system yields (bushel-crops)		at the grain price per bushel of (thalers)	or at a distance from the market of (miles)
10	8·4	1000 bushels −381 thalers	0·381	34·7
change with (1)	(0·84)	(−152 bushels +27 thalers)		
9	7·56	848 bushels −354 thalers	0·417	33·3
8	6·72	696 bushels −327 thalers	0·470	31·5
7	5·88	544 bushels −300 thalers	0·552	28·6
6	5·04	392 bushels −273 thalers	0·697	23·6
5	4·20	240 bushels −246 thalers	1·025	13·3
4½	3·78	164 bushels −232½ thalers	1·418	2·2
General formula for 10−x bushel-crops	$(10-x)\frac{84}{100}$	1000 bushels −381 thalers −152x bushels +27x thalers	$\frac{381-27x}{1000-152x}$	
Hence for 5·4 bushel-crops	4·53	—	0·854	18·6

118

The degree of fertility which		The land rent		The land rent of both systems will become equal	
in the improved system yields (bushel-crops)	in the three-field system yields (bushel-crops)	of the improved system is	of the three-field system is	when the bushel of rye fetches (thalers)	or the distance from the market is (miles)
10	8·4	1710 bushels −747 thalers	1000 bushels −381 thalers	0·516	29·9
9	7·56	1439 bushels −694 thalers	848 bushels −354 thalers	0·575	27·8
8	6·72	1168 bushels −641 thalers	696 bushels −327 thalers	0·665	24·7
7	5·88	897 bushels −588 thalers	544 bushels −300 thalers	0·816	19·8
6	5·04	626 bushels −535 thalers	392 bushels −273 thalers	1·120	10·5
5	4·20	355 bushels −482 thalers	240 bushels −246 thalers	2·052	
4½	3·78	220 bushels −455½ thalers	164 bushels −232½ thalers		
General formula for 10−x bushel-crops	$(10-x)\dfrac{84}{100}$	1710 bushels −747 thalers −271x thalers + 53x thalers	1000 bushels −381 thalers −152x thalers + 27x thalers	$\dfrac{366-26x}{710-119x}$	
from this we find for 5·4 bushel-crops	4·53	—	—	1·5	0
for 6·3 bushel-crops	5·3	—	—	1·0	14

THE THREE-FIELD SYSTEM

119

Yields (in bushel-crops) at equivalent levels of fertility		Limits of the three-field system, in miles from the Town		Extent of the three-field system, miles
under the improved system	under the three-field system	begins at	ends at	
10	8·4	29·9	34·7	4·8
9	7·56	27·8	33·3	5·5
8	6·72	24·7	31·5	6·8
7	5·58	19·8	28·6	8·8
6	5·04	10·5	23·6	13·1
5·4	4·53	0	18·6	18·6

A close look at this table shows that at a given price of grain, more fertile soil will be more highly[1] utilised by the improved system,

[1] Thünen means "more widely".

less fertile soil by the three-field system. It would thus be perfectly rational to have both systems side by side in a district where the fertility of the soil varies, even though the price of grain is the same in all parts of this district.

For instance, where the price of rye is 1 thaler the bushel, the land rent of both systems is in balance when the plot has the fertility to produce 6·3 bushel-crops in the improved, and 5·3 bushel-crops in the three-field, system; and here it would not matter which system were adopted, provided that all plots with a higher yield were farmed in the improved system, and all plots with a lower yield in the three-field system. But soil fertility is a variable, depending mainly on the farmer. Thus even when the grain price does not change, a rise in fertility will render a more intensive system suitable and profitable on the same holding.

120

The soil throughout the Isolated State is of one and the same basic fertility. If its yield were 5·4 instead of 8 bushel-crops, the three-field system would oust the improved system even at the price of 1·5 thalers the bushel of rye and would indeed stretch right up to the walls of the Town—were it not possible to raise the fertility of the ring immediately surrounding the Town by an intensive application of Town manure.

We conclude that low grain prices and low fertility have the same effect on the pattern of cultivation: both lead to the three-field system.[1]

---

[1] That is, they encourage a less intensive use of the land and therefore favour the three-field against the improved system.

CHAPTER 14B

EXPLANATIONS[1]

I HAVE assumed that throughout the Isolated State:

1. all properties are rationally managed;
2. soil fertility remains constant on all the farms;
3. all soil, with the exception only of the ring of free cash cropping, has the fertility to produce 8 bushel-crops after the bare fallow in a seven-course improved system.

It follows that for soil of the quality we have postulated and conditions resembling those obtaining in the Isolated State it would be as unprofitable to improve the soil beyond the point where it yields 8 bushel-crops as to allow the fertility to sink below this level.　121

It is well possible that these assumptions are mutually contradictory, and that, in particular, it might still prove worthwhile to upgrade soil with a yield of 8 bushel-crops. But at this point of my argument a close discussion of these matters would confuse two distinct problems and obscure the clarity which we are seeking; it belongs properly to Part Two.

Here, in the first part of my work, I mean to discover and compare the revenue of the various farming systems when these are applied to soil of the same quality and at the same level of fertility—always assuming of course that these systems remain stationary[2]—for only when this problem has been solved are we able to ask: Under what conditions and to what point is it profitable to improve the soil?

Before I could embark on my investigation, I had to postulate a definite yield for soil; and not wishing to stray too far from the normal average conditions of the world around us, I assumed the soil yield in the Isolated State to be 8 bushel-crops. For our present purposes, 8 bushel-crops must therefore be accepted as a yield consistent with rational farm management.

[1] This chapter was added in 1842.　　　[2] *im beharrenden Zustand.*

The only possible soil yield in the Isolated State is 8 bushel-crops; and if for soil of this fertility the tables on p. 73 list a series of yields ranging from 5 to 10 bushel-crops, it is necessary to explain the apparent discrepancy.

122   Around us we see soil very like that of the Isolated State and existing in generally similar conditions, but which yields an output of only 5 bushel-crops. This soil, if rationally farmed, would grow progressively richer, eventually to yield 8 bushel-crops, and the improved system would replace the three-field system. But where rational management is absent—as in reality it often is—and the soil rests at a lower level of fertility, the three-field system will yield larger profits than the improved system.

The tables on p. 73 list soils of different yields: in the Isolated State there is only one possible yield—8 bushel-crops. These varying yields refer to existing farms, which, in conditions very like those obtaining in the Isolated State, remain stationary, and which are therefore not subject to the law of rational development.

However, even rational cultivation will not produce a uniform yield of 8 bushel-crops on soils which differ in quality from the one we have postulated.

If we assume for the Isolated State a series of different soils, and compare the findings for them, we shall see that rational management will here produce a wide range of yields.

Since the different soils incur a wide range of cultivation costs, it becomes necessary to calculate these costs for each soil separately; and the resulting findings will show considerable differences between the land rent for these soils and that given in our tables for a soil

123   of the same yield per unit area. On the soil postulated in our tables the three-field system will, in a situation where rye fetches 1·5 thalers the bushel, stop producing land rent where the output sinks to 3·75 bushel-crops; whereas in fact it is possible that on sandy soil this same system will still prove profitable at the same price for rye and a soil yield of only 3 bushel-crops.

In practice we see three-field farms with a yield of only 2·5 bushel-crops; though here the farmer will generally have some other occupation to supplement his income. The question we invariably have to ask is this: Does tillage still repay the interest on the buildings and equipment? Is the land rent still positive?

CHAPTER 15

THE RELATION BETWEEN MANURE PRODUCTION AND THE AREA UNDER GRAIN IN THE IMPROVED AND THREE-FIELD SYSTEMS

I HAVE already stated what is basic to all my inquiry: that I am discussing only those improved and three-field systems where fertility is kept at a constant level without the addition of supplementary manure from outside the system.

In the three-field system, the arable land—and thus grain production—derives no benefit from half of the manure produced by the pastures; and the pastures themselves produce little. Because the three-field system produces so little manure, it can, if its level of fertility is to be maintained, put only 24 per cent of its total area under grain.

The improved system, on the other hand, utilizes all the manure from its better pastures, and here 43 per cent of the land may be cropped with grain without any loss of fertility.

Thanks to its greater output of manure, the improved system 124 can therefore put a far larger portion of its land under grain than can the three-field system. Nevertheless, the latter will become more profitable when the price of grain is very low; and in conditions where the improved system yields a negative net product, and has to be abandoned, the three-field system may still be able to survive.

When the price of grain is very low, the improved system is no longer able to carry the cost of its higher manure output from the product of its larger area in grain; in other words, the manure comes to cost more than it is worth.

In the opposite case, where the grain price is high or the soil exceptionally fertile, but particularly where both these factors are combined, improved farming yields a far higher land rent than the three-field system. At a yield of 10 bushel-crops and a grain price of 1·5 thalers, 100,000 square rods produce a land rent

    in the improved system of   1818 thalers
    in the three-field system of   1119 thalers

In these conditions, the improved system brings 699 thalers more than the three-field system, and the cost of producing the manure is more than balanced by the rise in grain production.

CHAPTER 16

FARMING SYSTEM WITH A HIGHER
MANURE OUTPUT

WE MAY conclude that when the price of grain is very high and the soil very fertile, the point will come where a still higher manure output than is possible in the improved system would be profitable. But we know that the possibility of an even higher output of manure exists, because:

1. The improved system keeps a bare fallow which, though useful in many respects, yields only a fifth as much manure as is obtained from the same area in pasture, and which consequently adds but little to the total stock of manure.
2. The pasture in the improved system is far less productive than it might be, invariably being introduced into plots which have carried three grain crops since manuring and which in consequence have lost some of their fertility.

The chief advantages of the fallow are as follows:

1. It prepares the ley for the winter-seed at the lowest labour cost; for although the ley may equally well be pulverised by means of the spring tillage, this demands far more labour, and costs thirty to fifty per cent more than the normal summer cultivation of the fallow—where the decomposition of the grasses does so much to further tillage.
2. It activates the manure and humus present in the soil far more effectively than any green crop could.

To give an example: a soil that yields 6 bushel-crops of rye after the fallow will yield only 5 bushel-crops after tares. Though some years and some varieties of soil may prove to be exceptional, the rule nevertheless holds that the fallow is the best preparation for winter grain, although the ratio when expressed in figures (here given

125

126

as 6 : 5) will vary greatly, depending on differences in soil quality, in the manner of its cultivation, and in the climate.

Following on a tare crop, rye will produce a lower yield than after a fallow, even though for both the soil contains the same amount of manure. This is due to the fact that a plot is less thoroughly worked for tares than it is in the fallow, so that a smaller portion of its content of manure and humus is converted into plant food. (This I call "the diminished efficacy of manure".) The lower yield of the rye crop when this is reaped directly after tares is thus due not only to the drain on soil fertility caused by this crop.

The advantages of the catch crop consist in the following:

1. The value of the feed it produces.
2. The manure the feed yields above what its production costs the plot; which makes it possible to extend grain production.

On its debit side we have:

1. The higher cultivation costs.
2. The cost of sowing.
3. The lower yield of winter grain which follows directly on the catch crop.

The question that invariably arises at this point is this: At what price for grain and soil yield (per unit area) will the advantages and drawbacks of the catch crop be in balance?

Where the data for such a calculation are provided, it is doubtless just as easy to determine this point with precision as it was to determine the boundary line dividing the improved from the three-field system. However, the calculation would prove to be extremely complicated; and it is not possible for me at this point to undertake the task, which would require a far more accurate knowledge than I possess of the fertility extracted by the green feed, and also far more time than I can spare. Therefore I shall merely indicate a few basic points which, I believe, would emerge from such a calculation.

Where the soil is of middling fertility, it will only become profitable to do away with the bare fallow at a very high price indeed for grain; for although, when this is done, the greater cost of the labour is soon repaid by even a slight rise in the grain price, the lower yield of winter grain that will ensue will affect the total net product so adversely that any extension of grain production—to say, half the total acreage—would, even when the price of grain is very high, be only barely able to cover the resulting loss.

In[1] the conditions we have postulated for the Isolated State, the value of the extra feed which is produced will do but little to offset this loss, because the competition of the uncultivated regions at the outskirts of the plain has depressed the price of animal products to the point where stock farming yields little or no rent.

Matters are different where the soil is very fertile. As a soil comes to contain more manure the yield per unit area rises to a certain point.

But whereas the amount of manure contained in a soil may be increased indefinitely, the grain output per unit area is limited—given the most generous allowance of plant food the crop is incapable of attaining more than a specific size and output. If the soil has reached the stage where a crop yields its maximum output, further increments of manure are not merely useless, but positively harmful, since they will cause the crop to lodge, thus reducing the yield.

128

Suppose that a given plot has a maximum rye yield of 10 bushel-crops. If manuring raises the fertility of this plot by one-fifth, so that it will produce 12 bushel-crops (assuming of course that the crop is capable of such an increase), the crop will lodge after the bare fallow. But if the grain crop is preceded, not by the bare fallow, but by tares, the efficacy of the manure that is left in the soil is reduced to the point where the yield will once again be 10 bushel-crops.

Here, then, the catch crop does not harm the succeeding winter grain, and on its debit side we have only the greater outlay on seeding and on cultivation, which, even at an only moderate price for grain, is easily repaid by the larger quantity of manure produced and the resulting rise in grain production.

There is no doubt that in these circumstances the fallow will rationally be abolished—assuming of course that soil and climate do not render it imperative.

But doing away with the fallow changes the entire pattern of the improved system. In order to prepare the ley for the catch crop it now becomes profitable to leave the ley in pasture for only one or at most two years, not for three as hitherto. And since a soil which is farmed in a course without a bare fallow is liable to deteriorate, good care must now be taken to arrange the crop order in such sequence

129

---

[1] Insubstantial amendments were made to this and the following two paragraphs for the 1842 edition.

that it produces the very best crops in succession. Each crop will be put into soil prepared for it, and each harvest will leave the soil in the very best condition to receive the following crop. A similar concern with the crop order, although useful in improved farming also, is less important there and may have to give way to other considerations. In short, high fertility combined with a good grain price converts the improved system into the more intensive system of crop alternation.[1]

In the seven-course improved system any rise in fertility would be wasted on a soil with a maximum average rye yield of 10 bushel-crops (which presupposes a mean fertility of 373° per 1000 square rods), because the grain crop would lodge, and the output fall in consequence. In these circumstances the farmer who considers the improved system the peak of intensive farming will either make no use of the stock of marl and mould present in his soil or will immediately rob it of these valuable contents by sowing more grain. Either way he will fail to invest a larger amount of productive capital in his property.

With crop alternation a far higher level of mean fertility is profitable. In the first place, the more regular distribution of fertility over the whole of the land calls for a higher level of average fertility if a 10 bushel-crop yield is to be produced; in the second place, the rye course, in order to produce the maximum yield of 10 bushel-crops, has here to be considerably more fertile than in the improved system, because the catch crop reduces the efficacy of the manure.

130

Because of the first reason, a six course-crop alternation system requires a mean fertility of 425° if the rye course is to have 500° after tares (Chapter 9); because of the second, a 10 bushel-crop yield requires 600°.

With potatoes and green feed the maximum yield is not as limited as with grain, and their production is most profitable on soil with a fertility of over 500°. If the courses are to maintain the same fertility among themselves as given in Chapter 9, then at a rye yield of 10 bushel-crops the potato course will maintain a fertility of 600°, and the mean fertility will rise by one-fifth, from 425° to 510° (425 × 1·20).

And as in the system of crop alternation soil fertility is less effective than in the improved system only for winter grain, but not

---

[1] *Fruchtwechselwirtschaft.* The German term conveys the sense of *continuous* rotation of *crops* without a fallow—a point important to keep in mind in what follows.

for potatoes, summer grain, or green feed, it follows that this system will produce a very much higher net product than the improved system with a yield of 10 bushel-crops.

Crop alternation can therefore utilise an average fertility of 510°; the limit in improved farming is 373°. In other words, crop alternation produces interest at a mean fertility of 510°; improved farming at 373°.

In countries where production just meets consumption, and grain is neither imported nor exported, the relation between the population and the amount of food produced is necessarily close. But the improved system produces far more food from a given area than does the three-field system, though less than the system of crop alternation. Given that the rye yield per unit area is the same for all three systems, and that the improved system with a yield of 10 bushel-crops can feed about 3000 people to the square mile, the three-field system will produce enough to feed only about 2000 people, whereas crop alternation will support 4000 people to the square mile. 131

* * *

Thünen then considers the advantage of replacing the grass ley completely by cultivated feed crops which can be fed to the cattle indoors. He thinks that cultivated feed crops, such as red or white clover, deplete the soil, not enrich it as some writers have asserted. But even allowing for the cost of manure to make good for this depletion, the advantage lies with the feed crop. On the credit side there are (1) increased feed output; (2) increased manure output from the stall-fed stock, and hence an increase in grain production, from 50 per cent of the area to 55 per cent and even (in warmer countries where an intermediate feed crop is possible between grain harvests) to 60–70 per cent. On the debit side, there are: (1) the greater cost of sowing the feed crop compared with the costs of sowing a grass ley; (2) increased cultivation costs; (3) increased costs of bringing the feed to farmstead; (4) the cost of taking the manure from the stalls to the fields, which does not exist with the grass ley. Because of these costs, crop alternation with stall-feeding will be found only on fertile soil; and because of costs (3) and (4) it will only be found, even on fertile soil, relatively near the farmstead. Where then the fertility of the soil justifies the widespread adoption of crop alternation with stall-feeding, the average farm will be small or at most medium-sized. 131-136

* * *

CHAPTER 17

RESULTS OF A COMPARISON BETWEEN THE BELGIAN AND MECKLENBURG SYSTEMS OF FARMING

FOR both systems we assume a soil for which the relative exhaustion caused by rye is one-sixth.

The crop sequence of the Belgian system we are now looking at is as follows:

1. Potatoes
2. Rye plus a root crop sown in the stubble of the rye
137   3. Oats
4. Clover
5. Wheat plus a root crop sown in the stubble of the wheat.

The sequence of the Mecklenburg system on which this comparison is based is the normal sequence of the seven-course improved rotation discussed already.[1]

FERTILITY AND YIELD OF THE BELGIAN SYSTEM
(EACH COURSE AT 10,000 SQUARE RODS)

		Degree of fertility	Yield
Course 1.	Potatoes	7680°	11,500 bushels
Course 2.	Rye	6974°	1056 bushels
	Roots	—	6500 centners[2]
Course 3.	Oats	7650°	1650 bushels
Course 4.	Clover	6910°	3150 centners hay
Course 5.	Wheat	7349°	1056 bushels
	Roots	—	6500 centners
50,000 square rods contain which is 7313° for 10,000 square rods		36,563°	

---

[1] i.e.: 1. Fallow, 2. Rye, 3. Barley, 4. Oats, 5. Ley, 6. Ley, 7. Ley.

[2] *Centner* (Zentner). Thünen uses this throughout to mean a unit of 100 Hamburg lb (106·79 English lb or 48·42 kg.) and not the prevailing unit in Mecklenburg at the time, which was 112 lb.

FERTILITY AND YIELD OF THE MECKLENBURG SYSTEM
(EACH COURSE AT 10,000 SQUARE RODS)

	Degree of fertility	Yield
Course 1. Rye	6336°	1056 bushels
Course 2. Barley	5280°	1056 bushels
Course 3. Oats	4488°	1267 bushels
Course 4. Pasture	3854°	898 centners of hay
Course 5. Pasture	4145°	898 centners of hay
Course 6. Pasture	4435°	898 centners of hay
Course 7. The fallow (in spring)	4726°	180 centners of hay
Add the manure from the straw	1552°	
70,000 square rods contain which is 4973° for 10,000 square rods	34,816°	

With the same yield of winter-grain (in bushel-crops), the mean fertility of the Mecklenburg compared with the Belgian plot is as 4973° to 7313°, or 100 to 147.

The final results of my calculations give the following survey of costs and land rent:

A. OF THE BELGIAN SYSTEM PER 100,000 SQUARE RODS

	Sowing costs (new thalers)	Cultivation costs (new thalers)	Costs of harvesting and manuring (new thalers)	General farming costs (new thalers)	Total costs (new thalers)	Gross yield (new thalers)	Land rent (new thalers)
At the yield of 10·56 bushel-crops	672	2060	2382	3188	8302	11,081	2779
At 10 bushel-crops	672	2060	2256	3046	8034	10,494	2460
(Variation per bushel-crop)	0	0	(225·6)	(254·4)	(480)	(1049·4)	(569·4)
At 9 bushel-crops	—	—	—	—	—	—	1890·6
8	—	—	—	—	—	—	1321·2
7	—	—	—	—	—	—	751·8
6	—	—	—	—	—	—	824·4
5·68	—	—	—	—	—	—	0

138

B. OF THE MECKLENBURG SYSTEM PER 100,000 SQUARE RODS

	Sowing costs (new thalers)	Cultivation costs (new thalers)	Costs of harvesting and manuring (new thalers)	General farming costs (new thalers)	Total costs (new thalers)	Gross yield (new thalers)	Land rent (new thalers)
At the yield of 10·56 bushel-crops	612	814	754	1357	3537	5137	1600
At 10 bushel-crops	612	814	714	1296	3436	4865	1429
(Variation per bushel-crop)	0	0	(71·4)	(109·7)	(181·1)	(486·5)	(305·4)
At 9 bushel-crops	—	—	—	—	—	—	1123·6
8	—	—	—	—	—	—	818·2
7	—	—	—	—	—	—	512·8
6	—	—	—	—	—	—	207·4
5·32	—	—	—	—	—	—	0

1

First of all it ought to be noted that the Belgian yield of winter grain is almost the same as the average wheat yield at Tellow. At Tellow, the attempt to increase the average wheat output had to be abandoned, because the crop lodged, producing thus a yield lower than the initial one. We may therefore regard the Belgian mean yield of 10·56 bushel-crops as the highest possible average yield for good arable soil.*

* At Tellow the average yield from 100 square rods (in Berlin bushels) was:

For the years	wheat	rye
1810–20	10·93 bushels	9·65 bushels
1820–30	11·37 bushels	11·30 bushels
1830–40	10·03 bushels	11·10 bushels
30-year average	10·78 bushels	10·68 bushels

The smaller wheat yield in the last decade as compared with the two previous ones was due in part to the lower efficacy of marling and in part to a change in the sequence of the crops—more wheat than formerly now being sown in the stubble of the preceding crop.

2

In the improved system a land rent of 1600 new thalers is associated with a yield of 10·56 bushel-crops; and as it is impossible further to raise this output, even the standard improved system, with a bare fallow receiving all the manure, cannot produce a higher land rent. With the same output in bushel-crops the Belgian system on the other hand produces a land rent of 2779 new thalers; or, at 10·56 bushel-crops, the land rent of the Mecklenburg is to that of the Belgian system as 100 to 174.
The gross yield of both systems is as 5137 to 11,081, or 100 to 216.

Suppose now that there are two states of identical size, the one 141 farmed mainly on the Belgian, the other on the Mecklenburg system: these two states must differ greatly in their wealth, population, and power.

Density of population is probably closely, though not directly, related to gross product. We assumed above, though of course this was a mere supposition, that the improved system with a 10 bushel-crop yield can feed 3000 people to the square mile. It would follow that at 10·56 bushel-crops this system could feed about 3200 people to the square mile; and since the gross yield of the Belgian system is as 216 to Mecklenburg's 100, it follows that the state which adopts the former system will be able to support 6900 people to the square mile.

It is worthwhile to compare this hypothetical estimate with reality, and where necessary to qualify it.

Hassel's *Manual of Geography and Statistics* gives the following population figures for the provinces of the Netherlands for 1817.[1]

Province	Area (square miles)	Population	Inhabitants per square mile
Hainault	79·38	430,156	5419
South Brabant	66·24	441,222	6660
Antwerp	47·88	287,347	6001
East Flanders	49·10	600,184	12,223
West Flanders	68·04	519,400	7634
Dept. of the North	109·90	871,990	7932
	420·54	3,150,299	

[1] *Hassels Handbuch der neusten Erdbeschreibung und Statistik* (Berlin 1816), *passim*. The figures actually refer to the western part of Belgium and to the *Département du Nord* in France.

142   These six provinces, the heart of Belgian agriculture, contain in
420·54 square miles a population of 3,150,299, which is 7491 to the
square mile.
          To the best of my knowledge Belgium generally has no need to
import grain. If this is correct, and she can indeed feed her own
population, our estimate falls far short of reality.
          When a nation's wealth stops rising and becomes stationary, the
unproductive section of the population will consume the land rent.
The number of unproductive subjects a state is able to support
depends, consequently, on its total land rent.
          But the army, too, belongs to the unproductive section of the
population; the larger the land rent of a state, the greater therefore
is the army it can muster and maintain—i.e. the more powerful this
state will be in the realm of international affairs.

                                    3

          What is it that gives the Belgian system this predominance? Does
it depend on climate, soil, or geographical location, or is it within
the power of any farmer to introduce into his property a similar—
if not entirely identical—system of intensive cultivation?
          Before we can answer this question we have to compare the fertility
of a plot farmed in the Belgian system with that of a plot farmed in
the Mecklenburg system.
          From estimates given at the beginning of the present chapter we
know that whereas the Belgian system requires a mean fertility of
731·3° per 1000 square rods, the Mecklenburg system needs only
497·3°—the Belgian system thus needing 234° more.
143   For a plot of the same size and at the same output of winter grain,
soil in the Belgian system is thus nearly 50 per cent more fertile than
soil in the Mecklenburg system.
          The Belgian system therefore obtains its larger land rent from the
same area but not from soil at the same level of fertility; and no
matter what the share of climate, soil type, crop order, national
character and so on in helping to produce the higher Belgian yield,
the extremely high fertility of the soil is the prerequisite without
which none of the other factors could begin to operate.

4

COMPARISON OF BOTH SYSTEMS AT LOWER LEVELS OF FERTILITY

When we take a closer look at the land rent of the two systems (cf. tables, pp. 85-6) we see that with declining yield per unit area the vast advantage of the Belgian system tends more and more to disappear. At 6 bushel-crops, the improved system is already producing a larger land rent than is the Belgian system; at 5·68 bushel-crops, the Belgian land rent sinks to zero, whereas in Mecklenburg it only disappears at 5·32 bushel-crops.

This finding becomes even more striking when we recall that at the same yield per unit area Belgian soil possesses a far higher degree of fertility than does Mecklenburg soil.

In order to produce a yield of 10·56 bushel-crops, the Belgians require a fertility of 73,130° per 100,000 square rods; which is 6925° per bushel-crop.

In Mecklenburg the production of the given yield from the given area takes only 49,730°, or 4710° per bushel-crop.   144

At a yield of 6 bushel-crops:

the Belgian system therefore contains 41,550° (6 × 6925)
and the Mecklenburg system,   28,260° (6 × 4710).

At a yield of 6 bushel-crops, the Belgian system, with a fertility higher by 13,290°, therefore produces a lower land rent than does the Mecklenburg system at this yield.

At 5·68 bushel-crops, when Belgian land rent sinks to zero, the Mecklenburg cropland retains a fertility of 39,334° (5·68 × 6925).

In the improved system, the land rent only disappears when the soil yield sinks to 5·32 bushel-crops and the fertility of the soil is reduced to 25,057° (5·32 × 4710).

A course of 100,000 square rods, which in the Belgian system has a fertility of 39,334° and yields no land rent, will in the improved system produce an output of 8·35 bushel-crops (39,334/4710) and a land rent of 925·1 (818·2 + (35/100) × 305·4) thalers. If the Belgian system were to be introduced into soil at this level of fertility, it would wipe out the entire land rent of 925·1 thalers which the improved system produces here.

This might well serve as a warning against adopting alien farming systems without a precise knowledge of all the factors operating in their native parts and a profound understanding of the basic principles of agriculture.

It may explain, moreover, why the attempts to resettle farmers from Belgium and the Palatinate have almost invariably come to grief. In general these people were given a type of land very different in quality from that they were accustomed to at home, land which, for successful cultivation, would have required the adoption of the local farming practices; and the story of these settlers, far from encouraging our German farmers to embark on agricultural experiments, instead served to set their minds against all innovation.

Even today there are large tracts of uninhabited heathland in North Brabant. This land is not among the worst; it carries heathland scrub, and some oak; it is part of a plain just above sea level and it is, moreover, surrounded by large towns, near to which land is usually valuable. It must strike any agriculturist as curious that even Belgian enterprise has not yet tamed such land.

What can explain this failure?

It is certain that the costly Belgian system would not pay on land of this quality, and just as certain that the Belgian crop order, when applied to poor soil, would prove to be not enriching, but utterly exhausting. If—as seems indeed to have been the case—the Belgian farmers tried to cultivate this land by a system resembling (even if not identical with) the one adopted on their rich land, failure was inevitable.

And here the Mecklenburg farmer might have succeeded where his Belgian colleague failed. Had the improved system been known —and accepted—on the banks of the Meuse, then perhaps (and I am inclined to say "probably") these wastes would long ago have turned into good farming land.

The improved system at a yield of 10·56 bushel-crops and the Belgian system at 7·18 have the same degree of fertility: 49,730° per 100,000 square rods.

At this level of fertility the improved system produces a land rent of 1600 new thalers, and the Belgian system one of 854·3 new thalers.

Thus on soil of the same fertility the improved system yields far larger returns than does the Belgian system, and the latter becomes profitable only where the soil has grown so fertile that under the improved system grain would lodge.

5

Sixty per cent of the total acreage of a Belgian enterprise may be cropped with grain without loss of fertility: in Mecklenburg, the farmer who wants to maintain the fertility of his soil without having to bring in supplementary manure from outside the system can crop only 43 per cent of his land with grain.
This result the Belgians achieve by:

1. putting clover, first among the manure-producing crops, into soil that is as rich in plant food as the soil awaiting winter grain —in Mecklenburg the farmer takes his pastures into plots which, after three grain harvests, have lost a good deal of their fertility;
2. keeping the livestock off the clover course (grazing would nearly halve the clover crop and reduce manure output by about a third), and cutting the clover for use as indoor feed. In consequence one Belgian clover course—20 per cent of the total acreage—yields nearly as much manure as do three Mecklenburg pasture courses: 43 per cent of the total acreage;
3. in one and the same year raising roots in the stubble of the winter grain. Thus after the exhausting grain crop the Belgian farmer reaps a crop which returns more manure than it takes from the plot.

147

I should like at this point to have subjected to the critical opinion of my reader my calculations on the revenue and the costs of the various courses and on their respective rates of exhaustion and replacement. However, as this would call for numerous explanations and discussions, and would take up a good deal of space, I shall confine myself to stating the general findings of these calculations. First: out of the total value of potatoes grown for feed on a course of 10,000 square rods, a surplus of only 25·5 thalers remains when the labour costs are deducted. Second: the replacement the potatoes yield by way of animal feed is only 46·2° above what their harvest costs the plot.
It would appear from this that the bare fallow could replace potatoes without reducing either the manure output or the revenue,

and that in both these respects potatoes might be regarded as a neutral crop. But where potatoes are cultivated, the tillage of the fallow becomes for the most part unnecessary—and it is this which adds so considerably to the costs of the improved system, for whereas, after potatoes, one ploughing only will prepare the soil for rye, four are required in the fallow. This saving on the fallow tillage gives to potato production its prominence in helping to achieve the high net product of the Belgian system.

It is not that in Belgium—unlike in other countries—the cultivation of feed crops yields a large net product. But just as clover and root crops are necessary and important to the Belgian system in producing the manure which alone makes large-scale grain production possible, so potatoes, in rendering unnecessary the cultivation of the fallow, are vital to this system.

148

6

From the tables on fertility and yield given at the beginning of this chapter we find:

That the production of	Requires a fertility per plot of	
	(a) in the Belgian system	(b) in the Mecklenburg system
1 bushel of wheat	6·96°	—
1 bushel of rye	6·6°	6°
1 bushel of oats	4·64°	3·54°
1 bushel of barley	—	5°
1 bushel of potatoes	0·667°	—
1 centner of clover hay	2·2°	—
1 centner of pasture grass	—	4·3°
I assume that in the Mecklenburg system the requirement is:		
1 bushel of wheat		6°
1 bushel of potatoes		0·667°

149   In the Belgian system the production of one bushel of winter grain (taking wheat and rye together) requires a fertility of 6·78°

($(6\cdot96+6\cdot6)/2$); in the improved system one bushel of winter grain requires a fertility of only $6°$.

Following on a bare fallow, a fertility of $6°$ is therefore as effective as $6\cdot78°$ is after a previous crop. The efficacy of manure after the bare fallow is related to its efficacy after a previous crop as $6\cdot78$ to $6 = 11\cdot3$ to 10. In other words, whereas the soil yield is $11\cdot3$ bushel-crops after a bare fallow, it is only 10 bushel-crops after a previous crop.

With less intensive cultivation than in Belgium the harmful effect of a previous crop on the activity of the plant food present in the soil becomes progressively greater; and for normal cultivation the ratio of $12:10$ assumed above is probably fairly accurate.

Oats never come into the fallow, and for them the soil fertility should therefore be as effective in Belgium as in Mecklenburg. But we find that whereas it takes the Belgian system $4\cdot64°$ to produce one bushel of oats, it takes the Mecklenburg system only $3\cdot54°$. The explanation lies in the different farming methods. In Belgium, the large quantity of manure for oats in which clover is to be sown is ploughed in only with the seed furrow, which means that the manure has almost no effect on the oats themselves. This the Belgian farmers probably do intentionally, in order to prevent the oats from lodging —and thus smothering the clover—and to ensure that the clover enjoys the entire benefit of the manure.

That the Belgians with the same degree of soil fertility manage to obtain nearly twice the clover yield achieved in Mecklenburg is due in part to their climate, which is far kinder than is our own to clover, mainly however to the different feeding methods. Whereas in Mecklenburg the animals graze down the clover courses, in Belgium the clover is allowed to grow undisturbed, between regular intervals of cutting.

150

7

By subtracting the cost of the seeding from the product of the green crop and the potatoes and comparing what is left with the labour cost incurred by these crops, we shall discover how much per bushel in labour costs (i.e. not including general farming costs) each crop cost to produce.

My calculations produce the following results:

The production of	Costs (in wages)	
	(a) in the Belgian system (new shillings)[1]	in the Mecklenburg system (new shillings)
1 bushel of wheat	19·7	—
1 bushel of rye	18·7	25·9
1 bushel of barley	—	15·3
1 bushel of oats	13·4	11·5
1 bushel of potatoes	3·3	—
	costs (in seed and wages)	
1 centner of clover hay	4·3	—
1 centner of root crops	1·3	—
1 centner of grass expressed in hay (grazed down, not cut)	—	0·7

151   It should be noted that this calculation is based on a rye price of 1 new thaler, 12 shillings the Berlin bushel, and that, since labour costs vary with the grain price, the calculation is valid only for this particular price.

The labour costs of producing one bushel of rye come to 25·9 shillings in Mecklenburg, but to only 18·7 shillings in Belgium; which shows the great superiority of potatoes over the fallow in reducing labour costs.

Rye, following on potatoes, constitutes a bad crop sequence, yet the Belgians over an average of several years harvest a maximum rye crop: on rich soil, extremely careful tillage may therefore nullify an error in the sequence. Such an infringement of the laws of crop rotation would bring about dire retribution on a poorer soil.

*   *   *

151–   NOTES AND EXPLANATIONS

154   *Thünen explains that he was stimulated to make this comparison after a close study of Schwerz's work on Belgian agriculture.*[2] *Some of*

[1] 1 shilling (Schilling) = 1/48 new thaler.

[2] J. N. SCHWERZ, *Anleitung zur Kenntniss der Belgischen Landwirthschaft* (3 vols, Halle, 1807–11). The actual farm Thünen used to represent the Belgian system was at Edegem, south of Antwerp: data *ibid*: Vol. 2, pp. 395–404.

the Belgian data for a comparison were lacking; here Thünen had to use the data from Tellow. Further, some assumptions had to be made, such as those about the exhaustion and replacement value of crops and green feed.

Thünen explains the considerable difference between the Belgian market price for feed crops and the feed value he assumes. The difference lies in the value of the crops in manure production.

The Mecklenburg data about prices and rents differ very slightly from those used elsewhere. In addition, the calculations for the Belgian system are not based on the same set of conditions as Thünen's previous calculations, so they cannot serve to indicate the area which the Belgian system would occupy in the Isolated State.

* * *

CHAPTER 18

SOME FURTHER CONSIDERATIONS IN THE CHOICE OF A FARMING SYSTEM

WE have discussed how the two factors, grain price and soil fertility, affect the choice of a farming system. But these, although the most important, are by no means the only ones to influence this choice; and to establish their precise effect we had to separate them from the other factors and consider them as the only variables, holding the others constant.

155 But under different conditions, or studied from another point of view, one or more of the factors we held constant could be varied—thus enabling us to study the effects of their increase or decline on the farming system.

A detailed study of these varied conditions is not strictly part of my inquiry; but to prevent misunderstandings I shall mention some of the more important ones.

A. SYSTEMS WITH RISING FERTILITY

When two farming systems are compared, the one which enriches soil and raises output from rotation to rotation is generally held to be the better system.

But it is not a necessary function of the one or other system to enrich or exhaust the soil—the improved and crop alternation systems may exhaust soil as much as may the three-field system. Like a seven-course improved rotation with four grain crops, a six-course crop alternation system with four grain crops is an exhausting system; a seven-course crop alternation with three, and a six-course improved rotation with two grain courses, are both enriching. Whether a system proves to be enriching or exhausting depends not on the crop sequence or indeed on the system itself, but on the ratio of the manure-producing crops to those which exhaust soil, the "seed-ratio" in short.

A comparison of two imaginary properties farmed by different 156 systems, one with an enriching, the other with an exhausting seed-ratio, cannot tell us which is the better system (it is immaterial for this purpose whether we derive our findings from experience or from calculation); it can only establish whether a soil enriched by careful husbandry will ultimately be more valuable than poor soil which has not been improved. And to this the answer is self-evident: the holding with the more enriching seed-ratio will invariably win.

Comparisons between different farming systems will give rise to basic confusion unless the following questions are sharply distinguished:

1. Which system yields the larger revenue if the object is to maintain a constant level of fertility without the addition of supplementary manure from outside?
2. In what conditions is it profitable to increase fertility at the expense of revenue; and to what point may fertility be profitably raised?
3. If the object is to raise fertility, not to obtain the maximum revenue, which system will achieve this at the lowest cost?

I shall attempt to answer only the first of these questions; for 157 although I have compared plots at various levels of fertility, I have always had to assume that the fertility of any given plot remains constant. The second and third questions—more important perhaps even than the first—await their solution from future advances in the field of agricultural statics.

B. THE RELATION OF THE HAY PRODUCED BY THE MEADOWS
TO THE TOTAL ARABLE ACREAGE

Where a farm run on the improved or on the three-field system has no meadows, and the sheep and dairy cattle are fed on straw throughout the winter, the animals will lose so much weight that most of the grass they subsequently consume on pasture will go into recovering their former weight, and little of it into the production of milk or wool. In these conditions the gross product of the animals will be so low as barely to cover the cost of their keep, and neither feed-straw nor pasture will bring a return,

If the pasture is to furnish a return it becomes necessary to help the livestock through winter by feeding them grain, or straw that has been only part-threshed.

It is however obvious that the draught animals must always be in a state fit to perform their task; and on farms which produce no hay they will have to be fed grain feed.

When we compare the production costs of clover-hay and potatoes with those of grain we find that grain is a far dearer feed than either of the other two.

* * *

Thünen gives numerical examples. The costs of oats, potatoes and clover used as feed are respectively 100 : 58 : 40.

* * *

It follows that three-field and improved farms which produce little or no hay should not adopt grain feed, but instead should cultivate feed crops. And as feed crops are more cheaply produced in a more intensive system, all such farms will have to put into crop alternation a section of their land sufficiently large to supply the hay, potatoes, etc. to keep the animals through winter—even though the price of grain has not reached the level or the soil attained the fertility to render this the appropriate system over all the arable land.

But the production of feed crops is profitable only on rich soil. On poor soil, clover fails utterly, and potatoes yield a crop so meagre that their production easily costs double the sum we have estimated.

This gives rise to an interesting new problem.

Where a farm has few meadows and the soil is of middling or even poor quality, would it pay to manure a portion of the land intensively and to introduce into it crop alternation—assuming that this section can be enriched only at the cost of the remaining, larger section?

I am not qualified to give a definite answer to this problem, though I do believe that on closer inquiry it would turn out to be "yes".

But the poorer the arable land as a whole, and the worse the soil, the greater the difficulty of producing feed crops. This explains why meadows are so valuable in districts where inferior soil predominates, and why it is almost true to say that they are, in such districts, the prerequisite of cultivation.

We assumed that in the Isolated State the cropland is associated with sufficient meadowland to supply the hay required for the improved and three-field systems, and that the manure from the meadows benefits only the section lying in a special course, not the entire arable area. We took no further notice of this special section, concentrating on the larger section, which manages to maintain a constant level of fertility without the addition of supplementary manure, and which obtains its meadow-hay by paying for it and by returning the manure this hay has produced.

We might equally well have assumed—and this might perhaps have clarified the matter—that no meadow is associated with the cultivated section, but that the arable land of each farm lies in two distinct sections, the smaller in crop alternation, producing winter feed, the larger farmed by whatever system adapts itself most profitably to changes in the level of fertility and the price of the product.

C. INDOOR FEEDING

Experience tells us that a cow fed on good and plentiful feed yields far more milk than one that is poorly kept.

Indoor feeding normally keeps the cows in abundant feed in winter as well as summer.

A comparison of the net and gross milk yields of a cow well fed winter and summer with those of a pasture cow, well fed only in summer, illustrates the great superiority of indoor feeding.   161

But meagre winter keep is not an intrinsic feature of pasturage. In fact, there is no reason whatsoever why winter feed should be less plentiful with grazing than with a system that keeps its animals indoors the whole year round.

Hence, in comparing indoor feeding with grazing, we have to distinguish very carefully between the following points:

1. What part of the higher milk yield of the stall cow is due to abundant regular feeding the whole year round?
2. If the pasture cow is equally regularly and well fed, what advantages are left to indoor feeding?

It is vital that the livestock be kept on a regular and abundant diet the whole year round. This is easily achieved where the cattle are stall-fed in summer, provided there is enough green feed. With grazing, the difficulties are greater. In May and June the grass shoots up so fast that the animals cannot consume it all and part will run to seed. In July and August the growth slows down, and where they depend wholly on the ley the animals will generally go short of feed.

162

This may be dealt with by occasionally bringing fresh pastures into the stubble of the clover or into once-cut meadows, or by taking green feed to the pastures.

Where regular feeding is ensured in this way and the pasture cows are as well fed during winter as are the stall-fed cows, there is no reason why they should not produce the same yields in milk and in butter.

This is why, in discussing indoor feeding in Chapter 16, I did not assume higher returns from a given quantity of feed for the stall-fed as compared with the pasture cow, and considered only the essential and inherent advantages and drawbacks of the system.

It is a basic condition of indoor feeding that the soil be sufficiently fertile to produce clover to be cut for feed, instead of only grasses and pasture clover.

Where this condition is met, the chief advantage of indoor feeding is that the clover is not grazed down but is cut; which means that any given area of land yields nearly double the amount of feed it would in pasture, and far more manure. In other words, on a given area of land and soil of the same fertility, indoor feeding yields a larger surplus of replacement over exhaustion than does grazing.

For many years I was not certain that stable manure is of greater value than the manure produced on the pastures, especially as the latter is always associated with an appreciable quantity of animal gases and exhalations, which are of great nutritive value for soil. But longer experience has now convinced me that even where there

163

is no change at all in the grass yield, the soil does not gain twice as much wealth in a two-year pasture as it does in one year; and in a three-year pasture the benefit is proportionally even less. I have noticed, also, that the longer cow-droppings are exposed to the weather (i.e. the later the ley is ploughed in) the greater the loss of efficacy in the manure.

On the other hand, grazing avoids certain labour costs which are associated with indoor feeding; such as bringing the feed to the farmyard, or carting the stall-manure to the plots.

Whether indoor feeding or grazing proves to be the more profitable system depends entirely on which is higher: the value of the extra feed and manure obtained from indoor feeding, or the total extra costs incurred.

This in turn depends on the price of manure and feed; thus again we find that the price of agricultural products is second only to soil fertility in determining if, when, and where, indoor feeding has the advantage over grazing.

D. MODIFICATIONS OF THE VARIOUS FARMING SYSTEMS

Our discussion has shown that the three different systems—three-field, improved and crop alternation—are appropriate to different levels in the grain price and in soil fertility.

For the purpose of our present argument the characteristic features 164 of these systems are as follows:

1. *The three-field system*

   (*a*) One section of the arable land is permanently in pasture.
   (*b*) Each year one-third of the tillage is in bare fallow.
   (*e*) All the manure is taken to this fallow.

2. *The improved system*

   (*a*) All the arable land is alternately in grain or pasture.
   (*b*) Each rotation has one bare fallow.
   (*c*) All the manure is taken to this fallow.
   (*d*) Grain and leguminous crops are cultivated in succession without interruption from tares or clover; and after the grain harvest the courses having suffered the greatest loss of fertility are put in pasture.

3. *The crop alternation system*

   (*a*) This has no bare fallow; all the arable land is cropped.
   (*b*) All the manure it produces is spent on feed crops, which are grown on the courses richest in plant food.
   (*c*) Grain and feed crops alternate.

But any one of these three systems may undergo many modifications if one of its characteristic features is replaced by one from either of the other systems. Thus mixed systems arise, standing halfway between the pure examples, and forming transitional stages from the one to the other.

165   It is scarcely possible to mention the innumerable gradations by which the mixed systems may approach to, and deviate from, the pure forms, let alone incorporate all the gradations in a theoretical framework. It is however possible to cast a brief look at some of the more important modifications.

1. Pure three-field system.
2. Three-field system in which the pasture is broken up from time to time (on average once every nine years); where several grain crops are taken from this section without manuring; and where the land is then allowed to revert to pasture. This system repays the cost of cropping the ley, for although the grain crop may itself not fully cover these costs, the straw it produces yields additional manure for the tillage, and the pasture is rejuvenated.
3. Improved system with a soft as well as a ley fallow, and where subsequently the land is left in pasture for more than three years. Such is the twelve-course improved rotation with the following sequence: 1. ley fallow, 2. winter grain, 3. summer grain, 4. soft fallow, 5. winter grain, 6. summer grain, 7. summer grain, 8–12 pasture. In retaining the soft fallow and leaving the land in pasture for several successive years this system still bears traces of the transition from the three-field system. By restricting the ley to one-twelfth of the total area it reduces the cost of the ley tillage, though it has the disadvantage of obtaining little grass and manure from its fourth- and fifth-year pastures.

166   4. Pure improved system with a ley fallow, but no soft fallow.
5. Improved system in which the fallow as well as a section of the preceding and the succeeding course is manured. This, though it looks exactly like the pure improved system, embodies one essential feature of crop alternation: the pasture comes not into poor but, at least in part, into rich soil. We must regard it therefore as a transitional stage to the pure crop alternation system.
6. Pure crop alternation.

We shall find these modifications even where all the arable land, from farmstead to farm boundary, is of the same fertility. But new modifications will appear where the outlying fields are poorer than those near the farmstead—as generally happens in reality.

The greater cost of cultivating the outlying plots is in itself sufficient to give rise to a tendency to farm the two sections by different systems; and if, in addition, the sections differ in their level of fertility, it will definitely pay to treat the nearer and the farther divisions of the land as distinct entities. This is the so-called "in-field, out-field" variation of the improved system. In the two sections the proportion of cropland to pasture will differ, the grain plots being larger in the in-field, and smaller in the out-field, than they would be if both sections were farmed in the same system. The in-field is thus predominantly devoted to grain, the out-field to pasture.

In Chapter 14 we saw that in the Isolated State the three-field system will pay when rye fetches 0·470 thalers the bushel, and that the improved system will only yield a larger net product than the three-field system where the rye price is at least 0·665 thalers. If none but the pure systems existed, only the three-field system would be able to utilise arable land at a rye price of between 0·470 and 0·665 thalers the bushel. But in fact, a rye price of between 0·470 and 0·665 thalers the bushel makes profitable a higher manure output than is possible under the three-field system—provided that the cost of its production is not as high as in the pure improved system. In other words, a mixed system will arise.

We also saw, in Chapter 16, that the pure improved system is only able to utilise soil of a mean fertility of 373° per 1000 square rods, whereas crop alternation can make good use of a mean fertility of 510°. If, with rising soil fertility, a holding farmed in the improved system were suddenly to adopt crop alternation, the soil would not be sufficiently fertile to support the new system, and the net revenue would fall. But an improved system in which the final grain course is manured can easily utilise a higher mean fertility than 373° without incurring costs higher than those of the pure improved system; thus it becomes a useful bridge from the pure improved system to the system of crop alternation.

Now suppose that instead of the steady state we have a gradual but continuous rise in grain price and soil fertility—as normally happens in practice. In due course we would see one single holding pass through all the modifications we have been looking at as isolated prototypes.

For if the two factors, grain price and fertility, have risen to the point where it will pay to adopt a system with costs which, though not as high as those of the pure improved system, are yet higher than those of the three-field system, a mixed system will arise. And because mixed systems may approach one or other of the pure forms by way of innumerable modifications, we shall find, for every stage in grain price and fertility, a corresponding farming system. Given rational cultivation, a slight rise in both factors will bring about a slight change in farming methods, until ultimately the pure improved system will set in.

If both factors continue to rise, there will be momentary pauses, but neither rest nor constancy.

Where manure production is rising, the system that has reached the level of fertility beyond which the fallow cannot usefully absorb any additional manure will use the surplus to manure its final course —the third grain course, which is to carry clover. Where this is done clover, instead of coming into the poorest soil, is put into soil so enriched by seven years in pasture that it needs little or no manure. In consequence the section of the final grain course which can be manured will progressively expand from rotation to rotation, fully utilising all the surplus manure. Further increases of fertility will eventually lead to the abolition of the fallow; and with the end of the fallow, the improved system vanishes, to be replaced by crop alternation.

169

In mountainous districts only the valleys are cultivated, and the mountain slopes serve as pastures. Here the improved system cannot extend over the entire area of a farm; and with rising grain price and fertility the transition from the three-field to the crop alternation system, by way of the improved system, cannot take place as in the plains.

And if the arable section in the valleys is so small, compared with the mountain pastures and meadows, that despite the exhausting three-field system soil fertility continues to increase, we arrive at the problem of how, and at what level of fertility, this part of the farm will adopt crop alternation?

Since my own calculations do not cover this particular example, I am unable to give a theoretical answer to this problem. It has however long been solved in practice: a section of the fallow, or even all of it, is cropped with potatoes, clover, peas, flax, and such-like crops. But a cultivated fallow ceases to be a fallow, and with it the three-field system loses its essential features. In having no fallow and farming all the arable land, this system is identical with crop alternation, without however enjoying any of the advantages of a rational sequence of crops. It is evident therefore that in these conditions crop alternation will be more profitable than a three-field system with a cropped fallow; and in fact since Thaer, that great teacher of scientific agriculture, introduced crop alternation to us as a system worthy of the attention of every serious farmer, it has been adopted on many a three-field holding in the mountains of Silesia, Moravia and Saxony.

170

Our discussion has been based on the assumption of soil at different levels of fertility but of the same physical quality throughout. We find, however, that on practically every existing farm the soil varies in quality. It would not serve my purpose to go into this at length; I mention it merely to underline the difficulty of choosing a system of cultivation when for every single farm we have to consider not only the varying distance between the different plots and the farmstead, but soils of different physical quality and at different levels of fertility. However sophisticated agricultural theory may one day become, the farmer who is not content with routine methods, who wishes constantly to be aware of all the manifold factors that may affect his conduct, can never act mechanically, but must give deep and serious though to everything that might affect his interests, and to conditions in society at large.

Having reached this point, we can return to the Isolated State, in order to determine the various rings that form around the Town.

CHAPTER 19

SECOND RING:
FORESTRY

THE plain of the Isolated State has to provide the Town not merely with food but with all its needs in fuel,[1] building timber, charcoal and so on. Which section of the Isolated State will produce all these varieties of wood?

Suppose that beech logs to be used as fuel sell at 16 thalers per cord[2] (224 ft^3) in the Town, and that the cost of taking one cord to the Town comes to 2 thalers the mile. In these conditions fuel cannot be brought to the Town from farther than eight miles—even though the wood could be produced at no cost and the land on which it is produced did not have to carry land rent.

It follows that the outlying districts cannot supply the Town with wood, which must therefore be produced near the Town.

If now we assume that only the grain price is known (1·5 thalers the bushel of rye), and try to discover what, given this assumption, wood will cost in the Town, our task becomes very much more difficult.

Wood and grain have no common measure of use-value: the one cannot replace the other.

"But why," it might well be asked, "may wood not cost 40 thalers the cord though rye fetches only 1·5 thalers the bushel? And if this should indeed be possible, it invalidates your conclusion that fuel has to be produced near the Town: on the contrary, it could then be brought from very far afield. Your argument that such a price-relation occurs nowhere in reality is not conclusive. Practically

---

[1] *Brennholz.* "Firewood" is the most exact translation, though it may convey the wrong impression in coal-using countries. Thünen is referring to wood used as basic fuel, which would certainly have been true of the Mecklenburg of his day and even much later.

[2] *Cord (Faden).* This unit of 224 Mecklenburg cubic feet equalled 194·7 English cubic feet, or 18·1 cubic metres.

everywhere around us we see the remnants of our ancient forests; and where these have vanished, other countries can supply us from their primeval forests. These forests cost man no labour, effort, or capital to create, and however high their use-value, their exchange value, at the place where they are found, can scarcely be much higher than that of water. In the Isolated State however, conditions have reached their final stage of development and are not subject to change, and here, where the primeval forests have vanished long ago, each wood and forest is man-made. If you want your findings to be valid, you have to prove the necessary connexion between the price of grain and that of wood.''

We have to admit the logic of this challenge, and try to make a satisfactory reply.

Suppose the Town price for one cord of wood is unknown, or equal to y thalers.

Suppose now that there is a beechwood of 100,000 square rods, divided into a hundred stands[1] of which one is felled each year. If this wood is efficiently administered, there will be one stand with one-year trees, one with two-year trees, and so on, to one with trees a hundred years old.

Let the product of the felled stand be	500 cords	173
Let the product obtained from thinning the younger stands also be	500 cords	
total product	1000 cords	

Suppose that the costs of managing this wood (administration, sowing or replanting the felled stands, replanting seedlings which have failed to grow, etc.) come, after deduction of the receipts from the game reserves and the chase, to 500 thalers per annum.

In our examination of agricultural costs we did not count the total net product of a farm as land rent, but only as much as was left after the interest on the buildings and valuable equipment had been deducted. This applies also to forestry: we cannot treat the total product of a forest as land rent or the yield of the soil as such, but

---

[1] *Stand (Kavel). Kavel* was a North German word meaning a "lot"; here Thünen uses it to mean 1/100 part of an area of 100,000 square rods, or 1000 square rods (5·35 English acres, or 2·17 hectares).

only the portion that is left after the interest on the capital embodied in the timber stock has been deducted.

Land cannot be farmed unless capital is invested in buildings, tools, etc.; forestry requires that the woods consist of trees from one year old to a hundred years or more.

Given a sufficiently large market it would be possible to fell at one time the entire stock of a hundred stands, sell the wood, and invest the money thus released; and only in so far as the annual net product from the forest exceeds the interest thus to be gained may we ascribe a value to the land.

Now suppose that the hundred stands contain a timber stock equal in value to 15,000 cords of mature wood. At a 5 per cent interest rate, the value of the return on the capital embodied in the trees would be equal to 750 cords. Subtracting this interest from the annual product of the forest, which is 1000 cords, we find that the land as such produces a yield of 250 cords.

If all the trees were felled and converted into capital, none of the costs of managing the forest would be incurred: the extra product of 250 cords must therefore carry the extra costs of management which it incurs.

If the annual outlay is 500 thalers, the production costs incurred by the standing timber (that is not including the costs of felling and sawing the wood) come to 2 thalers the cord.

The production costs, in my sense of the term, do not contain land rent, because according to my definition land rent is merely the surplus of price over cost of production.

If the cost of felling and cutting up the wood comes to half a thaler the cord, one cord will cost 2·5 thalers at the place where it is produced.

But this price, like every other price expressed in money, is valid only for one particular set of circumstances, and it will change with any change in the price of grain. A satisfactory answer to the problem we have posed requires however that our propositions remain valid for every standpoint in the Isolated State.

It follows that we must adopt the methods used in calculating farming costs: expressing the production costs one-quarter in money and three-quarters in rye.

When this is done, one-quarter (0·62 thalers) of the production costs per cord (2·5 thalers) will be given in money, and three quarters (1·88 thalers) in grain. If the calculation according to which the cord costs 2·5 thalers is based on a situation where rye sells at 1·291 thalers the bushel, then 1·88 thalers will be equal in value to 1·46 (i.e. 1·88/1·291) bushels of rye. Expressed in general terms, the production costs of one cord of wood therefore come to 1·46 bushels of rye plus 0·62 thalers.

According to Chapter 4 we can calculate the rye price for every standpoint in the Isolated State: for at x miles from the Town, one bushel of rye costs $(273 - 5·5x)/(182 + x)$ thalers. At this price for rye, 1·46 bushels plus 0·62 thalers are equal to $(511 - 7·4x)/(182 + x)$ thalers; in other words, in the district x miles from the Town, the production costs are $(511 - 7·4x)/(182 + x)$ thalers the cord.

A further question now poses itself: What will be the transport costs per cord if wood is supplied from a district x miles from the Town?

The cost of carting one load of 2400 lb over a distance of x miles comes to $199·5x/(182 + x)$ thalers (Chapter 4).

If one cord constitutes two full loads, its freight costs will come to $399x/(182 + x)$ thalers. 176

If the wood is produced on land which yields no land rent, it can be supplied to the Town at a price which covers merely the cost of its transport and production.

In the improved system—whose land rent must here be our measure—the district 28·6 miles from the Town does not yield rent. If, in the formula for the production and transport costs of wood, we substitute 28·6 for x, we shall find that in the Town one cord will cost 55·6 thalers.

As the Town cannot do without wood it will have to pay even this exorbitant price unless it can manage to obtain cheaper wood from a somewhat nearer district.

Wood that is produced near the Town becomes progressively cheaper to transport, though it will occupy land which yields rent. Its price must therefore cover, in addition to the cost of transport and production, the cost of the rent.[1]

The land rent from 100,000 square rods arable land at x miles from the Town comes to $(202,202 - 7065x)/(182 + x)$ thalers (Chapter 5). 100,000 square rods yield 250 cords of wood; one cord will consequently (omitting the small fractions) carry a land rent of $(809 - 28·3x)/(182 + x)$ thalers. 177

[1] i.e. a rent sufficient to displace the crop there produced, in this case grain.

In this situation the three constituents of the Town timber price come to:

(a) Production costs $\dfrac{511-7\cdot4x}{182+x}$ thalers

(b) Transport costs $\dfrac{399x}{182+x}$ thalers

(c) Land rent $\dfrac{809-28\cdot3x}{182+x}$ thalers

Total $\dfrac{1320+363\cdot3x}{182+x}$ thalers

In the Town the price per cord must therefore come to $(1320+363\cdot3x)/(182+x)$ thalers, and if for x we now substitute other values, we shall see which part of the Isolated State can supply the Town with the cheapest wood.

When x, (the distance from the Town) is	y, (the Town price per cord) is
28·6 miles	55·6 thalers
20 miles	42·5 thalers
10 miles	25·8 thalers
7 miles	20·4 thalers
4 miles	14·9 thalers
1 mile	9·2 thalers
0 miles	7·2 thalers

178   Suppose for the moment that firewood is produced in a district where the land does not yield rent. Here the Town would have to pay 55·6 thalers the cord. But the people of the districts nearer to the Town would soon realise that forestry would bring them greater profit from their land than farming; they would supply the Town with cheaper wood, and drive the remote producers from the market. This process would continue until the only districts producing fuel for the Town would be those very near the Town, which can supply the cheapest wood.

But the production of a crop that yields a full harvest only one hundred years after the time it was sown cannot suddenly shift from one district to another. Thus it is scarcely surprising that around us we see districts bare of trees which are ideally located for timber production and possess the right type of soil.

If we want to establish the price wood will fetch in the Town, we have to know the volume of the demand. The size of the Town's needs determines the area under timber; and the cost at which the remotest producer in this area can supply the Town is the norm for the price at which wood will sell in the Town. Thus if timber production had to extend up to seven miles from the Town, one cord would cost 20·4 thalers.

In these conditions, land at the outer edge of this ring will yield   179
the same—or rather an only very slightly higher—land rent from forestry than it would in agricultural use. But thanks to the savings on the very considerable freight costs of timber, an equivalent area of land only one mile nearer to the Town yields already a very much higher land rent. With falling distance from the market, the rent from land producing wood rises therefore at a much faster rate than it would if the land were producing grain in the improved system.

We have now come to the point where we can prove the price-relation of two products—grain and fuel—which are not substitutes for each other.

The rise or fall in the price of products which are substitutes for each other, that is, products with a common measure of use-value, will be parallel, and between them the price-relation will hardly alter, if at all.

Where commodities lack a common measure of value, a change in the demand for one may bring about a major change in the price-relation.

Take, for example, the invention in the Isolated State of a fuel-saving stove. If this reduces the demand for fuel to the extent that in future an area five instead of seven miles in radius could provide the Town with fuel, the price would fall by about four thalers the cord, or 20 per cent.

The outer fringe of the forestry ring, no longer required for fuel   180
production, will now turn to grain. But as this area is extremely small when compared with the total area of grain production, the result will be a minor, barely noticeable, fall in the grain price.

If the cord of fuel used to cost about as much as fourteen bushels of rye, it will now fetch no more than about twelve bushels of rye.

Inventions and improvements in production techniques have effects very like those of a fall in consumption.

For the foregoing calculation the author was not able (as he had been in discussing farming costs and product) to take his basic data from experience, but had to make a rough estimate as to the basic figures. But however internally consistent its findings and results, a calculation based on estimates and assumptions can show only the likely outcome of the assumptions, not their relevance to actual conditions.

However, if we can define the limits within which the assumed figures are likely to deviate from existing facts, and if we can establish that given these limits our findings remain valid, then we have proved our results correct.

181 Let us now extend these limits as far as possible, beyond the bounds of probability, and assume that in the one instance the production costs of timber come to eight times, and in the other to one-eighth the sum we have assumed.

First case. The production costs are eight times the sum we have assumed.

An increase in production costs may be due to two different causes: (1) a rise in the total costs of forestry where the timber yield remains constant, or (2) a fall in the yield where costs remain constant.

(*a*) Let the costs of forestry be eight times the sum we have assumed, the timber yield remaining constant.

In this case:

$$\text{Production costs} = 8\,\frac{(511-7\cdot4x)}{(182+x)} = \frac{4088-59\cdot2x}{182+x}\ \text{thalers}$$

$$\text{Transport costs} = \frac{399x}{182+x}\ \text{thalers}$$

$$\text{Land rent} = \frac{809-28\cdot3x}{182+x}\ \text{thalers}$$

$$\text{Total} \quad \frac{4897+311\cdot5x}{182+x}\ \text{thalers}$$

When x (the distance from the Town) = 20 miles, the price per cord is 55 thalers.

When x (the distance from the Town) = 10 miles, the price per cord is 42 thalers.

When x (the distance from the Town) = 0 miles, the price per cord is 27 thalers.

(b) Let the timber yield be one-eighth the quantity we have assumed, the costs remaining constant.

In this case:

Production costs	$= \dfrac{4088 - 59 \cdot 2x}{182 + x}$ thalers
Transport costs	$= \dfrac{399x}{182 + x}$ thalers
Land rent	$= 8 \dfrac{(809 - 28 \cdot 3x)}{182 + x} = \dfrac{6472 - 226 \cdot 4x}{182 + x}$ thalers
Total	$\dfrac{10{,}560 + 113 \cdot 4x}{182 + x}$ thalers

182

When $x = 20$ miles, the price per cord is therefore 63 thalers.

$x = 10$ miles, the price per cord is therefore 61 thalers.

$x = 0$ miles, the price per cord is therefore 58 thalers.

Second case. The production costs are one-eighth of what we have assumed them to be.

(a) The costs fall to one-eighth while the output remains constant. Here we find that

Production costs	$= \left(\dfrac{511 - 7 \cdot 4x}{182 + x}\right) \div 8 = \dfrac{61 - 0 \cdot 9x}{182 + x}$ thalers
Transport costs	$= \dfrac{399x}{182 + x}$ thalers
Land rent	$= \dfrac{809 - 28 \cdot 3x}{182 + x}$ thalers
Total	$\dfrac{870 + 369 \cdot 8x}{182 + x}$ thalers

When $x = 20$ miles, the price per cord is 41 thalers.

$x = 10$ miles, the price per cord is 24 thalers.

$x = 0$ miles, the price per cord is 5 thalers.

(b) The output increases eight-fold while the total costs remain the same. Here

183

$$\text{Production costs} = \left(\frac{511-7\cdot4x}{182+x}\right) \div 8 = \frac{61-0\cdot9x}{182+x} \text{ thalers}$$

$$\text{Transport costs} = \frac{399x}{182+x} \text{ thalers}$$

$$\text{Land rent} = \left(\frac{809-28\cdot3x}{182+x}\right) \div 8 = \frac{101-3\cdot5x}{182+x} \text{ thalers}$$

$$\text{Total} \quad \frac{162+394\cdot6x}{182+x} \text{ thalers}$$

When   x = 20 miles, the price per cord is 40 thalers.
         x = 10 miles, the price per cord is 21 thalers.
         x = 0 miles, the price per cord is 1 thaler.

The invariable conclusion to be drawn from all the cases we have here examined is this: the Town can be supplied with far cheaper wood where this is produced nearby and not in the more distant regions. And since we may be certain that where forestry is rationally conducted neither costs nor yield will fall outside the limits we have set (irrationality of course knows neither rules nor limits), we have proved the proposition that wood must be produced near the Town.

We have now obtained a formula which will not only enable us to determine the price of wood but which is of such general validity that from it we can work out the price of every product in the Isolated State and the area where it is best cultivated; assuming that production costs, land rent and demand are known.

184   Let us ask for instance, "At what price can one bushel of rye be supplied to the Town and where will it be most profitable to grow it?" and try to find the answer.

From the data in Chapter 5 a plot of 100,000 square rods has a gross product of 3144 bushels of rye; since one load contains 28·6 bushels of rye (2400/84), 3144 bushels equals 110 loads (3144/28·6).

For this harvest, the production costs come to 1976 bushels of rye plus 641 thalers, which, distributed over 110 loads, amounts to 18 bushels of rye + 5·83 thalers a load.

Given the price of $(273 - 5 \cdot 5x)/(182 + x)$ thalers the bushel of rye, the production costs per load equal $(4914 - 99x)/(182 + x) + 5 \cdot 83$, which is equal to $(5975 - 93 \cdot 2x)/(182 + x)$ thalers. For 100,000 square rods of arable land or 110 loads of rye, the land rent is

$$(202,202 - 7065x)/(182 + x)$$

on one load it is therefore $(1838 - 64 \cdot 2x)/(182 + x)$.
For one load of 28·6 bushels of rye the costs are therefore distributed as follows:

Production costs	$\dfrac{5975 - 93 \cdot 2x}{182 + x}$ thalers
Transport costs	$\dfrac{199 \cdot 5x}{182 + x}$ thalers
Land rent	$\dfrac{1838 - 64 \cdot 2x}{182 + x}$ thalers
Total	$\dfrac{783 + 42 \cdot 1x}{182 + x}$ thalers

Hence the following relations obtain: 185

when $x = 20$ miles, 1 load of rye costs 42·9 thalers, which is 1·5 thalers per bushel.
   $x = 10$ miles, 1 load of rye costs 42·9 thalers, which is 1·5 thalers per bushel.
   $x = 0$ miles, 1 load of rye costs 42·9 thalers, which is 1·5 thalers per bushel.

The answer to our question is this: all parts of the Isolated State where grain production yields land rent can supply the Town with rye at 1·5 thalers the bushel, and the production of grain is equally profitable in all parts of the Isolated State.

This finding follows from our assumptions, for the calculation of the land rent for the various districts rests wholly on the supposition that in the Town rye fetches 1·5 thalers the bushel. The calculation hence does not provide us with any deeper insight into the problem, though it confirms that the methods we are using are correct. It is however of the utmost importance, since for every crop for which we

know the production costs and land rent in relation to those of rye
it will now be possible to determine the price it will fetch in the Town
and the district where it must be cultivated.

APPLICATION OF THIS FORMULA TO VARIOUS OTHER CROPS

First crop: carrying the same land rent as grain but with only
half the production costs.

Production costs $\dfrac{2987-46\cdot6x}{182+x}$ thalers[1]

Transport costs per load $\dfrac{199\cdot5x}{182+x}$ thalers

Land rent[2] $\dfrac{1838-64\cdot2x}{182+x}$ thalers

Total $\dfrac{4825+88\cdot7x}{182+x}$ thalers

186   When $x = 20$ miles, one load costs 32·7 thalers
$x = 10$ miles, one load costs 29·7 thalers
$x = 0$ miles, one load costs 26·5 thalers

The district near the Town can therefore supply this crop more
cheaply than the more distant one. The price the crop will fetch in
the Town can be determined as soon as we know how far the area of
its cultivation must extend to satisfy the Town's needs.

Second crop: same land rent as for grain, with double the production costs.
Here the total costs come to $(13{,}788-51\cdot1x)/(182+x)$.

When $x = 20$ miles, one load costs 63·2 thalers
$x = 10$ miles, one load costs 69·2 thalers
$x = 0$ miles, one load costs 75·7 thalers

This crop will be grown at some distance from the Town.

---

[1] In all German editions this is misprinted as 46x.
[2] Thünen here introduces the land rent applicable to a load of grain lifted off the
same plot, because this "displacement rent" is a cost that must be carried by the
cultivator of the alternative crop. This idea of "displacement rent" has already been
introduced in the discussion of forestry (p. 109 above). For a further analysis see pp.
xxxiv–xxxvi of the Editorial introduction.

Third crop: same production costs as grain, half the land rent. The total production costs for this crop come to

$$(6894 + 74 \cdot 2x)/(182 + x)$$

When $x = 20$ miles, one load costs 41·5 thalers
           $x = 10$ miles, one load costs 39·7 thalers
           $x = 0$ miles, one load costs 37·9 thalers

This crop will be grown near the Town.

Fourth crop: same production costs, half the land rent. Total costs $(9651 - 22 \cdot 1x)/(182 + x)$.   187

When $x = 20$ miles, one load costs 45·6 thalers
           $x = 10$ miles, one load costs 49·1 thalers
           $x = 0$ miles, one load costs 53·0 thalers

This crop will be grown far from the Town.

A close look at these four examples reveals the following general laws:

1. Where production costs per load are the same, the crop which has to carry the higher land rent will be grown farther from the Town.
2. Where the land rent incurred per load is the same, the crop with the higher production costs must be grown at the greater distance from the Town.

Problem. At what price can the Town be supplied with a commodity which, in comparison with rye, costs fourteen times as much to produce per load and twice as much to transport, if this commodity need not yield land rent?

In this case the production costs amount to $\dfrac{83,650 - 1305x}{182 + x}$ thalers

Transport costs to $\dfrac{399x}{182 + x}$ thalers

Total costs $\dfrac{83,650 - 906x}{182 + x}$ thalers

When x = 30 miles, one load costs therefore 266 thalers, which is
5·3 shillings a pound

x = 10 miles, one load costs therefore 388 thalers, which is
7·8 shillings a pound

x = 0 miles, one load costs therefore 460 thalers, which is
9·2 shillings a pound

188   The district thirty miles from the Town can therefore supply this product at nearly half the price the area immediately around the Town would have to charge. And if the distant parts can satisfy the Town's demand, it follows that the cultivation of this product would create considerable losses for the districts that lie nearer.

But let us return now to our discussion of forestry.

For our calculations we took the annual timber product to be 1000 cords, and the entire timber stock contained in all the stands to be equal in value to 15,000 cords. Hence in value the annual increment is to the total timber stock as is 1 : 15; it is 1/15th, or 6·66 per cent, of the entire stock.

But experience has shown that in buying a property it is extremely dangerous to assess the value of its timber from the total stock of timber it contains, and to buy on the basis of such an estimate. Many a buyer has suffered considerable losses in this way; some have lost their entire property. For subsequently it appeared that the timber failed to yield the full current interest rate; that its annual product was not 1/20th of the entire timber stock, but only 1/30th or even 1/40th, and that the capital spent on buying the wood yielded an interest rate of only 3·33 or 2·5 per cent.

We know of woods where the annual timber increment is assessed at only 1/40th part of the total timber stock.

189   Now if we suppose that these experiences derive from the essential nature of the tree, which restricts the annual increment to 1/30th or 1/40th part of the total stock, and if we develop this theory to its logical conclusion, we arrive at some most curious results.

1. Not only does the land under timber yield no land rent, but its product is in fact negative, because the interest on the stock of timber amounts to twice the annual product.

2. Everyone who owns a wood or forest, and knows his own best interest, will promptly fell all his trees, sell the timber, and

invest the capital thereby released. In so doing, he will not merely obtain double the interest he derived from the wood, but will also be able to sell the land on which the trees were standing. Should the market be too limited to let him sell his entire timber at once, he will not bother to replant the stands when they are felled each year, and eventually the entire wood will disappear, more slowly to be sure, but just as certainly.

3. This gradual destruction of the woodlands must raise the price of timber. But—and here we come to the special feature of this particular case—however much the price of timber rises, it cannot render forestry profitable or save the woodlands from their ultimate destruction: because the capital contained in the timber stock will rise with the rising price, and the interest on this capital when it is released and reinvested will always produce double the interest it would in forestry. Rising timber prices will merely make the destruction of the forests all the more profitable and alluring. Only a fall in the interest rate, to less than 2·5 per cent, could halt this process. But if the interest rate does not fall, and such an indispensible commodity as firewood is not to vanish from our earth, the governments will have to take steps to deprive private citizens of their right to dispose as they choose of their woods, forcing them to make do with only half the potential revenue from their forest property. Yet even such an infringement of the rights of property would not be able to stem the process of destruction for more than a little while—for in these circumstances the forests would be managed by their owners with the utmost negligence.

190

When, however, we look at the growth of a young tree, say a young pine, we find that a two-year old tree contains perhaps ten times as much wood as a one-year old; that a three-year old tree has about seven times the volume of a two-year old; and so on. The annual increment, we find, is not a fraction of the timber volume of a tree at the beginning of the year, but several times as high. As the tree matures, the absolute increment rises from year to year, but the relative increment, i.e. the annual increment measured against the tree's total volume at the beginning of the year, decreases,because the total quantity of timber with which it is compared is constantly becoming larger. Thus if in the fifth year the annual increment is equal to the timber content of the tree at the beginning of the year, in the sixth year it will be only about 90 per cent, and in the seventh perhaps only 80 per cent.

With this gradual fall in the relative increase of the timber volume, the point must ultimately arrive where the tree's annual increment is only 5 per cent of its timber volume at the beginning of the year.

191   If instead of a single tree we take an entire stand, containing trees all of the same age, the time must also come when for this entire stand the annual increment in value is equal to precisely 5 per cent of its total timber stock.

If the stand is felled at just this point in time, and the timber product thereby obtained is compared with the total timber stock of all the stands, ranging from those with one-year trees to those with mature trees ripe for felling, we shall see that the annual product is more than 5 per cent of the total timber stock.[1] For since the increment is 5 per cent on the stand ripe for felling, but considerably more on all the other stands with younger trees, it follows that the average increment—that is for all the stands taken together—must be larger than 5 per cent.

And if it is established that Nature grants trees a larger annual increment than 5 per cent, but many woods exist where this is only 2·5 per cent, it follows that all such woods are grievously mismanaged.

In woods where 100- and 200-year-old trees stand side by side with those of 10 and 20, and trees which have ceased growing occupy the space the younger ones need for their development, the absolute increment will naturally be very small (being a proportion of the very large total stock), and may quite easily sink to 2·5 per cent or less.

Such forest management, or rather lack of management, is justified
192   only where the land itself is of such little value that it would not pay to clear the soil for agricultural use.

This may well have been true for large stretches of Germany in past centuries. Conditions have meanwhile changed a good deal, but forestry has not universally undergone the development appropriate to the changed conditions, and we see many woods and forests managed by methods that have long ago become outmoded and irrational.

But even where the better modern practices prevail, it is a long, slow process to wean the woods from their natural condition, for

---

[1] This is confusing. In this case the *product* is much less than 5 per cent of all the timber. Thünen appears to confuse product and increment.

since the life-span of a tree exceeds by far that of a man, it takes several human generations to bring an entire forest area under the right methods of management.

When the right methods are adopted, only trees of the same age will stand together; and they will be felled before the relative increment in their annual value sinks to 5 per cent—the rate of interest I have assumed to prevail throughout the Isolated State.[1] With very tall timber, the trees will not be permitted to attain their full maturity and the forestry cycle will be far shorter than the proper life-span of a tree, and it is possible that the beechwood cycle, which we assumed to be one hundred years, will on these grounds be somewhat less.

Because fuel taken from more mature trees commands a higher price than that from younger trees, the growth cycle may be extended beyond the point where the relative increment is 5 per cent. This, however, can only happen for a few years, for the increase in the value of the fuel will not be able to outweigh for long the increase in production costs due to the loss of interest on the capital.

193

This is not so with building timber. Such timber, to be at all useful, must have a given toughness, and the trees cannot be felled until they have attained this toughness. Their growth will therefore take much longer than that of trees for fuel, which adds considerably to the production cost of building timber. But as such timber is essential, a given quantity, say one cubic foot, will fetch a higher price the tougher the timber, and timber prices will correspond to the costs of growing wood of every grade.

At a given weight, building timber will therefore fetch a higher price than timber for fuel, and relative to its value the former will cost less to transport than the latter.

Building timber will thus be grown in the section of the ring most distant from the Town.

In the shape of firewood the waste from building timber would not repay the cost of sending it to the Town; converted into charcoal it becomes a fuel of a lower specific weight which can still make a profit in the Town. The outer fringe of the forestry ring will therefore supply the Town with charcoal as well as building timber.

[1] Although marred by a curious arithmetical slip, this passage marks Thünen's first approach to the principle of marginal revenue productivity, which he was to treat in greater detail in Part II of *The Isolated State*. "Cultivation" of the trees was to be pursued until the marginal point, where their annual increment in value was just equal to the return from an alternative investment of the capital employed.

It may be profitable, in the innermost fringe of the ring of forestry nearest the Town, to produce trees with a very fast growth rate, for although their timber will not be as valuable, weight for weight, as for instance beechwood, a given area of land will yield a larger annual product. The outer fringe, on the other hand, cannot afford to supply the Town with any but the most expensive grade of fuel.

Inside the forestry ring we would therefore find further subdivisions or concentric rings, producing different grades of timber.

The forestry ring will supply only the Town and the ring of free cash cropping with fuel. The districts at a greater distance from the Town will produce fuel for their own use, but being too remote to send any to the Town they do not concern our inquiry; and forestry will not be mentioned when we come to study the systems of the other rings.

Suppose the cord of fuel timber fetches 21 thalers in the Town: what is the land rent in the different sections of the ring of forestry?

One cord fetches 21 thalers, or

$$21 \left(\frac{182+x}{182+x} \right) = \frac{3822+21x}{182+x} \text{ thalers}$$

Production costs per cord are $\dfrac{511-7\cdot4x}{182+x}$ thalers

Transport costs are $\dfrac{399x}{182+x}$ thalers

When both types of cost are subtracted from the revenue we find that the land rent of the area producing one cord of wood is

$$\frac{3311-370\cdot6x}{182+x} \text{ thalers}$$

On 100,000 square rods yielding 250 cords the land rent therefore comes to

$$250 \left(\frac{3311-370\cdot6x}{182+x} \right) \text{ thalers}$$

When x (or the distance from the Town in miles) is	The land rent is
0	4548 thalers
1	4017 thalers
2	3492 thalers
4	2458 thalers
7	948 thalers

At the outer edge of the forestry ring, timber production yields the same land rent as does the adjacent farming land. Thanks however to the enormous savings made on transport, the land rent from timber rises rapidly with proximity to the Town, until, very near the Town, it is 4548 thalers. At this point the improved system, if managed as in the remoter districts,[1] would yield a land rent of only 1111 thalers.

[1] See below, p. 142.

CHAPTER 20

A LOOK BACK AT THE FIRST RING, WITH SPECIAL REFERENCE TO POTATO PRODUCTION

THE discussions in the last few paragraphs have shown that fuel must be produced near the Town, and that in comparison with agriculture forestry yields a land rent which rises very rapidly with approach to the Town.

But earlier we said that the ring of free cash cropping would occupy the area immediately around the Town, giving some reasons for this statement without however developing these sufficiently to prove our point. Hence we must take the subject up once more.

196 Free cash cropping and forestry compete for the same land: both lay claim to the district nearest to the Town. But since these systems cannot exist side by side in one district, we must endeavour to discover which of the two will oust the other.

But because each district will adopt the system making the highest use of its soil, this question leads back to another, namely: Which system will produce the larger land rent very near the Town?

We must see, then, whether there is any crop which near the Town will yield a larger land rent than does timber. This brings us to the potato.

THE PRICE OF POTATOES IN THE TOWN

Rye and potatoes may both be measured by a common standard—nutritive value. If we assume, as indeed we must, that people have no preference for one or the other, then the prices of these two products will be precisely related to their nutritive value.

But chemical analyses and the findings of agriculturists are virtually unanimous in holding that in terms of flour content as well as nutritive value three heaped bushels of potatoes are equal to one bushel of rye. We take it therefore that in the Town one bushel of potatoes fetches one-third the price of one of rye, or half a thaler.

The following calculations on the yield and cultivation costs of   197
potatoes rest on the discussion of the Belgian system in Chapter 17,
where we assumed that on the same area and with the same level of
fertility soil which yields one bushel of rye will yield nine of potatoes.
We found that 5·7 bushels of potatoes cost no more labour to
produce than one of rye.[1]

A crop which from the same area of land produces three times the
nutritive value of rye, and rewards human labour with twice the
quantity of nutriment, is indeed so extraordinary, and its widespread
introduction is so likely to bring about a revolution in agriculture
that we would have to devote some space to it, even if it did not
enter into the problem of determining the boundaries of the first
ring.

We have previously excepted the ring of free cash cropping from
the assumption that soil throughout the Isolated State will yield 8
bushel-crops of rye after the bare fallow, endowing it, thanks to its
purchase of Town manure, with a far higher level of fertility. In
the following calculations we assume that this ring has the same
fertility as the Belgian system described in Chapter 17.

If the potatoes are fed to the livestock, the manure they return
will easily repay what their production costs the soil. Matters however are very different where they are not used as feed, but are sold.

In grain production not all the arable land can be cropped with   198
grain. To make good the loss of nutrient extracted by the grain, some
of the land must carry crops that will return a larger quantity of
manure than they consume. The same holds true of potato production for the market.

If we want to calculate the quantity of potatoes that a given area
of say, 100,000 square rods, can annually produce, and to compare
the nutritive value of this harvest with one produced on the given
area by grain, we have first to discover how large a section of the
land can carry potatoes without any loss of fertility.

Straw is a by-product of every grain harvest; but though this straw
restores a portion of the plant nutrients extracted by the grain crop,
it cannot make good all the exhaustion. In a seven-course improved

[1] *Supra*, pp. 92, 94. Thünen does not give these figures directly in Chapter 17: they can
be read from the tables. Actually, the first comparison works out at one bushel of
rye = 9·9 bushels of potatoes. In a Note (Note 5 at the end of the text in the 1842
edition), not reproduced in this edition, Thünen wrote that the yield of a good quality
potato would be only two-thirds as great as that of the rather coarse potato produced
for human consumption in Belgium.

rotation with the following sequence: (1) fallow, (2) rye, (3) barley, (4) oats, (5) pasture, (6) pasture, (7) pasture, there are as many pasture as grain courses.

If this particular system maintains a constant level of fertility on a good soil, it follows that the fertility extracted by one grain course is equal to the fertility returned by one pasture course plus the manure produced from the straw.

199   If the potato haulm is left on the plot, the harvest will produce no straw, and manure-yielding crops will have to be raised to make good the fertility extracted by potatoes.

To obtain a better picture of the problem let us take as our measure one pasture course and ask: How many pasture courses must be associated with one potato course in order to produce enough manure to cover the fertility extracted by the potatoes?

But the absolute exhaustion caused by potatoes is greater the richer the soil on which they are grown and the larger their yield; and the amount of manure produced from the pastures is also larger on rich than on poor soil. Where the pasture is set on poor soil it will take more pasture courses to cover the exhaustion caused by one potato course than where it is set on rich soil.

The findings of my calculations are as follows.[1]

1. Where the soil for the potato course is as fertile as for the barley course, but the soil for the pastures has the same fertility as for the pastures in the improved system, it takes $2\frac{3}{4}$ (to be precise 2·76) pasture courses to make good the fertility extracted by one potato course.
2. Where the soil for the potato and pasture courses has the same level of fertility, one potato course must be associated with $1\frac{5}{6}$ pasture courses.
3. Where potatoes are grown on soil so rich that it produces clover for indoor feeding, and clover and potatoes are set on soil of the same fertility, it will take $1\frac{1}{2}$ (1·46 to be precise) clover courses to make good the fertility extracted by one potato course.

200   We will now compare the relative nutritive yield of potatoes and grain in case (1). On a soil yielding 10 bushel-crops in the improved system, three grain courses, each of 1000 square rods, will yield 235 bushels of rye-equivalent. By comparison, one course of potatoes

[1] In Note 5 of the 1842 edition (not reproduced here) Thünen wrote that these data needed to be supplemented from experience elsewhere.

(at the same fertility as a barley course) will produce 720 bushels of tubers, which is equivalent to 240 bushels of rye. For grain, three grain courses have to be associated with three pasture courses in order to maintain soil fertility; for potatoes, 2·75 pasture courses suffice for one potato course. 235 bushels of rye therefore take six courses to produce; whereas 720 bushels of potatoes—240 bushels expressed in rye equivalent—take only 3·75.

On a course of 1000 square rods grain yields 39 bushels of rye (235/6), and potatoes the equivalent of 64 bushels of rye (240/3·75). The relative nutritive value of these crops is as 39 to 64, or as 100 to 164.

On closer examination we must thus greatly modify our first, superficial assumption that compared with rye potatoes yield three times the amount of nutriment from a given area. Nevertheless, potatoes do retain a very significant advantage.

However, where a farm need not produce its own manure but can buy as much as it requires to replace the fertility extracted by the potato crop, the proposition remains absolutely valid that on a given area potatoes yield three times the amount of food for human consumption yielded by rye.

Thus it becomes necessary to look at two further aspects of potato production: (*a*) where a farm produces all the manure required for potatoes, and (*b*) where this is bought. 201

(*a*) Suppose the potatoes are produced on a farm which manages to maintain a constant level of fertility by associating for this purpose 1·5 clover courses with one potato course.

For such a system my calculations show that per load of 24 bushels of potatoes:

1. Production costs $= \dfrac{489 - 4\cdot7x}{182 + x}$ thalers

2. Transport costs $= \dfrac{199\cdot5x}{182 + x}$ thalers

3. The revenue[1] 12 thalers or $12\left(\dfrac{182 + x}{182 + x}\right) = \dfrac{2184 + 12x}{182 + x}$

On deduction from the revenue of the transport and production costs, a land rent remains of $\dfrac{1695 - 182\cdot8x}{182 + x}$

---

[1] *Einnahme*, i.e. gross product.

This is the land rent for an area annually producing one load of potatoes for the market. But in my calculations I found that an area of 100,000 square rods—40,000 producing potatoes and the rest in clover—can supply the market with 1440 loads a year (the small potatoes fit only for feed being discounted).

100,000 square rods therefore produce a land rent of

$$1440 \left(\frac{1695 - 182 \cdot 8x}{182 + x} \right) = \frac{2,440,800 - 263,232x}{182 + x}$$

202

Hence when x, the distance from the Town in miles, is	100,000 square rods yield a land rent of
0	13,411 thalers
1	11,899 thalers
4	7462 thalers
7	3165 thalers
9·3	0 thalers

(b) Where the manure required for potato production is bought from the Town.

Here the situation is very different from that on the first farm, where only 40 per cent of the total acreage can grow potatoes. On this farm it is possible to crop all the land with potatoes, and 100,000 square rods can in consequence supply the Town with 3600 instead of only 1440 loads.

On the other hand this farm incurs the following costs which the first one does not have to bear:

1. The cost of bringing the Town manure to the plots.
2. The cost of buying it.

According to my estimates, the production of 24 bushels of potatoes costs the plot 0·94 loads of manure, which I shall call one load for short. For every load of potatoes taken to the Town one of manure must therefore be brought back.

If every wagon taking potatoes to the Town were to bring back one load of manure, the transport of the manure would need no special journeys, although the horses, having to pull a full load each way, would suffer far greater strain. Since I possess no comparative figures for this, I shall assume that the freight cost per load taken on

the return journey comes to half the ordinary freight; so that the
cost of fetching one load of manure comes to:

$$\frac{199 \cdot 5x \div 2}{182 + x} = \frac{99 \cdot 7x}{182 + x}$$

What here is the price of one load of manure in the Town; and
how is this determined?

Adam Smith divides the price of products into wage, return to
capital, and land rent. My own studies lead me to divide the price
of agricultural products into production costs, transport costs and
land rent; and although transport and production costs may in
turn be subdivided into wage and return to capital, I have not as yet
found it necessary to distinguish quite so finely.

Strictly, the substance we are now discussing cannot be called
either "a commodity" or "a product". It would be absurd to ask
what part in its production costs is played by wage, return to capital
or land rent; what are its costs of transport and production; what
land rent is incurred on its production. It is involuntarily produced;
its quantity will neither rise nor fall with any rise or fall in the
demand; and since the owner must be rid of it at any cost, its value
is for him negative. This commodity is so exceptional that its price
cannot be determined by any of the laws I have discussed. The
determination of its price is thus a question of some interest.

But we cannot yet answer this question, and so must assume that
the price of one load of Town manure is unknown, or equal to a
thalers.

According to my calculations, for the farm which buys manure
from the Town the price of one load of potatoes is made up as
follows:

1. Production costs $\dfrac{526 - 7 \cdot 5x}{182 + x}$ thalers

2. Transport costs (potatoes) $\dfrac{199 \cdot 5x}{182 + x}$ thalers

3. Transport costs (manure) $\dfrac{99 \cdot 7x}{182 + x}$ thalers

4. Cost of buying the manure a thalers

           Total costs $\dfrac{526 + 291 \cdot 7x}{182 + x} + a$

The revenue is 12 thalers or

$$12 \left(\frac{182+x}{182+x} \right) = \frac{2184+12x}{182+x}$$

When the expenses are subtracted from the revenue, the land rent per load is

$$\frac{1658-279 \cdot 7x}{182+x} - a$$

On 100,000 square rods, yielding 3600 loads of potatoes, land rent therefore comes to

$$3600 \left(\frac{1658-279 \cdot 7x}{182+x} - a \right) \text{ thalers}$$

Farmers living in the ring of free cash cropping have the constant choice of producing their manure or of buying it from the Town; they will only do the latter if this comes cheaper than producing it.

We have worked out the land rent of both kinds of farm enterprise; by equating the two figures we shall discover the price at which it becomes profitable to buy manure.

Let the land rent of farm A equal that of Farm B, where A is a farm that does not buy manure and B is one that does.

$$\overset{A}{\underset{}{1440 \left(\frac{1695-182 \cdot 8x}{182+x} \right)}} = \overset{B}{\underset{}{3600 \left(\frac{1658-279 \cdot 7x}{182+x} - a \right)}}$$

therefore

$$\frac{6780-731 \cdot 2x}{182+x} = \frac{16,580-2797x}{182+x} - 10a$$

or

$$10a = \frac{9800-2065 \cdot 8x}{182+x}$$

therefore

$$a = \frac{980-206 \cdot 6x}{182+x} \text{ thalers}$$

When x or the distance from the Town in miles is	a or the value of one load of manure is
0	5·4 thalers
1	4·2 thalers
2	3·1 thalers
3	1·9 thalers
4	0·83 thalers
4·75	0 thaler

It appears that the farmers living directly next to the Town can buy manure at 5·4 thalers the load without paying more than it would have cost them to produce it, but that with greater distance the price the farmers can afford to pay falls rapidly. At 4·75 miles they can still afford the cost of fetching the manure but can no longer pay its purchase price.

Thus very different factors influence the price of this commodity. The Townsmen must be rid of the manure even if they receive nothing for it or if indeed they have to pay for its removal; farmers who live near the Town can pay more than those living at a distance. Which of these interests will finally determine the price?

Here we must distinguish between two alternative situations:

1. where the Town has so much manure that not all of it can be used by the farms inside a radius of 4·75 miles;
2. where it has less than is required by the farms inside this radius.

Take the first situation. Once the entire area inside a radius of 4·75 miles has been supplied, some manure will remain and will have to be removed. If in such a situation the Town demanded some payment for its manure, say 0·83 thalers a load, the farmers living more than 4 miles away would stop fetching manure, and the Town's surplus would grow, together with the cost of its removal. Unless the Town means to act against its own interests it will have to make a free gift of the manure to farmers living more than 4 miles away. But is it possible to charge the farmer who lives near the Town for his manure when his colleague from afar can obtain this free of charge? Can he who sells a commodity fix its price by the benefit it brings the buyer, and sell cheap one day and dear the next? Such a policy would require arbitrary restrictions; and we have therefore to assume that in the given situation farmers from every district of the State will be able to get Town manure free.

In the second situation, where there is not enough manure to supply the whole area which might profitably use it, farmers living at different distances from the Town will compete for it. If at first manure is to be had for nothing, some of it will be taken to remote farms, and the farmers who live near the Town, for whom this manure is very valuable, would not get all they need. To protect their supply the farmers near the Town will have to pay enough for the manure to make it unprofitable for their distant colleagues to continue fetching this. Given that the Town has enough manure to

206

207

meet the needs of a ring four miles in radius, the farmers living in
this area will have to pay 0·83 thalers a load; if they paid less, say
half a thaler a load, the farmers from the outer districts could still
buy and fetch Town manure at a profit, and those from the nearer
parts would suffer.

Our calculation of land rent is based on this last supposition.
We assume that in the Town, or rather at its gates, manure fetches
0·83 thalers a load.

When we substitute 0·83 for a in the formula we have given, we
find that 100,000 square rods of tillage on farm B yield a land rent
of

$$3600 \left(\frac{1658 - 279·7x}{182 + x} - 0·83 \right) \text{thalers}$$

When x, or the distance in miles from the Town, is	Land rent is
0	29,808 thalers
1	24,126 thalers
2	18,504 thalers
3	12,948 thalers
4	7467 thalers

That land rent inside this ring rises so disproportionately with
approach to the Town is due to a combination of two factors: (1) the
local products are expensive to transport relative to their price, and
(2) the cost of transporting the manure falls in direct ratio to falling
distance from the Town.

But our calculations give such an inordinately high rent for land
directly next to the Town that we must pause to see if we can find a
single similar example in the real world.

It should not surprise us if we fail to do so. In the first place, our
calculations are based on soil which not only has the highest useful
level of fertility but is of exceptional physical quality; such soil is
rarely found in large, continuous tracts. And secondly, there is no
considerable and certainly no very large town that is not built on
navigable water, which, as we shall shortly see, extends the ring
supplying the Town with potatoes to such an extent that the price
of potatoes falls to less than one-third the price of rye, bushel by
bushel.

But on closer investigation we find instances of even higher land rent.

In the first decades of the present century the rental of the pastures directly next to Hamburg was 1 Mark the square rod, which is roughly 37,000 thalers per 100,000 square rods.

Sinclair, in his Code of Agriculture[1] (p. 558), tells us that near London one acre of horticultural land yields

Rental	10 pounds sterling
Poor rates, tithes, and other duties	8 pounds sterling
making a total of	18 pounds sterling

which is approximately 58,000 thalers per 100,000 square rods.

Rental is not yet pure land rent: to obtain this we have to subtract from the rental the interest on the capital invested in the glass of the greenhouses, in the forcing-beds, fences, etc. But, though this interest is high, the intensity of land use will still be higher than in the Isolated State.

However much intensive utilisation may inflate the price of land near a large town, this is only a prelude to a far greater rise in land values inside the town. The man who wants to build a house outside the town walls, and buys a plot of land for the purpose, will pay for it only the value this land would have had for market gardening. Once the house is built the land rent this plot used to yield becomes ground rent; but at this spot the amount of both these types of rent will be identical. Still nearer to the town, ground rent will continue rising until, at the town centre or main market square, we find the bare plot on which a house might stand costing more than 100 thalers the square rod.

If we want to know the reasons for the disproportionate rise in ground rent with approach to the town centre, we shall find them in labour economies; in the greater general convenience of a central situation; in the time-savings to be made in trade and business: for one and the same law governs ground as well as land rent.

210

---

[1] SIR JOHN SINCLAIR, *The Code of Agriculture; including Observations on Gardens, Orchards, Woods, and Plantations* (London 1817). Thünen refers here to J. von Schreibers' translation, published in Vienna in 1820: the figures he gives are based on a table on p. 417 of the 1817 English edition. On page 426 Sinclair quotes a rent of up to £12 per acre for the best garden ground near Edinburgh.

At this point we ought to mention that although we have worked out the land rent from potato production, we do not yet know the actual land rent produced by soil in this ring; for in the first place, a given course can grow potatoes only in alternation with other crops, and secondly, this ring has to produce many other crops, some with a higher, some with a lower land rent than potatoes.

211

On each holding potatoes will consequently occupy only a portion of the land; and we shall only find the land rent of the total area from the aggregate net product of all the crops occurring in the rotation. Only a farmer living near a large town, who could draw the data from his own property, could undertake this calculation, a very difficult but instructive task, which would shed light on several obscure points in theoretical agriculture.

But at any rate potatoes will occupy a large section of the ring of free cash cropping; and we know enough about the land rent from potatoes to make a guess about the actual land rent which will be adequate to let us establish where in the Isolated State the rings of free cash cropping and of forestry will respectively be found.

Very near the Town the land rent of	thalers
farm *A*, producing the manure it needs for potatoes is	13,411
farm *B*, which buys manure for potatoes is	29,808
the forest enterprise, when timber fetches 21 thalers in the Town is	4548

Four miles from the Town the land rent of	
farm *A* is	7462
farm *B* is	7467
the forest enterprise is	2458

212

Because of the necessary alternation of crops a farm will have to raise some that utilise a given area of land less intensively than do potatoes. But, though in consequence the farm taken as a whole may yield only half the land rent yielded by the section carrying potatoes, free cash cropping will nevertheless, very near the Town, produce a land rent which is significantly higher than that produced by forestry.

And because soil in this district carries a very high rent, forestry is pushed out on to land with a lower rent.

Throughout the entire area four miles in radius—as far as manure is bought from the Town—free cash cropping remains unchallenged. Beyond, forestry would come into conflict with the system of farming as practised on farm *A* (which produces the manure it needs for potatoes), and it would have to recede even farther from the Town— were the soil to be still as rich as it is near the Town. But we assumed, and must continue to do so, that soil is of uniform fertility throughout the plain with the exception only of the district which is able to buy manure from the Town.

We have still to discover whether on a less fertile soil, yielding only 8 bushel-crops of rye after the bare fallow, potato production will inflate the land rent to the point where potato production ousts forestry. Should this happen, a new ring with its own peculiar farming system would arise between the rings of free cash cropping and forestry.

Before we try to tackle this problem we must discover how the labour costs of potato production will differ on soils of differing 213 yields.

The calculation I made for Tellow gave the following results:

If 100 square rods yield	One bushel costs
115 bushels of potatoes	3·8 shillings in labour costs
100 bushels of potatoes	4·2 shillings in labour costs
90 bushels of potatoes	4·6 shillings in labour costs
80 bushels of potatoes	5·1 shillings in labour costs
70 bushels of potatoes	5·7 shillings in labour costs
60 bushels of potatoes	6·5 shillings in labour costs
50 bushels of potatoes	7·8 shillings in labour costs

This is a less exact calculation than the one on the labour costs of grain production, partly because potatoes are not produced on a large scale, but mainly because my summary accounts do not specify the various operations of potato production. This means that when I differentiate between costs related to yield and costs related to the size of the cultivated area, some pure estimates are unavoidable. Nevertheless I believe that my findings will not differ much from those of an absolutely accurate calculation.

It is worth noting that the labour costs I refer to do not cover the entire production costs which, in addition to the direct labour costs, include the general farming costs.

At Tellow it was found that at a soil-yield of 115 bushels per 100 square rods one bushel of potatoes costs 3·8 shillings in labour; in the Belgian system at the same yield, one bushel costs only 3·3 214 shillings in labour (Chapter 17).[1] This discrepancy may in part be explained by the fact that my own calculations cover the storage

1 See *supra*, p. 94.

costs of potatoes (turning them, preventing their germination), which are not included in the calculations of the Belgian system, so that the one tells us what the potatoes cost at the time of their consumption, the other what they cost just on harvesting. It may well be true, however, that potatoes are more economically produced in Belgium, where they are grown on a far larger scale than in Mecklenburg, and where the labourers are adept in the techniques of their production.

The table on p. 135 shows that the labour costs of producing one bushel of potatoes rise rapidly with a decline in yield per unit area, and that on a soil with a yield of only 50 bushels per 100 square rods they are twice as high as on a soil yielding 115 bushels from the same area. If on a rich soil, 6 bushels of potatoes cost roughly as much in labour as 1 bushel of rye, then on a poorer soil, 3 bushels of potatoes will cost nearly as much as 1 of rye. Taking labour as our measure of value, we find that on a rich soil the same amount of labour produces nearly twice as much nutriment for human consumption if it is spent on potatoes instead of grain, but that on a poorer soil the labour spent on potatoes brings no larger nutritional return than that which is spent on grain.

Since potato production is so very much more expensive on a soil with a yield of 8 than on one with a yield of 10 bushel-crops, and since, moreover, we know that a soil of this yield not only produces no clover for indoor feed, but requires 2¾ pasture courses to restore the fertility extracted by one potato course, we realise that potatoes will only be able to occupy a small portion of the total tillage. It needs no detailed calculations to see that at four miles from the Town, potato production for the market will not produce a land rent of 2458 thalers on a soil so poor, and that potatoes will hence not be able to oust timber from this district.

The ring of forestry will follow directly on to the ring of free cash cropping.

Throughout this entire discussion we have assumed the price of potatoes as given, and have worked out the rent of land carrying potatoes from this. We must now determine the potato price where land rent is given.

Again the data are taken from the discussion of the Belgian system in Chapter 17.

The land rent of a Belgian enterprise which does not sell potatoes, hay or straw, but derives all its income from grain and animal products, is 3749 bushels of rye minus 2044 thalers.[1]

When rye fetches $(273 - 5{\cdot}5x)/(182 + x)$ thalers the bushel, the land rent expressed in money comes to $(651,469 - 22,664x)/(182 + x)$ thalers.

When potato production for the market as on farm A is introduced on soil which under ordinary cultivation yields this land rent, each of the 1440 loads of potatoes incurs

Land rent	$\dfrac{452 - 15{\cdot}7x}{182 + x}$	216
Production costs as at A	$\dfrac{489 - 4{\cdot}7x}{182 + x}$	
Transport costs	$\dfrac{199{\cdot}5x}{182 + x}$	
Total costs	$\dfrac{941 + 179{\cdot}1x}{182 + x}$	

Hence when x, the distance from the Town in miles, is	One load costs	One bushel costs
0	5·2 thalers	10·4 shillings
1	6·1 thalers	12·2 shillings
2	7·1 thalers	14·2 shillings
3	8 thalers	16 shillings
4	8·9 thalers	17·8 shillings
7·5	12 thalers	24 shillings

Thus the potato price is governed largely by the distance between the place of their production and the place of their consumption. Where this is 1 mile the price is 12·2 shillings the bushel; at 7·5 miles it has risen to 24 shillings.

Potatoes must be grown as near as possible to the place where they are consumed, and they will only be brought from remote regions where the demand of the Town is so large that the immediately surrounding district cannot meet it.

[1] This fact does not appear in Chapter 17. It comes from Thünen's calculations, the end result of which was the table on p. 138.

217

The size of the demand determines the potato price, which is much
higher in a large than in a smaller town. Should a town, however,
have a demand so large that potatoes come to cost more than one-
third the price of rye, grain would become a cheaper food than
potatoes, and the consumption of potatoes would fall to the point
where again they cost one-third as much as rye.

Where the demand is very large, the maximum potato price is
determined by the relative nutritive value of potatoes as compared
with rye; with smaller demand, the price is governed not by this
relation, but by the cost of bringing potatoes to the market.

But the Town of the Isolated State is so large that the ring of
free cash cropping cannot fully satisfy its demand for potatoes. The
potato price will consequently rise to its maximum, and here our
assumption that in the Town potatoes will cost one-third as much as
rye is justified.

It is worth noting that although potatoes provide very much more
nutriment from a given area of land than does grain, they are ill-
suited, without the supplementary aid of grain, to constitute the
staple diet of very large cities.

When we looked at farm A we found that on very fertile soil
potato production for the market stops yielding land rent at 9·3
miles from the Town, whereas grain, on far less fertile soil, continues
to yield rent up to 31·5 miles. If potatoes were the only edible
vegetable, arable farming would cease at 9·3 miles from the Town;
the Isolated State would be far smaller; and the Town itself would
have a smaller population.

Several further questions occur on the subject of potato production.
We might for instance ask:

1. What effect will the widespread introduction of potato production have on the grain price if the potatoes are grown for
   human consumption?
2. Where the potatoes are grown for feed, how will they affect the
   price of animal products and the size of the land rent from stock
   farming?

We lack the data necessary to solve these questions, though we
can make the following points.

We saw that in the Isolated State a small town can be provided
with potatoes at half the price they must fetch in the capital.[1] In

218

---

[1] Given that the large town had to draw its potato supplies from a 7·5 mile radius,
while the smaller town could draw them from within a mile.

practice towns are built on rivers, which reduces, though it by no means ends, this difference in price. Since potatoes are coming to be an increasingly important staple food, reducing the consumption of grain, the wage differential between the large and the small town must continue to increase. For even when the real wage—i.e. the total basic needs the labourer can satisfy with his earnings—is   219
the same in both, this wage expressed in money must differ with the differing cost of prime necessities.

Other factors being equal manufactured goods are most cheaply produced where the wage is lowest. The increasing consumption of potatoes will thus tend to prevent the aggregation of huge populations in large cities.

CHAPTER 21

THIRD RING:
CROP ALTERNATION SYSTEM[1]

So THAT we can decide whether the third ring is the right place for the system of crop alternation, it will be useful to summarise the conditions in the Isolated State which are of decisive influence in this respect.

1. Fertility is everywhere such as to yield 8 bushel-crops of rye after the bare fallow in the seven-course rotation; this level of fertility remains constant.
2. Rye sells at 1·5 thalers the bushel in the Town.
3. One ring is wholly given over to stock farming, which has such a depressing effect on the price of animal products throughout the State that only the first ring can profit from the production of feed. In all the other rings feed yields little or no land rent.
4. The mere alternation of grain and leaf crops does not constitute a system of crop alternation (Chapter 15): the bare fallow has to be abandoned in addition.
5. We worked out the product of the various systems on the basis of a particular estate (Tellow) where soil and climate are such that at a given level of fertility rye, after cut tares, yields only five-sixths its normal output after the bare fallow; i.e. the coefficient for rye, after tares, is 0·83.[2]
6. Plots near the farmstead are cheaper to cultivate than those at a distance; there is thus a tendency to farm the two under different systems, with more intensive tillage on the nearer land.

   This gives rise to the problem of getting the animals to the pastures; and in some instances this could be done only by

220

---

[1] This chapter was much extended and almost completely re-written for the 1842 edition.
[2] Thünen apparently refers to the discussion on p. 54 above. There however the "coefficient" would appear to be 0·88.

means of special walks. Hence we do not normally find a division into in-field and out-field unless the layout of the land allows for it.

We regarded this obstacle as insurmountable in the Isolated State, where all the land belonging to one farm is consequently cultivated in one system, instead of being divided into an in-field and an out-field.

7. This discussion is based on the assumption (see Chapter 15) that in order to produce the hay required for the three-field and   221
the improved systems, meadows are associated with the crop-land, though the manure from these meadows benefits only the section of the tillage lying in a particular course. We will not go into this at present.

Neither three-field nor improved system need therefore grow hay for winter feed on its tillage. These systems will only produce more hay on their tillage, thereby approaching the system of crop alternation, when the value of the additional manure and the net product from the extra animals kept cover the cost of producing the feed crops.

If we take these conditions—which are in part contained in our hypothesis and in part its consequence—as the basis for a discussion of the system of crop alternation (Chapter 16), it needs no specific calculations to realise that the Isolated State has no place for a crop alternation system which has no bare fallow and extends over the entire area of a holding.

The results of one careful calculation on the yield of the Belgian system show conclusively that only where the soil is very much more fertile than we have assumed it to be for the Isolated State, will an intensive system be more profitable than an extensive one.

But with a general rise in living standards crop alternation will in due course become the ruling farming system; and for this reason it ought to occupy the third ring and would in fact have done so but for several of our earlier assumptions—in particular the one that   222
soil is everywhere of the same fertility and not exceptionally rich.[1]

---

[1] This paragraph is ambiguous in the original German. Thünen could also mean that one day the system will occupy the *whole area* of the Isolated State.

CHAPTER 22

FOURTH RING: IMPROVED SYSTEM

WE KNOW that improved farming ends at 24·7 miles from the Town, giving way to the three-field system which from this point onwards is the more profitable (Chapter 14).

The improved system will prevail throughout this ring, but in the various districts of this large area it will assume different patterns, undergoing all the modifications listed in Chapter 18.

Very near the Town we shall find the pure improved system. With increasing distance from the Town and the falling value of grain, modifications introduced to economise on labour will appear until, at the outskirts of this ring, the system will have grown very like the three-field system of the following ring.

CHAPTER 23

FIFTH RING: THREE-FIELD SYSTEM

THE three-field system starts at 24·7 miles from the Town and ends at 31·5 miles, where the land rent from grain production dwindles to zero (Chapter 14).

At a Town rye price of 1·5 thalers the bushel the districts beyond this point cannot profitably produce grain to sell to the Town; so that the first five rings will have to grow enough to satisfy the Town.

223

CHAPTER 24

HOW IS THE PRICE OF GRAIN DETERMINED?

To FIND the answer to this problem we must for the moment assume that in the Town of the Isolated State (as we have depicted it) the rye price falls from 1·5 to 1 thaler the bushel.

At 31·5 miles from the Town production costs come to 0·47 thalers, and haulage to the Town to 1·03 thalers, the bushel.

A farm at this distance will stop sending its grain to the Town when the price falls to 1 thaler; as will all farms whose production and transport costs together total more than 1 thaler the bushel, i.e. all at more than 23·5 miles from the Town.

When all the farms at more than 23·5 miles distance cease to bring in their grain, the Town, unless its population and consumption pattern undergo a change, will be hit by a considerable shortage, which will again push up the price. In other words, in the given situation the price of 1 thaler is impossible.

224   The Town's needs can only be met if it pays a price which *at least compensates, for his outlay in producing the grain and bringing it to market, the most distant producer whose grain is still required.*

But the Town demand is so great that grain will have to be grown up to 31·5 miles. At this distance grain can only be produced if it fetches 1·5 thalers the bushel; so that the price cannot sink below this point.

In reality as well as in the Isolated State the price of grain is governed by the following law:

The price must be just so high that on the farm which incurs the highest cost in producing grain and taking it to market (but the product of which is still required to meet the demand) the land rent does not sink below zero.

It follows that the grain price is neither arbitrary nor haphazard, but is subject to strict laws.

But continual fluctuations in demand lead to continual fluctuations in the grain price.

Thus if consumption fell until the area 23·5 miles in radius could feed the Town, the mean grain price would sink to 1 thaler the bushel of rye.[1]

Should consumption rise however, the hitherto cultivated area would no longer suffice to meet the demand and the ensuing shortage would push up the price; and at the higher price, the remoter farms, which until now produced no land rent, would yield a surplus and hence a source of land rent, because the land beyond these farms could now be cultivated at a profit. In these conditions the area of cultivation would stretch to the farthest point where grain production continued to yield rent.

225

Once cultivation has reached this point, production and consumption are again in balance, though the grain price remains high.

The effect on the grain price of a rise in production is similar to that of a fall in consumption.

If soil-yield in the Isolated State rose from 8 to 10 bushel-crops, while the Town demand remained stationary, a far smaller area of production would meet the need, and the remainder of the plain would no longer be required for provisioning the Town. Given such a rise in yield, the area 23·5 miles in radius could feed the Town, and the rye price would sink to 1 thaler the bushel.

But if the rise in yield per unit area were to be accompanied by such a large increase in consumption that the grain price remained the same, the outcome would be a quite exceptional growth in population and national prosperity.

If a farm with a soil-yield of 8 bushel-crops can sell about 4 to the Town, one yielding 10 bushel-crops can sell at least 5·5. With rising soil-yield, cultivation will expand from 31·5 to 34·7 miles from the Town; the simultaneous increase in intensive and extensive cultivation will make possible a population increase of about 50 per cent; and this greater number will be as well nourished as was the smaller number before.

226

The Town's total consumption must in the long run be related to its total income. If the soil-yield were to remain constant, the rise or fall in the grain price would depend on the rise or fall in the income of the consuming classes in the Town.

---

1 Presumably Thünen means that grain prices will oscillate around this figure.

Scarcely ever does the market price of grain coincide with the average price; it fluctuates continually, depending on the current state of supply and demand.

The capital outlay on farm buildings and equipment is recovered only in the long run; in the same way one year's market price and the resulting revenue cannot determine whether the investment of capital has been sound.[1]

But because our discussion has always aimed at the final goal, the ultimate stage of all development, not at the manifold and confusing phenomena of transition, we were right to assume for grain a market price based on the average of prices for many years.

---

[1] Insubstantial changes were made in this paragraph for the 1842 edition.

THE SOURCE OF LAND RENT

IF RYE grown at a distance is brought to market at the same time as rye grown near the Town, that coming from a distance cannot sell for less than 1·5 thalers the bushel (its cost to the producer), although the farmer who lives near the Town could sell his grain at half a thaler and still recover all that he has spent on transport and production.

But he can neither be forced nor expected to sell his rye for less than the farmer who lives farther away when both products are of the same quality.

To the buyer rye grown near the Town is worth as much as that grown at a distance; it is a matter of complete indifference to him that the one cost more to produce than the other.

That which the farmer living near the Town earns over and above his costs is for him pure profit.

As this profit remains constant over the years, land near the Town yields an annual rent.

The land rent of a farm springs from its superiority, in soil or location, over the least favoured farm which is still producing for the market.

The degree of this advantage, expressed in grain or money, tells us the size of the land rent.

However, this explanation of the origin of land rent, which arises out of our previous discussion, is neither complete nor exhaustive, and in Part Two further arguments will be presented to show that even when fertility, distance from the market, and all other factors of influence on the value of the product are everywhere the same, land may nevertheless yield a rent—provided that free waste land is no longer to be had.

It follows that there must be a further, and more fundamental, explanation of the source of land rent than the fortuitous advantage of one farm over another; and though this realisation by no means invalidates the explanation we have given, it does imply that our present explanation has to be incorporated within a wider law.

In the world around us, where it is common to find land in cultivation which yields no rent, the superior location and fertility of one plot, compared with the least favoured plot in cultivation, is an adequate measure of the size of the land rent.[1]

---

[1] Insubstantial changes were made in the last three paragraphs of the chapter for the 1842 edition.

SIXTH RING: STOCK FARMING

In Chapter 23 we saw that where farming depends on the sale of grain, cultivation has to end at 31·5 miles from the Town. This however does not necessarily mark the absolute limit of farming; for if there were a product which, in relation to its value, were cheaper to transport than grain, it might still be produced to advantage in this area.

Stock farming answers this description; and we will now try to work out the product which dairy farming yields at this point. First, however, we have to work out the cost of taking butter to the Town.

The freight per load of 2400 lb is $199 \cdot 5x/(182 + x)$ thalers (Chapter 4). If we assume that x (the distance from the Town) is 31·5, we find that at this distance from the Town the cost of transporting butter comes to six-tenths of a shilling the pound.

But for several reasons butter is more expensive to transport than grain. In the first place, it is impossible to store it until winter, when the horses are in general available; it has to be taken to the Town fresh and in small quantities. Wagons are therefore frequently sent to the Town with only half a load; or carters are employed who, because it is their living, will come dearer than transport by the farm's own horses. And where carters are engaged, an agent has to be employed to sell the butter, adding extra costs of sale to the extra costs of transport. In the second place, butter has to be put in barrels, which cost money to buy and whose weight adds to the freight cost.

For these reasons we assume that the cost of transporting butter comes to one-fifth of a shilling the pound for a distance of 5 miles, one shilling for 25 miles, and one and a quarter shillings for 30 miles; i.e. it costs nearly twice as much as grain to transport. We will ignore that with distance from the Town the freight rate per mile will also vary and will assume that these rates are uniform throughout the state. Butter is so cheap to transport relative to its

229

230

value that this assumption will scarcely have a noticeable effect on the accuracy of our findings, while making the calculation far easier to understand.

When the market price for butter is 9 new shillings the pound[1]

over a distance of	the transport costs are	on the farm butter is therefore worth
5 miles	$\frac{1}{5}$ shilling	$8\frac{4}{5}$ shillings the pound
10 miles	$\frac{2}{5}$ shilling	$8\frac{3}{5}$ shillings the pound
20 miles	$\frac{4}{5}$ shilling	$8\frac{1}{5}$ shillings the pound
30 miles	$1\frac{1}{5}$ shillings	$7\frac{4}{5}$ shillings the pound
40 miles	$1\frac{3}{5}$ shillings	$7\frac{2}{5}$ shillings the pound
50 miles	2 shillings	7 shillings the pound

From Chapter 4 we know that rye is worth 0·512 thalers the bushel at 30 miles from the Town, or about one-third its market price. At this distance butter is still worth 7·8 shillings the pound, or nearly seven-eighths its market price.

In stock farming, the districts near the Town do not have the same advantages as in grain production; and these advantages, stemming from cheaper transport, are in the remoter areas offset by the lower cost of producing butter, meat, wool, etc.

231   The labourer's keep, the cost of building and maintaining the stables, and most other expenses incurred in stock farming depend, for the most part, on the price of grain, and where rye is worth only half a thaler the bushel they must be far less than where it fetches 1·5 thalers.

*   *   *

231–   *Thünen goes on to calculate the net product, or rent of land, as-*
255   *sociated with stock farming at varying distances from the Town. The results hinge upon the relation between the falling production costs away from the market and the rising transport costs. Basing his figures on the consumption of feed in the better Mecklenburg dairy farms in 1810–15,[2] he calculates annual production and the production costs per cow, and from this the variation in prices and costs at increasing distances from the Town, using a formula which breaks*

---

[1] Thünen explains that this is an 18-ounce pound.
[2] In Note 6 to the 1842 edition (not reproduced here) Thünen wrote that milk yields had greatly increased since then.

down the labour costs into a fixed money element and a decreasing rye element (decreasing, that is, when expressed in money).

For one cow producing 87·5lb of butter per year, general farming costs are taken at 20 per cent or 17·5 lb everywhere, leaving 70 lb for sale. The market price is taken at 9 shillings the pound, the prevailing Rostock price. As distance from market increases, the farm price decreases (because of transport costs) but the variable "rye" element in the labour costs declines even faster, so the net product increases to 30 miles, and even at 50 miles is still twice what it is at five miles:

Distance	Net Farm price/lb	Gross product	Labour costs:		Net product
			rye part	money part	
(miles)	new shillings	new thalers	per 70 lb butter new thalers		
5	8·8	12·83	7·72	2·53	2·58
10	8·6	12·54	6·68	2·53	3·33
20	8·2	11·96	4·76	2·53	4·67
30	7·8	11·38	3·01	2·53	5·84
40	7·4	10·80	2·83	2·53	5·44
50	7·0	10·21	2·83	2·53	4·85

On this basis the zone of stock farming would extend farther than fifty miles from the Town.

But this would mean a market surplus, which would be followed by a fall in market price until the net product of the marginal producer, 50 miles from the Town, was zero. The new market price, which satisfies this condition, is 5·67 shillings per lb.

Distance	Net product per cow at a market price of	
	9 shillings per lb	5·67 shillings per lb
(miles)		
5	2·58	−2·27
10	3·33	−1·52
20	4·67	−0·18
30	5·84	0·99
40	5·44	0·59
50	4·85	0

The result—that butter production is attended with loss in areas nearer the Town, and can be carried on with profit only at distances greater than 20 miles—follows from the general rules already developed in Chapter 19. A product whose production costs are fourteen times those of rye but whose transport costs are only twice those of rye—such a product is butter—can be produced near the town only when the price reaches 9 shillings the pound. The logical consequence would be that at a price of 5·67 shillings, areas near the Town should give up animal production and should cultivate grain. But Nature frustrates this logic. Even if they produce no direct return, animals must be kept to produce manure, so as to keep the soil fertile for grain crops. Thus if the prices of animal products fall, the nearer areas may be able to bear the losses, because their grain products yield a rent: the distant areas, which have no source of income but the animals, must abandon them as soon as they alone cease to be profitable. To determine the price of butter in the Town, which determines the areas of cultivation, it is necessary to know the demand and the area available for production.

In Chapter 26 B[1] Thünen continues his calculations. The general law is this: in conditions like those assumed in the Isolated State the land rent derived from animal products will sink below zero in the areas nearer the Town, with the exception of the ring of free cash cropping. But this has been based on the assumption of low milk yields: will it be true for higher yields? Re-working the calculations for double the butter yield (but for the same demand), Thünen draws nearly the same results as for the low yield. This seems paradoxical, even contradictory. But it merely illustrates a general law that a general increase in production through higher yield, consumption remaining the same, will lead to a fall in prices which will neutralise or even outweigh the effect of the increased production, so that the net product remains the same, or even declines. This does not apply to an increase on the part of one producer, which will not noticeably affect the market price. It is a rich source of error in economics, Thünen concludes, to generalise from individual cases.

In fact the high butter yield postulated in this section is never found in reality. The conclusion is that, even at a quite unrealistically high butter yield, the rule remains: in the Isolated State land rent from pastoral farming is negative in the nearer areas; with greater distances the production costs of butter fall (because of lower grain prices) faster than the transport costs of butter rise.

[1] New in the 1842 edition.

In Chapter 26 C[1] Thünen asks whether the price of meat, butter, etc., in relation to grain is determined not merely by the cost of getting them to market but also by their relative nutritive value. In reality meat is much more expensive than bread in all civilised countries though not in purely pastoral ones. This is because (1) most people prefer meat and everyone above the line of abject poverty will spend part of his income on it, (2) except in very large towns, vegetables and potatoes are much cheaper than bread and other farinaceous foods, though their nutritive value is not sufficiently concentrated to make them the staple food of the working class. But if vegetables are eaten together with meat, which has a far more concentrated food value than grain, then bread and farinaceous foods become redundant, and the worker can use the money he has saved on grain by buying vegetables or more expensive meat. Thünen makes calculations to prove this. He goes on to show that a field put down to potatoes will produce more food value (in potatoes themselves, and in potatoes used to produce meat) than if put down to rye. Thünen's calculation, for which he claims no general validity, shows therefore that potato cultivation will support a greater population than grain cultivation, though not as great as is often supposed.

* * *

Let us for the moment drop our assumption that farming in the Isolated State is in a steady state and that the soil of the wilderness beyond the cultivated plain is as fertile as that which is farmed, and let us suppose instead that the ring that has hitherto been devoted entirely to livestock is gradually ploughed under, to become arable, grain-producing land. Such an extension of the cultivated area will simultaneously increase the population and reduce the quantity of animal products supplied to the Town; as a result, the smaller quantity of animal products will have to be distributed among a greater number of consumers, and the portion available for each inhabitant will be appreciably smaller than it was before.

How will this affect the price of animal products? And how will the smaller amount be distributed among the different social classes?

With the scarcity, competition among consumers will raise the market price of meat. The poor man can afford to pay only as much

256

[1] Part of Chapter 26 in the 1826 edition.

as meat, compared with other foods, is worth to him; if the price rises, he will eat less or no meat. The rich man, on the other hand, can, and will, pay more for this tasty relish than its relative nutritive value compared with grain. By forcing up the price the rich man stops the poorer one from getting meat, and whereas his table will be as well stocked in meat as in the past, the working class will have to live on cheaper, and less wholesome, vegetable foods.

257 The extension of the area of cultivation thus causes a very unhappy reduction in the supply of habitual necessities to the working class.

But should the nation become even richer, the price of animal products will continue to rise until potatoes may profitably be grown for feed. There will then be sudden, and great increase in the quantity of animal products available, and the portion of each inhabitant will be considerably larger than it was before.

According to my calculations, one Morgen[1] of a given level of fertility will feed $2\frac{2}{3}$ times as many animals when cropped with potatoes as when put down to grass.

Where the wage is sufficiently high to enable the worker to pay more for animal products (which we have to assume for our present purposes, since working-class demand alone makes possible a high price for animal products), he will eat more meat, and live more comfortably.

There is yet another happy aspect to this situation.

In years of poor harvest, when the grain crop falls short of the demand, a part of the potatoes grown to fatten livestock will be sold for human consumption, and the animals will be slaughtered lean. When this happens, nearly five times as much nutriment is available for human consumption as in normal years, when most of it is converted into meat. It is therefore scarcely possible that a country which has reached this level of prosperity will ever suffer from famine.

258 It is quite otherwise in a land where the introduction of large-scale potato production brings about a great increase in the population, and the wage as a result falls to the point where the worker can buy only potatoes and comes to depend largely, or perhaps even wholly, on this vegetable, living entirely without meat. Such a country is to be pitied.

[1] *Morgen.* The Prussian acre, a unit equal to 117·86 Mecklenburg square rods or 0·226 ha, and thus equal to 0·63 of an English acre.

Unlike grain, potatoes cannot be stored from year to year, and the abundance of one harvest cannot provide against the shortage of the next. If in such a country the potato crop fails, the inhabitants cannot revert to a cheaper food, because none exists. Here we have the situation described by Malthus:

"But when their (i.e. the common people's) habitual food is the lowest in this scale, they appear to be absolutely without resource, except in the bark of trees, like the poor Swedes, and a great portion of them must necessarily be starved."[1]

Paradoxical though this may seem, the potato will, in these conditions, bring back the scourge of frequently recurring famine; perhaps today already Ireland provides an example of such a country.

Thus once again Nature has left it to the whim of man to choose whether to turn her superb gift into his scourge or his salvation.

STOCK FATTENING

Fat stock may be driven over long distances at no great cost, and the process of fattening may well be cheaper in the outlying districts than near the Town, where land yields a considerable rent. But since the driving of fat cattle over long distances involves many difficulties, and is associated with a significant loss of weight in the animals, it is possible that the fattening process will be started in the outlying districts, but finished nearer the Town.

259

RAISING YOUNG STOCK

Young cattle may be driven from place to place at little cost or trouble; therefore the sixth ring, with its low land rent and cheap feed, can supply young stock at such low cost that no other area of the Isolated State will be able to compete.

But in the ring of the improved system butter production yields far larger returns from land than does stock for slaughter; and this area will obtain all the young cattle it requires from the ring devoted entirely to stock.

[1] T. R. MALTHUS, *An Essay on the Principle of Population* (1817 edition), III, 248–9.

In practice it is sometimes worth a farmer's while, in countrie where location and all other conditions are favourable, to raise hi own young cattle, if he aims to obtain a better than average strain But in the Isolated State every farmer is as intelligent and a knowledgeable about the various breeds as the next, and here the only factor that determines whether or not stock farming is lucrative is the location of the farm.

---

260 Where the Town demand for animal products is such that stock farming stretches up to fifty miles from the Town, butter, as we have seen, will fetch an average price of 5·67 new shillings the pound in the Town, and the price of the other animal products—wool, fat meat, etc.—will be related to the butter price.

In a previous calculation we saw that the net product of a cow

in the district 30 miles from the Town is 0·99 new thalers
in the district 40 miles from the Town is 0·59 new thalers
in the district 50 miles from the Town is 0·00 new thalers

It follows that throughout this entire ring land rent is extremely low and that the product of the local farms consists almost wholly of the interest on the capital invested in the build ngs, equipment, and so forth.

This ring grows grain only to feed the men engaged in stock farm- ing. Very little straw is hence produced, and the number of animals kept is restricted to those that can be fed through winter on the small quantity of straw and on the hay produced by the natura meadows.

Because almost all the arable land of these farms is in pasture, summer grazing is so abundant that the cattle can consume only part of the grass, the rest of which will decay and go to waste.

Since the very low product from the animals would not repay the costs, feed and root crops cannot be raised to increase the stock of winter feed.

Here therefo e the number of animals kept is determined by the meadows, and we can ascribe entirely to the meadows the land rent of such a farm, low as it is.

261 Compared to its size, this ring sends a very small quantity of animal products to the Town.

The population too is scanty; and a farm large enough to support thirty families near the Town will barely find the work and food for three out here.

At fifty miles from the Town even stock farming ceases to yield land rent; and since the farms beyond this point will not repay the interest on the invested capital, this last, and lowest, branch of cultivation will cease.

———————

A few hunters will roam the forests beyond the cult vated plain, living virtually like savages. They will barter hides for their few needs which the Town can satisfy; but this will be their only contact with the cultivated plain.

This is the last outpost of the Town's influence on the plain. Beyond, there is only uninhabited wilderness.

———————

In the course of a few days a traveller passing through the Isolated State will see at work each of the farming systems we have described. He will come upon the various systems in regular succession, which will save him from the error of attributing to farmers' ignorance the less int nsive cultivation of the remoter regions. 262

The passer-by will find the more intensive systems striking and attractive, just because they are more complex and artificial and demand far greater skill and knowledge than the lower systems.

There is no doubt that where they prevail the intensive systems yield larger returns and utilise the soil more highly than do the other systems: it is easy thus to condone the error of those who think that all that is needed to introduce these higher systems into areas of less intensive farming is greater knowledge. This is, however, a dangerous mistake to make.

We saw that where the improved or the crop alternation system is adopted on a holding within the bounds of the three-field system, it will in due course vanish without a trace.[1]

Similarly, the three-field system, transplanted into a district where the improved or crop alternation system prevails, would not last long. This however is scarcely liable to happen: the idea is too unattractive, the drawbacks far too obvious.

[1] This follows from the discussions of Chapters 14a and 21.

The Isolated State presents, in its farming pattern, a picture of one and the same country viewed over several succeeding centuries. Only the three-field system existed in Mecklenburg a hundred years ago, and it alone suited the conditions of that time. Far back in the past, hunting and stock keeping provided probably the only means of getting food; and in the coming century crop alternation may prove to be as widespread as the improved system is today.

263

As a country grows in wealth and population, more intensive cultivation becomes profitable; and if conditions have reached the stage where a higher farming system is viable, the efforts of the farmer who first introduces it will prove permanent. The new system will prosper on his own land, and slowly, but irresistibly, it will spread throughout the country to become the ruling system.

This is what happened when the improved system was first introduced in Mecklenburg; this is what has happened in England, where the three-field and improved systems have given way to the system of crop alternation.

SECTION TWO

COMPARISON OF THE ISOLATED
STATE WITH REALITY

CHAPTER 27

A LOOK BACK AT THE COURSE OF
OUR INQUIRY

OUR picture of the Isolated State was based on Tellow, in that we showed how the farming system on this estate would alter when we mentally transplanted it to various distances from the Town—which is the the market.

In Chapter 5 we argued that the gross product of any given farm may be expressed entirely in grain, and that the price of animal products is related to the grain price.

If we are thinking of actual conditions in a developed country which is not surrounded by backward pastoral ones, this assumption is of course true and relevant. But our discussion of the Isolated State showed that even Tellow lies in an area where the influence of the primitive pastoral regions is considerably reduced, and that the relation between the grain price and the price of animal products cannot be the same in the Isolated State as it is at Tellow.

Hence we must discover how the economic pattern of the Isolated State will alter when the price of animal products is not governed by the grain price.

At Tellow butter costs 9 shillings the pound of 18 ounces, or, when the freight has been deducted, 8·6 new shillings. According to our calculations the only possible market price for butter in the Isolated State is 5·7 shillings the pound,[1] though here its value on the farm falls less rapidly with rising distance from the market than is true for grain. If we recast our calculations, substituting the price of 5·7 shillings for the Tellow price,[2] we shall find that near the Town the land rent is lower, but that it does not fall as rapidly with rising

265

---

[1] Thünen did not say this earlier: he assumed a surplus on the market sufficient to reduce the price from the Rostock price of 9 shillings (his first assumption) to 5·67 shillings. *supra* p. 151.
[2] In order to obtain comparability with earlier figures for the Isolated State. Thünen does not however show his new calculations here.

distance. Already at 25 miles distance it is higher than the rent found in our calculation,[1] because, regardless of its lower market price,[2] butter has here a higher value than where its price is governed by the local grain price.

Further, we postulated as the basis of our discussion conditions where farming costs have to be expressed one-quarter in money and three-quarters in grain; thus we were able to work out the farming system for the given estate appropriate to every change in the grain price.

We moreover worked out the variations in the grain price due to the varying distance from the market, depicting this in regional terms, and constructed the Isolated State on the basis of this assumption.

But the relative portion of costs to be expressed in money or in grain does not remain constant (Chapter 5) but changes with the location of the farm. Once again this is seen more clearly in the Isolated State than in reality.

266   The cost of the goods and materials which the farmer has to buy from the Town is not governed by the price of grain obtaining in the district where he lives; for in addition to the price these goods fetch in the Town he has to pay their transport to his farm.

The price of the articles produced by the craftsman who lives in the countryside consists of:

1. What he spends on food and other necessities while engaged on their production.
2. What he spends on raw materials.

If the artisan's raw materials come from the Town, iron for instance, then only a small portion of the price of his product will depend on the grain price obtaining in the district where he lives. If however the raw material is produced in the countryside, flax for instance, then the production costs of the article—linen—will depend almost wholly on the local grain price; because here the only portion of costs to be expressed in money is that covering what the weaver has to buy from the Town for his keep, furnishings and equipment.

---

[1] i.e. our original calculation for the Isolated State based on a new relation with the price of grain.
[2] 5·7 shillings a pound, the Isolated State price.

Hence the cost of what the farmer and the rural artisan who works for him buys from the Town is expressed in money.

Farms with the same volume of business will pay the same for the goods and materials they buy from the Town whether they are near the Town or at a distance. But the farmer of the Isolated State must in addition to the purchase price also pay the freight on any Town commodity brought to his farm. In other words, the cost of such commodities is higher in the country than in the Town by the freight (which includes marketing costs). But freight rates, a portion of which has to be expressed in money (Chapter 4), rise with distance from the Town; thus the remoter farms have to pay more in money as well as more in grain.

267

In transferring to the Isolated State a calculation which is based on the conditions obtaining at one actual estate we shall therefore meet with two important changes:

1. Stock farming yields a larger product in the remote districts than it does in our calculation.
2. The remote districts incur freight charges on the goods they buy from the Town.

As these deviations from our original findings work in opposite directions, the result will be very close to our previous finding.

But however much this may alter the land rent expressed in figures, the following, important findings of our inquiry remain absolutely unaffected:

When the price of grain is very low, a holding farmed in the improved system must adopt the three-field system, which is able to produce grain at lower labour costs.

When the grain price falls even further, the three-field system will also stop producing land rent, and will no longer be able to supply the Town with grain.

The ring of stock farming lies beyond the ring of the three-field system.

The findings and the conclusions I drew from them remain unchanged, though the extent of the rings and the location of the borderline between the two systems, expressed in miles, will vary.

268

However, the figures expressing these points serve merely to illustrate my theory and in no way affect the basic laws I have developed: for in this respect it is wholly immaterial whether the three-field system begins a few miles nearer to, or a few miles farther from, the Town.

The[1] difference in the findings, which arises from the fact that with increasing distance from the Town the value of grain does not fall at the same rate as that of animal products, can be entirely resolved by an alteration in the fraction giving the portion of costs to be expressed in money: as I do in the note below. Thus, even though the ratio of one-quarter, which was taken from observed reality, does not apply to the conditions of the Isolated State, we have justified our method of expressing in terms of rye the value of animal products, and have shown that this method can achieve correct results.

377   SUPPLEMENTARY NOTE TO CHAPTER 27[2]

In Chapter 6 animal products are reduced to their equivalent value in rye, and the receipts for them are expressed in bushels of rye.

This procedure is perfectly valid for any given situation. However, when this relation in value between rye and animal products is applied to other districts of the Isolated State, a discrepancy arises, because, in relation to their value, wool, butter, and the other animal products are cheaper to transport than rye.

This prompts the question: How large is the discrepancy due to this manner of calculation, and will it be possible to equalise this difference by an alteration in that portion of the cost that has to be expressed in money?

So that we may be able to work out this problem in terms of a particular example, receipts as well as transport costs have to be calculated separately for grain and animal products.

Not insisting on rigorous precision (which would be immaterial for our present purpose) we shall assume that for grain the freight costs per mile come to 1/50th, and for animal products to 1/150th, of the sale price.

---

[1] This paragraph was added for the 1842 edition.
[2] This originally stood as Note 8 of the long supplementary footnotes at the end of the text of Part I. In this edition the other notes have been omitted.

For a given farm let	bushels of rye	thalers	378
the total grain product be	6000		
the receipts from the livestock be		2400	
Total receipts	6000	2400	

After deduction of what the day labourers, the artisans, etc. (who work for the farm) pay for the grain they use, let the money costs be   2250

The grain costs in kind (including the grain used by the labourers, etc.) come to   3600

Total costs	3600	2250
Surplus remaining	2400	150

For a situation where on the farm itself rye is worth 1·25 thalers the bushel, 2400 bushels are worth   3000

Net product		3150

What will be the change in the net product when the farm lies at a greater distance from the market?

(a) When it lies 10 miles farther from the market

Here the value of rye falls by 10 times 1/50th, or one-fifth, from 1·25 thalers to 1 thaler the bushel, whereas for animal products the receipts fall by only 10 times 1/150th, or one-fifteenth.

For 2400 bushels of rye at 1 thaler the bushel	thalers
the receipts are	2400
and for animal products they are (2400 × 14/15)	2240
Total receipts	4640
Costs	2250
Net product	2390

379   *(b) When it lies 20 miles farther from the market*

	thalers
For 2400 bushels of rye at 0·75 thalers the bushel, the receipts are	1800
and for animal products (2400 × 13/15) they are	2080
Total receipts	3880
Costs	2250
Net product	1630

(c) When it lies 30 miles farther from the market

	thalers
For 2400 bushels of rye at 0·50 thalers the bushel the receipts are	1200
and for animal products (2400 × 12/15) they are	1920
Total receipts	3120
Costs	2250
Net product	870

With a rise in the distance of 10 miles, or a fall in the value of rye of 0·25 thalers, there is thus a regular decline of 760 thalers in the net product.

Comparison with the method of the present work

	bushels of rye	thalers
If the receipts for animal products are expressed in their rye equivalent, then for a situation where rye is worth 1·25 thalers the bushel, the receipts of 2400 thalers for animal products are worth 2400/1·25	1920	
The total receipts when expressed in grain come to 6000 + 1920	7920	
The total costs are:		
in grain, 3600 bushels of rye at 1.25 thalers		4500
in money		2250
Total costs		6750

	bushels of rye	thalers	
f of this money outlay three-quarters, i.e. 5062 thalers, is expressed in rye, then these 5062/1·25 =	4050		380
750 × 0·25 remain expressed in money, or		1688	
The total receipts are	7920		
Costs are	4050	plus 1688	

Net product	3870	minus 1688

	bushels of rye	thalers
At the price of 1·25 thalers the bushel of rye, 3870 bushels are worth 3870 × 1·25 =		4838
Deducting the costs of		1688

Net product	3150

When we adopt this method, how will the net product of the farm change with rising distance from the market?

a) *10 miles farther from the market*

	thalers
Here rye is worth 1 thaler the bushel	
For 3870 bushels of rye at 1 thaler the bushel the receipts are therefore	3870
the costs are	1688
The farm produces a net product of	2182

b) *20 miles farther from the market*

	thalers
For 3870 bushels of rye at 0·75 thalers the bushel	
the receipts are	2902·50
the costs are	1688
The farm produces a net product of	1214·50

(c) *30 miles farther from the market*

	thaler
For 3870 bushels of rye at 0·50 thalers the bushel the receipts are	193?
the costs are	168?
The farm produces a net product of	24?

381   When we use this method the net product falls by 967·50 thaler with a rise of 10 miles in the distance from the market; with th former method the decline in the value is only 760 thalers.

Here we therefore find a decline in the net product with risin distance from the market which is significantly larger than tha found by the previous method.

But even when we adopt the method of the present work th decline in the net product will be less if that portion of the outla which is to be expressed in money is assumed to be smaller tha we have assumed it to be; which prompts us to ask whether there i not a definite figure for the money portion at which the findings o both methods will be in agreement.

Let the portion to be expressed in money be $1/x$th of the tota outlay.

Expressed in grain the total costs are $3600 + 2250/1·25 = 540?$ bushels of rye.

The $1/x$th part of this cost is $5400/x$ bushels of rye, and this expressed in money, is $6750/x$ thalers where the price of rye is $1·2$ thalers the bushel.

Of the costs, $5400 - 5400/x = 5400\,(x-1)/x$ bushels have stil to be expressed in grain.

The gross product is $600 + 1920 = 7920$ bushels.

The costs are $5400\,(x-1)/x$ bushels $+ 5400/x$ thalers.

The net product is 7920 bushels $- 5400(x-1)/x$ bushels $- 5400/?$ thalers.

382   It follows that the net product

(a) at the price of 1·25 thalers the bushel
    $= 9900$ thalers $- 6750\,(x-1)/x$ thalers $- 5400/x$ thalers.

(b) at the price of 1 thaler the bushel
    $= 7920$ thalers $- 5400\,(x-1)/x$ thalers $- 5400/x$ thalers.

The difference $= 1980$ thalers $- 1350\,(x-1)/x$ thalers. The previous method produced a difference of 760 thalers. When both expressions for this difference are equated,

$$1980 - 1350\,(x-1)/x = 760$$
$$1220 = 1350\,(x-1)/x$$
$$1220x = 1350x - 1350$$
$$130x = 1350$$
$$x = 10\cdot4$$

When $x = 10\cdot4$, $(5400/x) = 520$.

	bushels		thalers
The portion of the costs to be expressed in money is therefore 520 bushels at 1·25 thalers each, or			650
The portion to be expressed in grain is $5400-520$, or	4880		
The gross product is	7920		
The costs are	4880	plus	650

The net product is therefore   3040 bushels minus 650 thalers

The application of this formula in calculating the net product of the farm at various distances from the market

(a) for the chosen standpoint,   thalers
    the receipts: 3040 bushels of rye at 1·25 thalers $=$ 3800
    the costs are   650

        The net product is   3150

(b) 10 miles farther from the market,   383
    the receipts: 3040 bushels at 1 thaler each $=$ 3040
    the costs are   650

        The net product is   2390

(c) 20 miles farther from the market,
    the receipts: 3040 bushels at 0·75 thalers each $=$ 2280
    the costs are   650

        The net product is   1630

(d) 30 miles farther from the market,   thalers
    the receipts: 3040 bushels at 0·50 thalers =   1520
    the costs are   650
                                                      ————

The net product is   870

Our results are therefore identical with those produced by method one.

From this we see that although the relative change in the value of grain and of animal products does not proceed at the same rate with rising distance from the market, it is nevertheless permissible to express animal products by their rye equivalent, and possible to obtain correct results thereby, because the discrepancy arising from the conversion may be equalised by an alteration in that portion of the costs which is to be expressed in money.

When this method is used, the larger the portion of the total receipts that is comprised by stock farming, the smaller must be assumed to be that portion of the costs which is to be expressed in money.

DIFFERENCES BETWEEN THE ISOLATED STATE AND REALITY

ACTUAL countries differ from the Isolated State in the following ways:

1. Nowhere in reality do we find soil of the same physical quality and at the same level of fertility throughout an entire country.
2. There is no large town that does not lie on a navigable river or canal.
3. Every sizeable state has in addition to its capital many small towns scattered throughout the land.
4. In reality the backward, pastoral regions hardly ever exert as depressing an influence on the price of animal products as in the Isolated State.

NOTE 1

In Chapter 14 we saw that low grain prices act in the same way as low fertility: both turn the improved into the three-field system; and if either factor continues to sink, the land rent will eventually drop to zero.

In Chapter 14 we assumed a variable price for grain and constant soil fertility. Equally well we might assume a constant price for grain and variable fertility, and apply this to reality.

This is, however, not necessary for our present purpose, since our previous findings enable us to indicate the situation of a farm of low fertility at a rye price of 1·5 thalers the bushel, as will be seen from the following sums.*

*   *   *

* Here we must remember the point made in Chapter 14b: that farms which, given the same soil and the same general conditions, produce different yields per unit area, are not subject to the assumption of rational management, and belong to reality, not to the Isolated State.

270–
273

Here Thünen gives examples of the effect of fertility under the three field system. For instance, assuming that the price of rye on the farm is 1·5 thalers the bushel, a farm on land with a fertility of 4·2 bushel-crops will yield the same land rent as a farm in the Isolated State at 26 miles from the Town; on land with a fertility of 3·72 bushel-crops land rent will fall to zero; on land with a fertility of 4·55 bushel-crops the three-field system yields a rent equal to that from the improved system.

*   *   *

NOTE 2

Once we know the relative cheapness of water as compared with land freights it will be easy to determine the economic situation of a farm which sends its grain to market by water.

Suppose that freight rates by water are one-tenth those by land. On a farm on a river, 100 miles from the Town, the value of grain (and all the values deriving from this) will be the same as on a farm in the Isolated State at 10 miles from the Town.

A farm 5 miles from the river incurs the same costs on 5 miles transport by land and 100 miles by water, and is in the same economic position, as a farm in the Isolated State which lies at 15 miles from the Town.

NOTE 3

274

Scattered throughout the land are many smaller towns which also require food; and as long as such local towns still have need of grain, the near-by farms will prefer to sell their produce locally than send it to the distant capital. The number of farms, or the area required to supply such a small town with food, we might call its region. Because it sends no products to the capital this region is lost to the capital; and in respect of provisions a small town affects the capital as would a barren desert. Were the plain of the Isolated State broken by many such deserts, the Town would have to draw its provisions from farther afield; and to supply its needs the rings would have to be extended. As a result, the cost of bringing in the grain from the remotest sector of the cultivated area would rise and the more costly transport would bring about an increase in the rye price in the capital.

In the small towns, however, the grain price is not governed by the assumption that they lie isolated inside their region; because the local farmers, who have the constant choice of sending their grain to the capital or to the local town, will only sell their grain locally if the small town pays for it the price it fetches in the capital less the cost of the transport; i.e. its value on the farm.

In the small town the price of grain is therefore governed by, in fact is entirely dependent on, the market price in the capital.

The situation is very similar if instead of small towns we take fairly large independent states. In conditions of free trade even such states will not be able to free themselves from the influence of the large town in determining the grain price.

NOTE 4

In practice distance or import tariffs weaken, and often wholly nullify, the influence exerted by the backward pastoral regions on the agricultural system of the more developed countries.

If Podolia[1] and the Ukraine lay west of the Vistula, and their animal products were allowed to enter Berlin freely, the land rent from stock farming would be extremely low in north-west Germany, even today.

But as this outside influence ceases to operate, or at any rate becomes less important, the price-relation between grain and animal products alters significantly, rising in favour of the latter; and in these conditions stock farming will still be everywhere able to yield a more or less appreciable land rent, which will have important effects on the boundary between the three-field and improved systems, and even more so on that between the improved system and the system of crop alternation. To endeavour to establish generally-valid laws to express this change would take me too far from my present theme; I shall do so in Part Two.

The principle on which the Isolated State was formed exists also in reality; though here, where numerous other factors enter into operation, it manifests itself in very different ways.

The geometrician works with points without extension and lines that have no width; neither exist in reality. We too may divest an

---

[1] The area lying south-west of the Ukraine and immediately north-east of the upper and middle Dniestr river.

operative factor of all its attendant details and all that is merely fortuitous: for only thus may we hope to discover its influence on the phenomena before us.

276 And as it is possible to locate, in the Isolated State, the precise point coinciding with the economic situation of any given real farm, we cannot deny—practical difficulties apart—that it must hence be possible also to draw up a map of an entire country, shading in different colours the regions where the various systems will prevail. Such a map would afford an interesting and instructive survey. The farming systems would not succeed each other in regular succession, as in the Isolated State, but would be jumbled up among each other: the farm of fertile soil, on a river, 100 miles from the Town would belong to the third ring, that 10 miles from the Town, with sandy soil, to the sixth.

We will now turn to an occupation which has natural affinities with farming, and consider several branches of cultivation not mentioned in Section One, where this would have interrupted the argument. All these are best studied with reference to reality.

CHAPTER 29

DISTILLING

THE ring of stock farming cannot provide the Town with grain, which at this distance is too expensive to transport. But if the grain is processed, and converted into a product cheaper to transport in relation to its value, the section of the sixth ring nearest to the Town will still be able to profit from its cultivation. Alcohol is such a product: the amount obtained from a hundred bushels of rye weighs   277
barely as much as do twenty-five bushels of rye.

The waste products from distilling can be most profitably used for stock feed; and as this ring depends on livestock anyway, and grain and fuel have here their lowest possible value, everything is in favour of distilling.

This ring is able to supply spirits at such a low price that unless restrictive regulations intervene no other district in the Isolated State will be able to compete, least of all the Town itself. For it is obvious that in the Town, where grain and fuel are three times as dear and where the nominal wage is far higher, the production of spirits would cost at least two or three times as much as in the stock-farming region.

In countries where artificial restrictions confine distilling to the Towns, the national income is bound to suffer from the labour wasted in bringing to the towns the grain and firewood. However, for quite different reasons it is unwise to sell alcohol at the lowest possible price; the state may therefore tax this product to the point where alcohol sells at the price at which the towns could have produced it. This increase in the price of spirits benefits the state more than does the alternative increase, caused by a misuse of resources which might have been productively employed in other, useful, occupations.

The alcohol-producing section of the ring of stock farming will be   278
farmed under the three-field system, which can supply the necessary grain most cheaply.

Where distilling is associated with stock farming, a far greater manure surplus is obtained than in a three-field system wholly dependent on the sale of grain: a far larger portion of the tillage can therefore carry grain without exhausting the soil.

If we were considering the various rings in terms only of their actual land use, we would have to include in the ring of the three-field system the area of distilling—and indeed, the entire ring of stock farming—where only a very small section of the arable land is in tillage. However, if we consider the systems in terms of their staple products (which for several reasons I prefer to do), we must distinguish between the district supplying the Town with grain and that supplying only alcohol and animal products. I have chosen to call only the former the ring of the three-field system.

At 31·5 miles from the Town the land rent of the grain-producing three-field system becomes equal to zero, whereas stock farming and distilling still yield land rent. The boundary between the fifth and sixth rings, between the three-field system and the district of stock farming, lies in the area where both yield the same amount in land rent. It follows, therefore, that the three-field system will not stretch as far as 31·5 miles, but will stop somewhat nearer the Town. However, as we do not know how much land rent is obtained from stock farming and distilling, we cannot give the figures for this distance.

*   *   *

CHAPTER 30

SHEEP FARMING

279–
286

With sheep farming, Thünen says, generalisations about land rent are for the time being impossible. Fine merino sheep have been introduced in Germany and their wool commands a very high price; at present the benefits enjoyed from sheep farming should be regarded not as land rent but as interest on the capital represented by the flocks and as a return to the owner on his industriousness. But when enough of the fine wool is produced, what will determine the price of wool and of its different varieties? Linked with this, where in the Isolated State will wool be produced? Once a stable equilibrium has been reached, the laws we developed to determine the price of other products will also apply to wool.

* * *

In following up the formula given in Chapter 19 we found: 286

1. that where, on a given area of land, two products yield the same output by weight, the one with the higher production costs will be grown farther from the Town;
2. that where production costs are the same, the product which from a given area of land yields the smaller output by weight will be grown farther from the Town.

Now one load of butter costs less to produce than the same weight in wool; and a given area of land produces very much more butter than wool. In the Isolated State the districts near the Town will therefore be given over to dairying, and the remoter ones to sheep farming.

Fine-wool sheep produce less wool than breeds with coarser wool,   287
but they require more nourishing feed and greater care. Since, in sheep farming, a given area of land yields less fine than coarse wool, and this smaller quantity of fine wool costs more to produce than the larger quantity of coarse wool, it follows that farms producing

177

the finer wool will lie beyond the ones with the coarser wool, that is, at a greater distance from the Town—*unless other factors come into play.*

And since the remoter districts yield less land rent than those nearer to the Town, the farms producing coarse wool will produce a larger land rent and higher profits than those with fine wool— even though the higher production costs of fine wool will always keep its price above the price of coarse wool.

I must repeat that this proposition rests on the following assumptions:

1. that all sheep farmers are equally intelligent and able;
2. that fine-wool sheep exist in such numbers that like the coarser breeds they can be bought for what they cost to rear; and that the proposition does not hold where these assumptions are not relevant.

In practice we may still be far from the situation we have just described; yet no-one will deny that the progress made in farming is bringing us continually nearer, and that thanks to the widespread struggle to improve husbandry we shall in time approach much closer to our goal.

288   Sheep farming is in practice still in a period of transition; in the Isolated State the process is completed, and we are looking at the final situation, subject to no further change.

Just now I said ". . . unless other factors come into play". It may well be, for instance, that on the unploughed pastures of the ring of stock farming the fine-wool flocks will degenerate and again produce coarse wool. Were this to happen, fine wool would have to be produced at the outskirts of the fourth ring, the ring of the improved system, and butter production would have to sacrifice as much of its land as is required to meet the demand for fine wool. In this section of the fourth ring farms with fine-wool flocks would then yield a larger land rent than those with coarse-wool flocks. But in the section nearest the Town dairy cattle will always be more profitable and yield a larger product than sheep, however fine their wool.

Whether the quality of the wool is affected by the quantity and quality of the pasture and the feed on which the flocks are kept becomes thus a question of great importance when we come to consider the ultimate objectives of sheep farming. Should we discover for instance that the production of the best wool is limited to certain

districts or particular farms, these farms and districts will always
yield a high rent, because the output of wool of this quality could not
be increased at will (cf. vineyards with outstanding wines).

We have shown that some day in the future, when fine flocks have   289
ceased to be the exception and wool production fully meets the
demand, fine flocks will give a lower product than dairy cattle and
perhaps even than coarse flocks; but there are several good reasons
why this knowledge should not deter us from endeavouring to
improve still further the quality of our flocks.

(a) Even if the present high profits from fine-wool flocks are a
phenomenon of a period of transition, which will cease once a steady
state sets in, experience has already shown that this process will take
a very long time. Saxony has been enjoying the fruits of this transition
for sixty years; the other provinces of eastern Germany for thirty
years; another thirty years may pass before the process is completed.*
For on the one hand, the consumption of woollens and the demand
for fine wool will increase with the falling price of wool, so that even
the increased output will not be able to satisfy this demand, and on
the other, the many mistakes that have been made in cross-breeding
flocks—and which are likely to continue being made in future—   290
will considerably slow down the increase in top-grade flocks.

(b) The eastern provinces of Germany are scarcely able to produce
enough fine wool to bring the price down to its natural level. This
will happen only when Poland, Russia, Hungary, Australia, etc.,
take up fine sheep farming on a large scale, and successfully—for
what the ring of stock farming is to the Isolated State, these countries
are to Europe. And should the fear that the fine flocks will degenerate on the steppes and on the permanent pastures of the three-field
system prove to be justified, Germany's eastern provinces will keep
their fine flocks for many years to come. For then the effective
transfer of fine-wool flocks to these foreign countries will depend on
the adoption, in these countries, of intensive cultivation, and the
replacement of the three-field by the improved system; and this
could happen only gradually. Some day these countries, too, will be
intensively farmed, and fine-wool flocks will then become more

---

* This conjecture, made in 1825, has since been proved mistaken. It is true
that in the intervening years the *average* price of fine, but especially of medium
quality wool, has remained above the production cost, but in the last few years
the price of fine wool has been sinking so rapidly that if this slump continues
dairy cattle will become more profitable on first class soil than fine-wool flocks—
as they already are in Mecklenburg.

profitable than with us, in countries where today soil yields a lower rent than in the eastern provinces of Germany.

But long before these gradual processes have reduced the price of fine wool to its natural level, fine-wool flocks will have ceased to be profitable in the richer and more intensively farmed countries of western Europe, especially in France. The increase of fine flocks in eastern Europe will thus depend on their decrease in the west; which must lengthen the period of transition.

291   (c) But even if all these conjectures were mistaken, if today already wool had sunk to the price which in conditions of free trade we might describe as its natural price, the embargo system ruling throughout Europe is forcing us to produce fine wool.

The London market is closed to all our agricultural products except wool.[1] Embargoes have torn asunder the bonds that once connected nations; none of the laws that govern the grain price in conditions of free trade can come into operation; every country tries to be an Isolated State.

By their embargo, the states of western Europe have forced the price of their domestic grain to unnatural heights: in the once grain-exporting eastern countries the price has sunk below its natural level. The London market, which used to rule the price of all our agricultural products, no longer determines the price of our grain, only that of our wool. Wheat, in London, fetches three times the price ruling in the Baltic ports; the London wool price is only higher than our own by the cost of transport; and while with us (being exporters) the price of grain, meat, butter etc. has dropped to practically zero, our wool sells at the price fixed by the mechanism of free world-trade.

This is the reason why sheep are so very much more profitable with us than cattle or horses; not only does it suggest that we should direct all our energy and attention to sheep farming: it forces us to do so.

292   Even in conditions of free trade, wheat, in the Baltic ports, fetches no more than two-thirds—or at best three-quarters—of its London price, because transport is so dear. This means that even if he does not enjoy artificial protection, the English farmer will find it very

---

[1] Written in 1826, when the 1815 Corn Law still prevailed in England. This law, which forbade the importation of grain unless the price rose above 80 shillings the bushel, could fairly be described as an "embargo". In 1828 it was replaced by Huskisson's sliding scale, which however made little difference. The Corn Laws were repealed in 1846, four years after the publication of the second edition of Part I.

much more profitable to grow grain than we can ever do; and in England grain production must yield a high rent. In wool production, however, the English farmer enjoys no similar advantage, because the gross product of the English sheep farm, in so far as it derives from wool, is larger than our own only by what the English farmer saves on transport to the London market. With us, sheep farming will therefore utilise a given pasture or a given quantity of feed nearly as highly as it does in England. But for the reasons which in the Isolated State determined that stock farming yields a negative land rent near the Town and a positive one at a greater distance, our net product will be very much larger than that of the English sheep farm; and in conditions of free trade England could never compete with us in this line of production. The greater the difference in the grain price, the greater England's loss from sheep farming for wool and the higher its profit with us: thus the embargo system, and the artificial rise it causes in the price of grain, must result in a decline of wool production in England and its success with us.

(*d*) Breeding high-grade sheep has its own attraction, because the methods of procedure are not as clearly settled as in other branches of husbandry, and are in part still to be discovered. And just as the product of sheep farming depends on the quality of the flock, so 293 the maintenance and further improvement of the flock depends on the farmer, on the attention he pays his sheep, and on the soundness of his ideas. It is however extremely doubtful that the skill and knowledge necessary to improve a flock will ever become common property, that mechanical acquaintance with the rules and slavish imitation of example will ever be enough. And if something more is indeed needed, the product of the best sheep farms will never become entirely land rent: a portion of this product will always remain the reward to the individual farmer's greater skill and insight.

CHAPTER 31

THE PRODUCTION OF
INDUSTRIAL CROPS

WE HAVE assumed, as already mentioned, that every farm is divided into two sections, cultivated by quite different systems; the first, and larger, section maintaining the same level of fertility without the addition of manure produced outside its own area, the other, smaller, section using the manure produced from the meadows.

We considered only the fomer in Section One of this work, when we were discussing the formation of the Isolated State and looking at the various systems in their pure and simplest form, and did not even mention the production of industrial crops.

But it is absolutely compatible with our assumptions to suppose that industrial crops are raised in the second division of any given farm; and we shall try now to discover where, in the Isolated State, we shall find such industrial crops as are required by the Town.

In Chapter 19 we stated the proposition that *with the same production costs the crop that has to carry a higher land rent must be grown farther from the Town.* Applying this to particular crops, we have to ask: How is the incidence of land rent on a given crop to be determined?

In the seven-course improved system each grain course is associated with one pasture course to replace the plant food the grain harvest has extracted from the soil. To simplify the problem, let us for the moment take a district where stock farming, and therefore the pasture course, yields no land rent, though it produces no loss. The grain course will have to carry the land rent falling on two courses, or in other words, the grain course has to carry double the land rent it incurs on its own area.

If we now compare with grain an even more exhausting crop, one that needs say two pasture courses to replace the lost fertility instead of only one, we find that this crop incurs a threefold land rent on the area of its cultivation. With the same output in weight, the crop causing the greatest exhaustion will always have to carry the highest rent, and it follows, from the law we have just stated, that the crop extracting the largest amount of fertility from the soil must be grown farthest from the Town.

If this already happens where the land rent of the pasture courses equals zero, it must happen all the more where these courses yield a negative land rent near the Town, and a positive one at a greater 295 distance; for the very exhausting crop will, if cultivated near the Town, incur not only a threefold land rent on the area where it is grown but also the loss on its two associated pasture courses, whereas, when this same crop is cultivated at a greater distance from the Town, the product of the two pasture courses is again subtracted from the threefold land rent.

In conjunction with the laws stated in Chapter 19 this produces the following propositions on the relative position of the different commercial crops:

1. Where production costs and yield in weight are the same, the crop extracting the most fertility from the soil must be grown farther from the Town.
2. Where yield and exhaustion are the same, the crop with the highest production costs must be grown in the remoter district.
3. Where exhaustion and production costs are the same, the crop which on a given area yields the smallest output in weight must be grown farther from the Town.

* * *

Thünen goes on to apply these propositions to various commercial crops. He stresses however that the data on soil exhaustion are in-conclusive for most of these crops. 295– 309

1. Rape

From various observations Thünen concludes that rape, provided it is not introduced on the same plot more than every twelve to fourteen years, exhausts the soil only about two-thirds as much as rye. But because of its low straw yield, rape still needs nearly the same replacement of manure as rye, i.e. the same size pasture plot has to be associated with it; therefore a rape plot must bear the same land rent as a rye plot. But taking into account that the yield of rape, in bushels, is lower, a single bushel of rape has to bear one and two-thirds as great a land rent as a bushel of rye. The production costs of one bushel of rape as compared with one bushel of rye are as 141·4 to 100. Transport costs are somewhat higher for rape, not because it weighs more per bushel but because it has to be transported at an inconvenient time of year.

From these data Thünen calculates the prices at which rape can be supplied from various districts of the Isolated State. He concludes that when rye fetches 1·5 thalers per bushel in the Town, one bushel of rape can be supplied from an area thirty miles from the Town at 1·9 thalers, but from a point near the Town only at 2·21 thalers. The distant district can supply the Town's needs for rape, so the price will fall to 1·9 thalers; rape cultivation nearer the Town will be abandoned.

In the real world this means that in free trade conditions richer states (soil fertility being equal) cannot compete with poorer ones in rape production; and in countries with low grain prices and low land rent rape production is more profitable than grain. Thus rape is not cultivated in England or on the best land of Belgium and Holland.

Thünen considers in some detail the influence of plant pests on rape cultivation.

2. Tobacco

309
In its demands on the soil, and in yield, tobacco closely resembles rye. But the production costs are higher, and so tobacco cultivation must be carried on farther away than grain, that is, in the pastoral ring.

3. Chicory

310
Data here are lacking, but Thünen concludes that the yield of roots is so great in weight that a load of chicory will bear only a low land rent, and probably also low production costs, so that production will take place near the Town.

4. Clover seeds

310
Production costs here are fairly high because much work is involved. Soil exhaustion is difficult to calculate. The yield from a given area is so low that one load has to bear a high land rent. Clover seeds will tend to be cultivated in the remoter parts of the ring of the improved system;

areas nearer the Town will find it more profitable to buy seeds than grow them.

5. Flax

The yield of flax from a given area is only one-quarter that of rye, it is twice as exhausting as barley, and the production costs are 7·5 times those of rye. Flax is therefore cultivated not merely outside the zone of cereal cultivation but outside the areas where tobacco and rape are cultivated.

310–
311

*   *   *

It follows that industrial crops will mostly be produced not near the Town but in the ring of stock farming. If it depended wholly upon stock farming, this ring would be extremely thinly populated; but distilling and industrial crop production add to the local source of income and thus to population. According to a calculation I have made, a day-labourer's family, growing flax in summer and spinning and weaving it in winter, can make a living on 300 square rods of good soil even though an annual rent of 25 thalers has to be paid for the plot. Widespread flax production can alone explain why East Flanders, which besides Ghent has no large towns, supports 12,000 inhabitants to the square mile.

The section of the ring of stock farming nearest to the Town is an interesting example of a fairly well-cultivated area yielding little or no land rent. The prices of the products grown here cannot rise sufficiently to yield an appreciable land rent; for if they did, the remoter section of this very large ring would take up the cultivation of these crops, which are very cheap to transport, and would thus depress the price. Hence almost the entire income of this ring consists of return on capital and wages.

311

312

In Chapter 5 we saw that the cost of producing one bushel of rye on soil with a yield of 10 bushel-crops is 0·437 thalers, and on 5 bushel-crop soil, 1·358 thalers; that grain production is thus very much cheaper on rich than on poorer soil. This applies to industrial crops also, but to a far greater degree. For most industrial crops require such extremely careful cultivation (hoeing, earthing up, weeding etc.), and so much of the type of labour whose amount is governed by the size of the cultivated area and not by the product of the harvest, that the larger harvest reaped from a rich soil is here only a little more expensive than the meagre harvest reaped from a poorer soil. The production of these crops becomes profitable only on a soil so rich that it would cause grain to lodge.

313   Let us now look at conditions in reality, bearing the production of industrial crops in mind. Obviously soil is not everywhere of the same fertility (which it is in the Isolated State). As a rule, dearer grain is in the more intensively farmed countries associated with more fertile soil; and conversely, the less intensively farmed countries combine low grain prices with a lower degree of fertility.

And if we ask in which type of country the production of industrial crops will be the more profitable, given free trade, we shall find that the advantage the poorer country enjoys in its lower wage and rent is offset in the richer country by the greater soil fertility. In the production of industrial crops the advantage of rich soil is however so decisive, that it outweighs the savings of the poorer country on wage and land rent.

It is this factor of soil which, in association with the greater industriousness of the population and its greater skill in handling these crops, explains why the relatively rich countries produce industrial crops for export as well as for their home market; flax, which of rights belongs in the less intensively farmed areas of eastern Europe, is still the staple crop in East Flanders, the garden of Europe. But one day, when the soil of the Baltic countries has become more fertile (and it is in the power of the local farmers to achieve this), flax production will decline in Flanders; this will happen all the faster if the government of the Netherlands[1] continues to increase the differential in the grain price between these regions

314   by levying high tariffs on imported grain.

In England, where wage and land rent are high, industrial crops are also grown and are promoted by duties on foreign imports. But the Corn Laws have driven the difference in grain prices to the point where the English are already finding it worth their while to buy our artificial manure (bones, oil-cakes etc.) instead of buying our grain. Should England retain the Corn Laws, her farmers will

[1] Belgium became independent from the Netherlands in 1830, but this was not altered in the 1842 edition.

discover that their manure has become too valuable to be spent on industrial crops with their generally high rate of exhaustion; they will leave the production of these crops to countries where grain is cheaper; and England will again permit their import.*

*   *   *

* Since this was written, the high import duty on rape has been abolished.

CHAPTER 32

AT WHAT PRICE CAN THE VARIOUS AREAS OF THE ISOLATED STATE SUPPLY THE TOWN WITH FLAX AND LINEN?

314–
318

Thünen makes estimates of the production costs and the land rent for flax production at various distances from the Town. He calculates the costs of manufacturing the flax into linen cloth; these costs vary greatly from one area to another, because labour costs vary with the price of grain. The conclusion is:

Distance from Town	Cost of producing and transporting 1 lb flax shillings	Costs of manufacturing 1 lb flax into linen cloth shillings	Total costs of linen cloth made from 1 lb flax shillings
0 miles	6·1	14·9	21·0
10 miles	4·9	11·9	16·8
28 miles	3·0	7·3	10·1*

* *Anomaly of 0·2 thalers due to reduced cost of transporting finished cloth as against flax.*

The inhabitant of the Town would therefore pay more than twice as much for linen cloth if the flax were cultivated and the cloth manufactured near the Town than when these things were produced in the zone 28 miles away.

* * *

318   Having applied to the production costs of linen the formula initially worked out for agricultural costs, we have to ask ourselves whether it may not also be possible to determine the exact district where each single trade and industry is best located to supply its product at the lowest price.

319

This would require a knowledge of the secrets of every factory, and sufficient insight into every industry to distinguish the exact amount of capital investment, wage, and entrepreneurial profit for each single product.

We would find, from such a calculation, not every factory and workshop located in the capital; many will be where their raw materials are cheapest. The Isolated State would thus contain, besides the central Town, many smaller ones.

This contradicts our very first assumption. But we had need of that assumption only to simplify our argument, for subsequently, in Chapter 28, we saw that the small town has no effect at all on agricultural prices which, if the capital is the chief market place where all farm products fetch their highest price, depend wholly on the capital. And where the Town (1) lies at the centre of the plain, (2) is the seat of government, and (3) has all the mines near by, this is bound to happen anyway.

Such a discussion of industrial location, to be of any use, would have to take account of the following points which, having no bearing on the determination of agricultural prices, were not mentioned when we discussed that subject.

1. In reality the interest rate is very much lower in the richer countries. For our present purposes it is immaterial whether this is inherent in the nature of the subject,[1] or springs from the division of the world into states. Now it happens that there are many factories and workshops where the interest on the capital investment represents the major portion of annual costs, and the wage and the outlay on raw materials only a relatively small portion. Every such concern will be found in the wealthier state, even though wages and raw materials are much more costly here. For our purpose it would therefore be necessary to divide the price of goods into wages, return on capital, and land rent.

320

2. The size of the market and of the demand for its product determines the scale any given industrial plant can attain in any given place; and the volume of business will in turn determine how far this concern can adopt specialisation of labour and the replacement of manpower by machines. But the division of

---

[1] "Ob dies nun in der Natur und dem Wesen der Sache selbst begründet ist"; Thünen's meaning is here obscure.

labour and the replacement of men by machines is of decisive influence on the price at which a product is supplied, as Adam Smith has shown so plainly.

For both these reasons, some industries which at first sight would seem to belong in the poorer country, where the raw materials are produced, will be more profitable in the richer country; and it will cost the poorer country less to buy than to produce the manufactures of these industries.

CHAPTER 33

RESTRICTIONS ON FREE TRADE

WHAT will be the effect on the prosperity of the Isolated State of edicts restricting the production of flax and linen to districts near the Town?

To better envisage this situation let us divide the Isolated State into two, separate states, and make the following assumptions:

1. The central Town with a surrounding ring fifteen miles in radius constitutes state *A*.
2. The rest of the plain as we have described it forms the other state, *B*, which, by comparison with the first, we will call the poorer state.
3. Each state is concerned only with its own interests, even when these are gained at its neighbour's expense.

Suppose now that, in the hope both of retaining in the country the currency which used to go abroad and of creating a domestic flax and linen industry, the richer bans the import of flax and linen. How will this affect the prosperity of (1) the richer state which is restricting imports, and (2) the poorer state?

To simplify our problem as much as possible we shall assume that in all other respects trade between the two states remains entirely untrammelled.

When they are no longer imported, flax and linen will have to be produced at the border of state *A*, fifteen miles from the Town. But the soil in this district yields an appreciable rent; and because grain is here much dearer, wages will also be much higher than in the district thirty miles from the Town. It follows that the new flax district will only be able to supply the Town with linen at a far higher price than its inhabitants have been used to pay. But linen is a basic necessity, and they will have to pay the higher price.

Despite the rise in the price of flax, the farmer of state *A* who has turned from grain to flax production will not profit from his new activity. In the first place, the grain price will not rise in consequence of the change, but will fall, as we shall see, so that the rent from grain production will at any rate not increase; and secondly, inside this ring flax will never yield a higher land rent than will grain—for all our previous discussions have shown that wherever grain prevails, the land rent is determined by this crop, and by no other. The introduction of flax will therefore change the crop produced on the land without affecting the intensity of the land use.

The flax-producing district cannot supply the Town with grain from the land now carrying flax. But since the Town had need of all the grain this district once produced, a shortage will arise.

323   Where shall we find the missing grain?

The districts of state B that used to grow flax cannot provide the Town with rye at 1·5 thalers the bushel, because the freight is too expensive at this distance. If the demand is to be met, the price of grain will have to rise until the flax-producing district—the district of distilling and rape production to be precise—is able to produce grain for the Town.

But does the Town possess an inexhaustible fund to pay this continually rising grain price; and where does the money come from?

Many of the inhabitants earn just enough to buy the bare necessities at existing average prices. But just as the remotest producer cannot supply rye for less than 1·5 thalers the bushel, so the working class in the Town cannot afford to pay a higher price; and just as a fall in the price of grain below the former average price makes it unprofitable to cultivate the outer fringe of the grain-producing ring, and turns this area to waste, forcing its inhabitants to emigrate, so a rise in the average grain price impoverishes the urban working class and forces some of them to emigrate, that is, if no new source of income is found.

324   But the embargo has created no income source to augment the labourer's wage and enable him to pay more for grain. On the contrary, the increase in the price of a staple food touches all; in particular the worker, who now has to spend more of his wage on linen, has less to spend on grain. If he is to survive, the price of grain must fall, not rise.

There is thus no possibility of increasing the grain price and none, consequently, of extending the area of its production. The district which used to produce flax cannot turn to grain or other crops, because the price of grain and of industrial crops makes it unprofitable to cultivate them at this distance from the Town. Land that was cultivated will remain untilled and tumble down to grass, and the people engaged in flax production will lose their livelihood, and will emigrate.

When the inhabitants have left the district where flax was hitherto produced there is no further demand for the goods they used to buy from the Town—ironware, cloth, tools, etc. The miners, the factory workers, and the artisans who supplied these products will lose their livelihood; and like the people of the now-deserted district they will have to choose between emigration and starvation.

Ultimately the effects of such a restriction on trade are as follows:

1. The flax-producing district of the poorer state disappears entirely, and with it all the people who made their living from flax;
2. The Town of A, the richer state, loses the labourers, the artisans, etc., who worked for this district; it suffers in size, wealth and population. 325

The wealthier state, which by its restriction inflicts a grievous wound on its poorer neighbour, harms itself no less severely.

It is worth noting that the embargo will have harmful reprecussions on the richer state even where its poorer neighbour takes no reprisals.

In economic theory it is difficult to give an exhaustive and correct definition of national wealth and to indicate with precision the signs of its growth or decline. In the Isolated State, however, the extension or contraction of the cultivated plain is a visible and unerring sign of the growth or decline of the country's wealth.

We have only demonstrated the effects of trade restrictions on the production of one single commodity, flax; but if we were to study any other branch of farming, we would obtain the same results and draw the same conclusions. The arbitrary transfer of sheep farming or of rape production to districts near the Town would invariably produce the same result: a shrinkage of the cultivated area, and of the Town.

Looking at Europe, we see differences between country and country in living standards, population density, grain price and land 326 rent, which are as great as those between the districts of the Isolated State.

Between the London region and the provinces of eastern Russia, along the Volga and the rivers of the Urals, there exists, in this respect, a difference that is perhaps even greater than that between the Town and the outer edge of the stock-farming ring in the Isolated State.

And just as in the Isolated State restrictions on trade not only cost the poorer state wealth and population, but harm its richer neighbour also, so restrictions between European countries that are at different stages of development harm not only the agriculture of the poorer countries, but the power and prosperity of the wealthier ones.

Yet embargoes and restrictions hamper trade throughout the whole of Europe.

No longer do we try to enforce the production of southern plants in the north: we have accepted the exchange of crops from different climates and think this good for national prosperity. But we do not yet seem to have realised that the exchange of products between countries in one part of the world but at different stages of development is no less natural, and no less profitable for the various nations, than the exchange of products which differ because they grow in different climates.

---

327   It is worth bearing in mind that the farmer of the Isolated State, who is constantly aware of everything affecting his position, will always know his best course of action.

To form and develop our picture of the Isolated State we needed only the assumption that every citizen knows his own best interest, and acts accordingly. And because the laws by which society is held together spring from the interaction of all its members, each intent only on his own interest, rightly understood, the interest of each individual must lie in the observance of these laws.

Man, thinking he is furthering his own concerns and nothing more, is the tool of a higher power, he is at work, often unawares, on the great and artificial structure of the state and of society; and his work and the laws he follows in creating it are no less admirable and significant than the phenomena and laws of Nature.

THE EFFECT OF TAXATION ON AGRICULTURE

THE Isolated State gained from the assumption of Section One that no taxation existed there; for the calculation of the net product of arable land in Chapter 5, which is based on data taken from reality, does not include taxes in the costs, and what we call land rent is there the net product of soil before deduction of taxes.

But suppose that this state, which till now has had no taxation, is saddled with all the duties customary throughout Europe. How will this affect agriculture and national prosperity?

———————————————

CHAPTER 34

TAXES RELATED TO THE SIZE OF
THE ENTERPRISE

A. IN THE ISOLATED STATE

Taxes on consumption, when levied on such basic necessities as salt, flour, etc., the poll tax, taxes on livestock, import tariffs, the stamp tax and many others, fall on farms in proportion to the size of the enterprise and regardless of the net product of the soil.

In the Isolated State a farm 30 miles from the Town will pay as much in taxes as one only 10 miles away if both enterprises are of the same size, that is, if both require the same input of labour and capital expenditure.

The farm 31·5 miles from the Town will adopt the three-field   329
system (Chapter 14) where only 24 per cent of the arable land is in grain (Chapter 8); the one 10 miles away will be farmed in the im-improved system, with 43 per cent of its acreage in grain. Because the improved system has on the one hand a very much larger portion of its land in grain, and on the other very much higher cultivation costs, than the three-field system (Chapter 10), the farm 31·5 miles from the Town will do only about half as much business as the one at 10 miles distance, given that both occupy the same area of land.

If on the nearer farm taxation comes to 200 thalers on 100,000 square rods, the remote farm will have to raise 100 thalers. From 100,000 square rods, the first farm derives a land rent of 685 thalers (Chapter 5); after paying his taxes, its owner will have 485 thalers left.

The owner of the remoter farm, whose land rent is equal to zero, whose total income is limited to the interest on the capital value of the buildings and equipment, has to take the tax money of 100 thalers from his capital.

But capital that continually shrinks soon ceases to be capital, and the owner will have to abandon the attempt to farm his land.

Some people may argue that the owner of such a farm, though he draws no land rent, enjoys the interest on the capital invested in the buildings and equipment and can take from this the money for the tax. To this we reply that no-one keeps his capital in an undertaking which yields no interest. The manufacturer will cease producing if lending out his capital promises to bring him larger profits; the farmer, in this situation, will spend no further money on the upkeep of his buildings, and when these threaten to collapse he will sell farm and livestock, and take up a different occupation, or emigrate.

Every farm that yields less in land rent than the tax it has to pay is in a similar situation; and taxation will produce the same result, albeit not so fast.

In the ring of the three-field system only the farm at 26·4 miles from the Town produces a rent of 100 thalers on the given area; the new tax will consequently put a stop to grain production beyond this point. The outer districts will not become entirely deserted: livestock will take the place of grain; but the outer edge of the stock-farming ring will be abandoned—a tax-made wilderness.

All the people who lived and worked in the now-deserted district will lose their jobs; and because, in its happier days, the state contained precisely as many inhabitants as were required to perform all necessary tasks, these people will not find employment in any other district of the country. With them, the townsmen who used to work and produce goods for the abandoned district, the craftsmen, factory workers, manufacturers, tradesmen, merchants, etc., will also lose their function and employment; and to escape misery and hardship all who have become redundant will have to leave their native country.

Once cultivation has shrunk to a narrower ring and everyone who has become redundant has left the country, equilibrium sets in again: though the state will have suffered in size and population and lost a portion of its capital and land rent.

Only when it is newly introduced does the tax have such drastic effects. Where it has remained unchanged since the early days of a state, potential development has been arrested: the soil has not been tilled beyond a certain point and the population has not de-developed beyond the number that is compatible with the impost, but everything is in perfect equilibrium, as in the untaxed state.

If every existing tax were to be abolished, suddenly and for good, the reverse would happen. Capital would accumulate, and would derive its value from the fact that it might profitably be employed in the reclamation of waste land; there would be food and work for more people and, as always happens in such a situation, the population would increase rapidly.

Hence taxation curbs the development of the state and restricts the growth of population and national capital.

B. IN THE REAL WORLD 332

In the Isolated State, a tax has its sharpest effect on the farm that lies farthest from the Town. In reality, distance from the market is not normally sufficiently great to depress the land rent to zero: here the farm with the poorest soil is the one to be hit first by taxes, and the one to suffer most.

But hardly ever do we find in practice that absolute uniformity of soil we have assumed for the Isolated State, for almost every farm has good as well as poor soil, or some land with a high, and some with a low, potential yield.

For various reasons the value of arable land may be extremely low and may approach to zero, i.e.:

1. The soil is poor in quality.
2. It is at a low level of fertility.
3. The plot lies far from the farmstead.
4. It has to be drained by many deep ditches.
5. It lies near the meadows, and almost at their level. Such land is difficult to farm and yields a meagre product.
6. It is cut by many ditches meeting in sharp corners, which slows down the work of cultivation.
7. It is stony.
8. It is surrounded by high timber, etc.

It would be difficult to find even a single farm, sections of which do not suffer from one or other of these defects and hence are of less value than the rest. Most farms have a great deal of such land; and in some districts poor land predominates and good land is the exception, to be generally found only near the villages. 333

Where such poor land still produces a small net product, a new tax will reduce its rent to zero or even less.

At the introduction of a new tax, every farm must, or should, abandon its inferior land and confine its tillage to the better section which, even after payment of the tax, will yield a rent.

Ultimately, the effect of taxation on the Isolated State is that the remoter districts are left uncultivated. In reality, the same effect appears in miniature on each single farm: its farthest or least fertile section will go out of cultivation.

But whether every fifth farm in the land is sacrificed, or whether each single farm abandons a fifth part of its tillage, is immaterial to the country's welfare: for the effect on population and on national prosperity will be the same.

In the second case we would find no deserted farmsteads, and the statesman might see no hint of the damage his tax is causing— although the annually diminishing yield of the levy should serve to warn him. For every new tax large enough to have such an effect, will bring its largest returns in the first year, but will yield progressively less, because the population and the wealth it feeds on are in decline. Only when the full effects have worked themselves out, and tillage is restricted to the districts where it is able to survive the tax, will the annual returns remain the same from year to year.

334

There is yet a further difference between the Isolated State and actuality. In our imaginary State, agriculture is invariably conducted in an entirely rational manner. In practice this is exceptional, particularly in periods of transition. We may trust the farmer of the Isolated State to adapt his system to any change in circumstance—he will cease cultivating a plot whose land rent has turned negative.

But in the world around us the local farming system is never the fruit of an all-embracing recognition of everything of relevance. It is the piecemeal work of centuries and generations; it has become what it is by slow, continuous improvements and constant adaptations to time and place, and as a rule the process has been more effective than is commonly believed.

But a system which has developed only gradually cannot adopt large and revolutionary innovations suddenly and overnight. If new factors enter into operation, a new tax for example, which render the existing system unprofitable, a long time generally elapses before the old and trusted methods are abandoned, and the system is brought into line with the new situation.

A new tax therefore does not immediately put a stop to the cultivation of a poor soil, which will continue being tilled as hitherto.

Now, however, the farmer is saddled with double the costs: for he has to pay not just the new tax, but the losses incurred on the continuing cultivation of the poor land; or, what comes to the same thing, the better soil must pay in addition to the tax levied on its own cultivation that levied on the cultivation of the inferior soil. **335**

The resulting loss of income means that the tenant who has leased the farm is no longer able to pay the rental, or the indebted owner to take the interest, out of the revenue; and frequently the missing money is taken from the working capital and equipment. But with less equipment, efficient tillage becomes impossible. Such, however, is the force of custom, that people will not usually see that poor land which still yields a noticeable gross product has ceased to produce a net product and is, in fact, producing a loss. In such situations, the farmer will generally prefer to till his whole land badly than to leave part of it untilled; a policy that may well wipe out the total income of a farm.

It takes several such experiences and many years before traditional methods adapt themselves to changed conditions, and only that land is cultivated which can pay its costs. This slow and fluctuating process of transition deprives the nation of far more capital than the tax was ever meant to raise.

In the actual world, where prosperity tends to advance by slow degrees, the operation of a new tax (assuming it is not excessive) is not seen clearly, for here it slows down, but does not arrest, the growth of national prosperity. In the Isolated State, where there is no **336** progress, where (unless outside influences intervene) everything is in stable equilibrium, we see, in the decline in wealth and population, the natural operation of the tax.

CHAPTER 35

THE EFFECTS OF TAXATION WHEN GRAIN CONSUMPTION REMAINS CONSTANT

WHAT we have been saying is valid only for the situation where a new tax reduces the consumption of grain. Where a nation is sufficiently prosperous to pay more for grain, and consumption remains constant, the effects are very different.

Suppose for instance that, as a direct result of the tax, the outlying districts of the Isolated State stop sending grain to the Town. The ensuing shortage will promptly raise the grain price—and the higher price will permit the remoter districts to resume grain production for the Town: equilibrium is re-established. And since the Town's needs are met only when the grain-producing ring stretches up to 31·5 miles from the Town, the grain price will continue rising to the point where the remotest farm within this ring recovers, in addition to its outlay on production and transport, the money it has paid in tax.

In these conditions the consumer of the grain will pay the entire tax levied on agriculture.

The physiocrats hold that every duty levied on trades is ultimately passed on to agriculture. The artisan who has to pay a 10 per cent duty on his business will, according to this theory, pay this sum in the first instance; but to survive in business he will raise the price of his product until the extra outlay is fully covered. It would follow from this that it would be far better to levy taxes on agriculture directly, than to adopt such devious means of obtaining the same revenue from what is, ultimately, the same source.

But, as we have seen already, where there is no change in consumption the taxes levied on agriculture are paid, not by the farmer, but by the consumer of the grain.

Farmers and artisans pass on their taxes. State employees, living on a salary, cannot raise the price of their work at will; and in addition to the taxes levied on them directly, they must now pay the higher cost of prime necessities. In these conditions the government service will cease attracting candidates; and eventually the state will be forced to adjust the salaries of its employees to the higher cost of living.

Thus it appears that with the sole exception of the people who live off the interest on their capital, every social group is indemnified against taxation, and that the state can push taxation to its utmost limit without endangering the welfare of the whole: for none of its active subjects will suffer; each advances the money for the tax, but never actually pays for it.

———————

This striking finding rests on the assumption that the introduction of the tax will in no way affect consumption. We still have to see whether this assumption is correct.   338

In Chapter 33 we mentioned that the price of grain depends not only on the cost of bringing it to market, but also on the consumer's ability to pay the price.

Many people, in the Town and in the rural districts, have an income only barely sufficient to satisfy their basic needs. With a rise in the grain price, their earnings or means will no longer suffice to buy all the grain they need. And however indispensable grain may seem, the poor consumer cannot give more for it than all his income. If this is too small, he must make do with less grain; and unless his fellow citizens support him from the poor box, he will eventually die of hunger.

Suppose now that as the result of a tax falling directly or indirectly on agriculture, the grain price rises in the Isolated State. Consumption will decline, because the poorer townsmen can no longer pay this price. But because at the time the tax is introduced production has not yet declined, there will be no actual shortage of grain, and the fall in consumption will create a surplus, which will again lower the price to the point where even the poor are able to buy all the grain they need. In other words, grain reverts to its former mean price.

But at this price, agriculture, saddled with the new tax, can no   339
longer be carried on as extensively as before; and now all the above-mentioned effects of the tax will set in: the cultivated area will contract; and the inhabitants of the district that has become redundant, together with the townsmen who worked for it, will have to leave the country.

Where a country is in a steady state, and everything within it is in equilibrium, the price the consumers can afford to pay coincides with the price at which the remotest producer can afford to supply his grain—which explains why we did not need to consider this twofold determinant of the grain price in Section One. But as soon as a new tax, or some other interference by the state, disturbs this harmony, the two determinants will cease to coincide.

The price the consumers can pay will then be either below or above that at which the remotest producer can deliver grain. Since the price the consumers can pay cannot be raised if, as we have assumed, there is no new income source, the producer's price, where this is higher, must fall until it again coincides with the people's means. This will come about when land which cannot profitably be cultivated at the lower price is abandoned, and tillage is restricted to land which can carry the tax even at this low price for grain. In the reverse situation, where the people are able to pay more for grain than the price at which it is supplied, the supply price will initially provide the norm, but in this situation population and consumption alike will increase rapidly, the area of cultivation will expand and the supply price will rise to the point where it corresponds with what the people can pay.

340

Hence we find that in all the richer countries grain is dear, and in all the poor ones it is cheap.

A grain shortage or a famine in northern Norway will not increase the price of grain in other European countries, or indeed in Norway itself, because the people are too poor to pay more for grain. But even a moderate increase in the demand for grain in London will raise the price throughout the whole of Europe; and when this happens, ships filled with grain set sail for this world market from every port of Europe.

———————

These days every European state strives by high tariffs and embargoes to ban foreign grain from its home market, seeking to promote domestic agriculture by raising the grain price to artifically high levels.

Without doubt, high prices for grain stimulate farming both intensively and extensively—as all our previous discussions have gone to show. But politicians forget that high prices are maintained only where the people obtain the extra income to pay for them.

Where there is no simultaneous increase in the people's income, the increase in the grain price is short-lived, and within a few years the price will have reverted to the point that coincides with the people's ability to pay. However, the artificial increase in the grain price will have driven trades and industries working for export into countries where grain is cheap: so that the measure has lessened,   341
not increased, the nation's means of exchange. The ultimate result of all such arbitrary restrictions must be, instead of the intended rise, a permanent fall in the price of grain.

———————————

The action of a tax at its first introduction must be carefully distinguished from its ultimate effect, for there is a great difference between the two.

When it is first introduced the new tax causes misery and hardship among the people, because the total common income, less the sum taken by the tax, has still to be divided among as many people as before. Those who become redundant and can no longer be fed will not automatically leave the country and a cut-throat struggle for survival will determine who is to emigrate.

Once emigration, or a fall in marriages, has restored the balance between the population and the people's income, there is no reason whatsoever why any member of the producing classes (I include the landowner in his role as farm manager, not as the recipient of the land rent) should fare worse, i.e. get a smaller return for his labour, than before the tax was introduced. To what extent a people will put up with hardship and privation before deciding to cut down on marriage or emigrating, depends on its disposition. And if the   342
people's character (which forms the basis of the wage rate) has not been affected by the tax (and such a change of character is not a necessary by-product of the tax), the producing classes, the artisans, day labourers, tenant farmers, etc., will not have less left after payment of the tax than formerly.

In the world around us we see these classes live as well in England, a country with high taxes, as in Russia, where these are negligible.

Thus, long-established taxes do not harm the ordinary citizen. But the state that levies them sets a limit to the expansion of its income and population; it fails to attain the power, wealth and population which, without taxation, it might enjoy.

———————————

CHAPTER 36

TAXES ON TRADES AND INDUSTRIES

WHENEVER the artisan or the manufacturer has to pay a large tax, he is doubtless inclined to recover his loss by raising the price of his product. At the higher price, many people will buy less of the product or will stop using it altogether; the lower demand will create a surplus; and the price will again fall.

Artisans and manufacturers who are not able to survive at this lower price will have to give up their occupation and move away. When this happens, the supply for the market grows less, and the price of the product rises once more; and as labour in this industry cannot permanently be paid at a lower rate than that in other industries, the price of the product will continue rising until it fully covers the new tax.

Because the price of some commodities required by the farmer, iron tools for instance, will rise as a result, farming costs will also rise, and the land rent of the farm which lies farthest from the Town will sink to zero. Ultimately, the effects will be the same as those, already mentioned more than once, of a tax levied on agriculture directly.

If we inquire for the ultimate effect of a new tax on the price of goods, that is, its effect after the period of transition is completed, we shall see that this is not at all the same for manufactured goods and grain.

The artisan and the manufacturer recover what they have to pay in taxes by raising the price of their product, which consists therefore not merely of wages, return on capital, and land rent, but of a fourth constituent, the tax. But in the previous chapter we saw that a tax will not raise the price of grain unless it is levied on agriculture directly, or on articles that will add to the production costs of grain.

We know from observation that if the people's character does not change, all the productive citizens, including the farmers, can obtain

343

as good a living after the tax has been introduced and all its consequences have made themselves felt as they did before. Where, then, does the farmer get compensation for what he pays in taxes if unlike the manufacturer he cannot raise the price of his product?

344

It is an essential difference between industry and agriculture that agriculture will reward human effort with very different quantities of output, depending on the different quality of the soil: in industry the same skill and effort invariably bring the same labour-product.

If it were possible to levy a tax on industries which these could not recover by raising the price of their products, or if man-made restrictions could permanently keep the grain price above its natural level, then everyone engaged in these industries would suffer equally (assuming equal skill and capacity for work), and if the imposition were great enough, all the industries would succumb together, and simultaneously.

A tax related to the size of a farm enterprise can only put a stop to the cultivation of the poorer farm (in the Isolated State, the one that lies farthest from the Town): it cannot ruin farms more fortunate in their soil and location. For here the farmer will be able to live as well as before the tax if he abandons the less fertile section of his land, and restricts his labour to the better section which, even after payment of the tax, will reward the efforts of the day-labourers, the tenant farmer, or the manager as generously as did the inferior soil before the tax was introduced.

When we look at the effect of the tax on the volume of industry and agriculture in the Isolated State we find that all suffer equally. If agriculture is reduced by 10 per cent, all the trades associated with agriculture will lose 10 per cent in turnover, capital and labour, and the result will be the same whether the tax is levied on one single basic trade, on all trades, or on agriculture alone.

345

No part of the human body can suffer injury without damage to the whole; and similarly no sector of industry or agriculture in the Isolated State can be burdened with a tax without affecting every other occupation.

In the real world things are somewhat different.

If in a free-trade state of Europe one industry is heavily taxed, the manufacturer will not be able to obtain compensation by raising his price, because his product is still produced as cheaply as before in other countries which do not have this tax, and is still imported at a price at which he is no longer able to supply it. In these conditions taxation may ruin one particular trade without affecting any other, and the decline in wealth and population caused by the tax is seen in one single limb of the body civil. In such isolated instances, the state may perhaps not lose more in absolute wealth and population than it would have done had the tax been distributed over all the trades equally. Nevertheless, the tax disrupts the harmonious ordering of the whole.

346 The prosperity of the different groups within a state depends not only on domestic taxes, levied locally, but also on the taxes levied in every country maintaining free-trade relations with this state. Take two states, *A* and *B*, which have always levied the same tax on a given commodity. If *A* abolishes this tax, or introduces an export premium, *B*, if it wishes to protect the prosperity of those of its subjects engaged in the production of this article, must also abandon the tax or introduce an import tariff.

To preserve its internal economic harmony, *B* must therefore adapt all its taxes and tariffs to those of *A*.

Whether it is worth making such a sacrifice to maintain the balance of prosperity between the different sections of the population, whether the poorer country will ever be able to enjoy an independent tax system or will always have to depend in this on the richer state is a problem of practical politics beyond the scope of my discussion.

CHAPTER 37

INDIRECT TAXES AND THE POLL TAX

INDIRECT taxes levied on non-essentials which are not bought by the poorer classes affect the pleasures of the rich without restricting cultivation or the productive investment of capital. Such taxes, which limit the consumption of luxury articles, injure only the people engaged in their production and supply, of whom some will lose their livelihood. This class of worker is however neither as numerous nor as important to the state as is the class engaged in the production of prime necessities.

347

Where such a tax is levied on articles imported from abroad, it will touch only the livelihood of the merchants and the people engaged in their shipment and distribution.

Indirect taxes levied on the common man's basic necessities cause far more damage than does the poll tax. On the one hand the levy of these taxes is so costly that it consumes a great portion of the money raised, so that the citizens lose far more money than the state requires—or indeed receives, and on the other, these taxes hit the people who are in real need and depend on the charity of others, whereas the poll tax is paid only by people in employment, who have a real income.

The poll tax is held to be the most unjust of all the taxes, because it takes equally from rich and poor regardless of means or income. Yet this tax, when it has existed for a long time, has no disturbing effects on national welfare. The labourer must earn enough to feed his family and pay the tax: his wage will therefore rise until it covers the tax; and he will ultimately be as well off as the labourer in the country that has no such tax.

When it is first introduced however, the effects of the poll tax are very different. This again is seen more clearly in the Isolated State.

348

The labourer, who practically everywhere earns just enough to buy his basic needs, but little else, will have to earn more to pay the tax.

But a rise in the wage will depress land rent on the remotest farm to below zero, putting a stop to cultivation at this point. The local labourers will lose their livelihood and become destitute; and matters will improve only when all the people who (thanks to this restriction) have become redundant have left the country.

Once this has happened the workers who remain will get their wage increase, and the farms still in cultivation, which yield land rent, will be able to pay this increase out of their land rent.

Every long-established tax, provided that it is neither arbitrary nor uncertain, attains a certain harmony with conditions in the state, or rather, the state adapts itself to the tax in such a manner that its inhabitants cease to feel its incidence. But every new tax, or every alteration in existing taxes, has the same effect on the state as an attack on property: some branches of industry or agriculture are restricted and the people they employ lose their livelihood—at any rate until they find another occupation. We conclude from this that taxes that are unequal are a far smaller evil than those that change frequently.

CHAPTER 38

TAXES ON LAND RENT

IF THE owner of a farm has to pay the state a portion of his land rent, nothing in the organisation or volume of his enterprise need change. Farms with a land rent of nearly zero contribute little to such a tax, which does not even touch the most remote or poorest farm. A tax on land rent will therefore have as little ill effect on the expansion of cultivation as on population, on capital investment, or on the quantity of goods produced. Indeed, even if the tax were to consume the total land rent, cultivation could continue as before.

In other respects, too, the disposal of the land rent seems to have no bearing on the welfare of a country, for capitalists and landowners are in general as unlikely to put it to productive use as are the rulers of the state.

Frequently, where the owner is deep in debt, the larger portion of the land rent goes to the capitalist in the form of interest.

But whether the landowner or capitalist wastes the land rent on grand retinues, stables, and such-like luxuries, or the state spends it on large military establishments, makes no appreciable difference to national prosperity.

Land rent does not spring from capital or labour, but from the fortuitous advantage one farm enjoys over others in the quality of its soil or its location; it may therefore be taken away without affecting in any way the use of capital or labour. 350

In the Isolated State agriculture has reached a level that is permanent and subject to no change, and every holding is managed with as much efficiency and skill as is the next.

This is not so in the real world. What, then, can we call land rent in reality, and how is its amount determined?

Because differences in farming enterprise and expertise are very great in practice, farms with soil of the same quality, at the same distance from the market, may yield very different net products. This however does not mean that we may ascribe a lower value and a lower land rent to the badly managed farm. The difference in the product stems from the farmer's personality, and will vanish when another takes his place. The value and land rent of a farm can only be determined by features that are permanent—location and quality of soil—not those that are fortuitous and passing, like a farmer's personality.

It follows that the net product of any given farm cannot determine the land rent of this farm, even though the land rent springs from the net product and is nothing more than the net product minus the interest on the capital invested in the buildings and other valuable equipment.

The potential net product or net product of a farm run on the customary local lines (assuming a neither exceptionally high nor exceptionally low degree of industry or expertise on the farmer's part) may serve as the norm for the determination of land rent.

351

But we can only discover the results of such an average degree of skill and enterprise from the total product yielded by the efforts of all the farmers of an entire province or country.

The total net product of all the farms in one country, minus the interest on the value of the buildings etc., gives us the total national land rent, and this, divided among the individual holdings according to their soil and location, tells us the land rent of each farm.

From this we can see how difficult it is to work out the land rent of any given farm; and if only for this reason it should not surprise us to find that nearly every such attempt has miserably failed in practice. Matters are still worse however, because such estimates are usually based on entirely false premises. People cannot accept that there may be land which, although cultivated, yields no rent; and by equating four or six square rods of the worst quality land with one square rod of the best, they imagine they are making great concessions. But six times zero does not make one, and six square rods of the worst land are less valuable than one square rod of the best. Furthermore, land rent is all too often confused with the interest on the capital invested in farming. But a farm which yields no surplus besides the interest on its buildings, equipment, working capital, etc., does not yield land rent, although its owner draws an income. Every tax levied on what is mistakenly supposed to be the land rent of such a farm has just as damaging effects on cultivation as has the poll tax, the tax on livestock, etc.

352

To obtain correct and precise estimates of land rent for the purpose of taxation, experts would be required who have made this their special subject, and who have spent their whole lives studying this and nothing else. This would however make these estimates extremely costly, and would partly annul the advantage of a tax on land rent: the cheapness of the levy, compared with other taxes.

In practice, land rent is not constant but variable. Every change in local farming practice, every change in the price of the product and in the interest rate, has a disproportionately large effect on the size of the land rent. If the tax on land rent is fixed and does not rise with increase in the land rent, it will, after a hundred years, yield a sum which bears no relation to current land rent, or the needs of the state. If the tax is to rise with the land rent, frequent valuations of the farms are necessary. This is very expensive, and what is worse, the farmer, expecting such a rise in tax, will not attempt to improve his property. Thus a tax that seeks to keep pace with land rent is an obstacle to agricultural progress.

In the Isolated State the soil yield remains constant, and the government may take away the entire land rent without injuring cultivation. But in the actual world we see a more or less continuous struggle to attain a higher yield, and almost everywhere the possibility of achieving this. But soil improvements which raise the yield almost invariably cost a lot of money; and in some instances the interest on the capital invested in such improvements is nearly as high as the resulting increase in the net product.

353

If they are lasting, improvements will permanently raise the land rent of a property. But the source of this kind of land rent is very different from that of the older kind of land rent. The one springs from the sheer advantage of one farm in its soil or its location, and owes nothing to the efforts of the farmer; the other, later, kind of land rent is bought at the expense of capital.

Many improvements, once made, are permanent, and can evade the tax as little as can the older type of land rent—the improvement of the physical quality of the soil by the addition of loam, the drainage of bogs etc. In that the tax on land rent cannot undo improvements that have been made, it is of course harmless. However, in deterring farmers from undertaking such improvements in the first place, it is in fact highly detrimental to a nation's welfare.

Doubtless there is no better way of employing capital for the greatest good of an entire nation than in improving its land and extending the area of cultivation: for we saw that when the soil yield in the Isolated State rises from 8 to 10 bushel-crops, the population of the Town can increase by about 50 per cent, without necessarily causing a parallel increase in the grain price.

354   Since a country's growth in wealth, power and population is directly related to its increase of intensive cultivation, a tax on land rent, which does not remain constant over long periods—a hundred years at least—but which falls and rises with the current land rent of a farm, hampers and impedes the betterment of the soil. Of all taxes this, perhaps, is the one that does most to check a nation's progress.

* * *

The original (in the 1842 and subsequent editions) contained 8 extended footnotes on points arising from various chapters of the text. As these are of limited interest they have been omitted from this translation, except for Note 8 on Chapter 27, which has been inserted immediately after Chapter 27 at pp. 164-170.

* * *

NOTES AND EXPLANATIONS ON THE FOLLOWING DIAGRAMS OF THE ISOLATED STATE

THESE diagrams, drawn by a friend of mine, are not essential to an understanding of the problem under discussion—and nowhere in the work have I referred to them. But since they afford a simple and convenient survey of the results of my inquiries, I feel they might be welcome to the student who has read my work attentively.

Moreover, they offer me the opportunity of adding a few reflections which in the main body of the work would have interrupted the flow of the argument.

FIG. I

This shows the Isolated State in the shape it must take from the assumptions made in Section One and the conclusions drawn from these assumptions.

According to Chapter 26 the stock-farming ring stretches up to fifty miles from the Town; to save space it has been drawn only as far as forty miles on the diagram.

This diagram—as all the ones that follow—shows only half the ring forming around the Town. The other half is not only similar to, but absolutely identical with, the first half, and may easily be imagined.

FIG. II

Here we see the Isolated State crossed by a navigable river.

The diagram rests on the assumption that water freights are one-tenth the cost of land freights.

Here the ring of crop alternation, which on Fig. I occupies only a narrow strip,[1] becomes very much larger, stretching along the

[1] Strictly, of course, it should not appear at all.

river to the state frontier. The ring of stock farming has contracted, and near the river it disappears entirely.

The effect of constructing highways is similar, if less marked. If highways are built to all the districts of the plain, the more intensively farmed rings will expand, retaining, however, their regular shape, as in Fig. I.

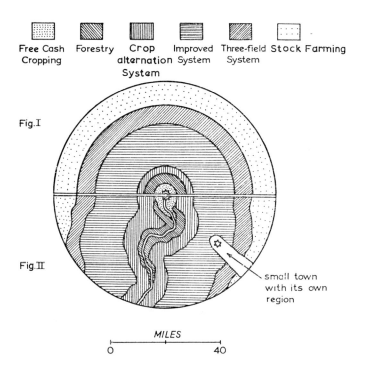

Free Cash Cropping Forestry Crop alternation System Improved System Three-field System Stock Farming

Fig. I

Fig. II

small town with its own region

MILES

0   40

On this diagram we see, at the edge of the plain, a small town with its own region. By "region" I mean the area that supplies this town with food, sending none to the capital (Chapter 28).

We may also think of this small town with its region as an independent state; in such a small state the grain price is governed wholly by the price obtaining in the central Town (see Chapter 28).

These small states are related to the central Town in much the same way as are the states of Europe to the wealthy country that can pay the highest price for grain, namely England, and particularly its capital, London.

Even where they neither import nor export grain, its price in all the European countries is governed by the London market, and when this market is closed, the grain price falls throughout the whole of   386 Europe.

FIG. III

Here the soil yield is 10 bushel-crops, and the grain price in the Town varies between 1·5 and 0·6 thalers the bushel of rye.

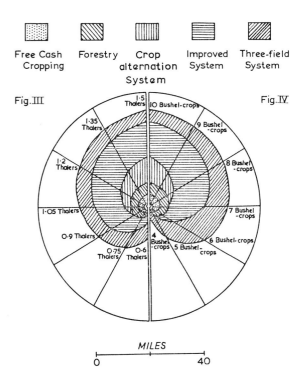

The diagram illustrates the effect of the Town grain price on the extension of the cultivated plain. Only the radius of the cultivated area and of the individual concentric rings is marked; so if we wished to draw a representation of the Isolated State for a given grain price, say 1·05 thalers, similar to that of Fig. I, we would have to measure the distance between the Town and point 1·05 with a compass, and draw a circle of this radius around the Town.

We would do the same to mark the individual concentric rings whose radii are measurable on a straight line between the Town and point 1·05 thalers.

Since the present work made no mention of the effect on the plain of the changed grain prices in the Town itself, I have to set down the formula on which the measurements in this diagram are based.

If we assume that rye fetches a thalers the bushel in the Town and b thalers in the country, and if we then apply the method used in Chapter 4 for the mean price of 1·5 thalers, we shall find that in the rural districts the value of one bushel of rye,

387

$$\text{or} \quad b = \frac{a(12{,}000 - 150x) - 136{\cdot}92x}{12{,}000 + 65{\cdot}88x}$$

$$\text{or} \quad b = \frac{a(182 - 2{\cdot}3x) - 2{\cdot}1x}{182 + x}$$

It follows that $\quad x = \dfrac{182(a - b)}{2{\cdot}3a + b + 2{\cdot}1}$

We know, from Chapter 14, that when rye is worth 0·38 thalers the bushel (0·381 thalers to be precise), the land rent of the three-field system with a yield of 10 bushel-crops equals zero. To let us determine the limits of the three-field system, let b be equal to 0·38 thalers.

If for a we successively substitute the values 1·5, 1·35, 1·20, and so on, we shall, from the formula stated above, discover the value of x for each different value of a.

When the price of rye per bushel is	The radius of the cultivated plain is
1·50 thalers	34·7 miles
1·35 thalers	31·7 miles
1·20 thalers	28·6 miles
1·05 thalers	25·0 miles
0·90 thalers	20·9 miles
0·75 thalers	16·1 miles
0·60 thalers	10·4 miles

The boundary separating the ring of the improved from that of the three-field system will be in the district where rye sells at 0·51 thalers the bushel (0·516 thalers, to be precise: Chapter 14). By substituting 0·51 for *b*, we shall be able to work out, by means of a similar calculation, the boundary of the improved system for the different values of *a* (the different average price obtaining in the capital).

The number of people living in the Town is necessarily directly related to the area of the cultivated plain and to the total quantity of food it can produce; with every contraction of the area of cultivation, the Town will therefore diminish in size.

388

As with the forestry ring, the area of the ring of free cash cropping is directly proportional to the size of the Town and thus to the area in cultivation. We assumed that at the price of 1·5 thalers crop alternation will stretch as far as 9·4 miles from the Town (although the point made in Chapter 21 remains valid[1]); with falling prices, this area will contract rapidly, and at 0·9 thalers it will become equal to zero.

Taking the rings of the improved and the crop alternation systems together, we see that when:

The bushel of rye costs	These rings extend for	Which is
1·50 thalers	21·4 miles	62% of the radius of the plain
1·05 thalers	13·4 miles	54% of the radius of the plain
0·60 thalers	1·6 miles	15% of the radius of the plain

Taken by itself, the ring of the three-field system:

When the price of rye per bushel is	Ring extends for	Which is
1·50 thalers	4·5 miles	13% of the radius of the plain
1·05 thalers	5·4 miles	21% of the radius of the plain
0·60 thalers	6·2 miles	60% of the radius of the plain

This shows that falling grain prices cause in addition to a shrinkage of the cultivated area (in reality the inferior land is abandoned) a simultaneous decline in intensive cultivation.

[1] That the crop alternation system does not occur in the Isolated State owing to the uniform standard of fertility of 8 bushel-crops.

389   If we suppose the area of the cultivated plain to be equal to 1000 units when rye costs 1·5 thalers the bushel, we obtain the following table from the measurements given in this diagram:

At the price of	The area of the plain is
1·35 thalers	844 units
1·20 thalers	687 units
1·03 thalers	525 units
0·90 thalers	367 units
0·75 thalers	217 units

With the exception of the last figure, the area varies almost as the square of the grain price.

If we suppose that:

1. a tax is levied on all the grain brought to the Town for sale;
2. the grain price in the Town remains at 1·5 thalers the bushel of rye,

we find that the effect on the farmer will be the same as of a fall in the grain price; Fig. III will therefore serve also to illustrate the operation of such a tax.

For instance, if a tax of 0·3 thalers the bushel of rye is introduced (no matter whether this is levied on milling or on entry into the Town) the farmer will receive only 1·2 thalers the bushel, and the radius of the cultivated plain will shrink from 34·7 to 28·6 miles.

Now suppose that this tax is progressively raised. The result will be a progressive contraction of the cultivated area. If the tax rises to 390   0·9 thalers the bushel, the radius of the cultivated plain will stretch only up to 10·4 miles; at an even higher tax, the entire state will eventually disappear. Here, then, we have a vivid illustration of how high taxes may convert fertile country into wilderness.

A state which raises taxes to the utmost limit will have nothing left to tax, and its coffers will ultimately be empty. A state which levies no taxes at all will attain its utmost possible expansion, but here too the treasury will be empty. There must be a point where taxation yields its maximum. What level of taxation produces this maximum in the following instances?

When the tax is	The area of the cultivated plain is	The relative yield of the tax is
0 thalers the bushel	1000	0
0·15 thalers the bushel	844	126·60
0·30 thalers the bushel	687	206·10
0·45 thalers the bushel	525	236·25
0·60 thalers the bushel	367	220·20
0·75 thalers the bushel	217	162·75

Here the tax of 0·45 thalers the bushel yields the highest revenue for the Treasury. Every further tax increases diminishes the total sum, and it is worth noting that a tax of 0·75 thalers the bushel produces no larger revenue than one of 0·22 thalers.

This shows that even a government that has ceased to represent the interests of its subjects, and merely uses them for raising revenues, would act entirely against its own interest by raising taxes to an excessive level.

FIG. IV   391

This diagram shows the effect on the Isolated State of a change in the soil yield when the price of grain remains constant (at 1·5 thalers the bushel of rye); though it is subject to the qualification stated in Chapter 14b (taking the present figures as a variation from the ones there given).

As for the various gradations in the grain price in the last diagram, so here again I give only the radius of the cultivated plain and of the various concentric rings for every yield in bushel-crop, from 10 to 4.

The measurements of this diagram are based on the calculations in Chapter 14; for the cultivated area they are as follows:

At the yield of	The cultivated plain has a radius of
10 bushel-crops	34·7 miles
9 bushel-crops	33·3 miles
8 bushel-crops	31·5 miles
7 bushel-crops	28·6 miles
6 bushel-crops	23·6 miles
5 bushel-crops	13·3 miles
4 bushel-crops	2·2 miles

Comparing this with the last table, we find that a fall in the soil yield causes a greater decline of intensive cultivation than a steady fall in the price of grain. When the price is halved, from 1·5 to 0·75 thalers the bushel of rye, the improved system still occupies 38 per cent of the radius of the cultivated plain; when the yield is halved, from 10 to 5 bushel-crops, it disappears entirely.

———————————

The Isolated State in its Relation to Agriculture and National Economy

THE NATURAL WAGE AND ITS RELATION TO THE RATE OF INTEREST AND TO LAND RENT

SECTION ONE

I. INTRODUCTION

I

Adam Smith taught me political economy, Thaer scientific farming.

They are the founders of two sciences, and many of their teachings will forever rank among the basic principles of science.

We accept in the writings and the lectures of outstanding men that which appears to be unquestionable, making it part of our own thinking; it ceases to be the object of our own inquiries.

That which, in the teachings of these two great men, appeared to me incomplete, which failed to satisfy my urge for a deeper understanding of the problems and drove me to make my own inquiries, may be summarised in the following questions, although the summary is not exhaustive.

1. How will a change in the price of grain affect the system of farming, assuming that cultivation is rationally conducted?
2. What determines the price of grain and of wood?
3. Does the more intensive farming system—the system of crop alternation—enjoy an absolute predominance over the improved and three-field system, or does it superiority depend on the price of agricultural products?
4. What is the source of land rent, and what determines its amount?
5. What is the ultimate effect of taxation on agriculture?
6. What is the natural wage, or what, in Nature's scheme of things, is the worker's rightful share of his product?
7. What determines the rate of interest; and what is the relation between this and the wage rate?
8. How does the stock of capital affect the rate of interest and the price of commodities?

9. What, at their first appearance, is the effect of important improvements in agriculture and inventions in industry, and what is their ultimate effect?

The concept of the Isolated State first came to me in my youth, when I was studying agriculture at Herr Staudinger's Institute at Flottbeck near Hamburg; and since that time I have always felt compelled to consider every problem of agricultural and political economy in the light of the principles that form the basis of the Isolated State: for I could see no hope of ever finding a solution to any of these problems but by freeing it from all the accidental and contingent phenomena that are associated with it in reality.

3

When I first took up farming, I did my best, by keeping exact and detailed accounts, to provide myself with data on the costs and net product of agriculture for the different yield in bushel-crops and for the different grain prices. After five years of such book-keeping, I grouped and summarised the data which, in this form, became the basis of the discussions in Part One.

My present object being to scrutinise the method of Part One, I feel that I am justified in reminding my readers as to the course of the discussion there, and some of its results.

II

The calculations in Part One, which are based on conditions at Tellow, show that when the value of rye falls to 0·549 gold thalers the Berlin bushel, the land rent of the improved system vanishes or becomes equal to zero on a soil yielding 8 bushel-crops of rye after the fallow, and that with the disappearance of the land rent, tillage also ceases (Chapters 5, 6).

But a change in the farming system may introduce economies into the running costs of an enterprise and the soil may consequently continue to be tilled and may continue to yield rent even when the rye price sinks to less than 0·549 gold thalers the bushel. The change in the system, adopted to reduce costs, gives rise to a pattern of cultivation which is identical with the three-field system.

4

With falling grain prices the point must therefore come where the three-field system becomes more advantageous than the improved system.

But with a continuing fall in the grain price, even the land rent of the three-field system will ultimately disappear. This will come about when the rye price sinks to 0·470 thalers the bushel (Chapter 14a); here land can no longer be profitably cultivated for grain production.

Looking on the other hand at the effect of rising grain prices, we see the point arrive where soil becomes too valuable and productive to permit any portion of it to lie idle. With the consequent break-up of the fallow, the *improved* system changes into the system *of crop alternation*, which at this stage will yield a larger land rent than the former system.

———————————

If from the price grain fetches in the town where it is sold we subtract the cost of its transport, we shall discover its value on the farm itself. With increasing distance from the market, the transport of grain becomes more costly, and its value on the farm itself diminishes. Increasing distance from the market has thus the same effect as a fall in the grain price where distance remains constant.

It is thus possible to depict the effect of the grain price on cultivation as a problem in space; and from such a representation the Isolated State developed.

When the problem is regarded in this way a second question becomes associated with the first: 5

With great or lesser distance from the market, how must the cultivation system change in order to maximise the net product?

The laws obtaining here are not discernable directly from experience and observation; for everywhere in reality we see differences in the quality of soil and in its level of fertility; the influence of navigable rivers; and so forth; and farms which are located at different distances from the great market towns will exhibit the combined influence of all these factors, assuming always that all farms are rationally managed.

To free one factor, distance from the market, from its permanent association with all the other factors, to see its working and ascertain its significance, we had to postulate a large town built, not on a navigable river, but at the centre of a plain whose soil is everywhere of the same inherent quality and at the same level of fertility.

This intellectual operation is akin to the experimental methods used in physics as well as agriculture: only the factor to be determined is raised quantitatively, while all the others are held constant.

Given these assumptions, concentric rings of regular formation will form in the plain of the Isolated State around the Town as we described it in Part One; and passing from the Town towards the border, we shall come in turn upon the districts where prevail respectively free cash cropping, forestry, crop alternation, the improved, and the three-field system.

With continuously rising distance from the Town we shall reach the point where the cost of producing and transporting grain is the same as the price the Town will pay for it. At this point land rent disappears, and—in so far as it depends on grain production—cultivation ends.

From this follows the law determining the grain price (Chapter 24).

Land rent springs from the advantage enjoyed by farms nearer the Town over those at the edge of the cultivated plain; and the degree of this advantage determines the size of the land rent (Chapter 25).

Beyond the point where cultivation for grain production ceases, the ring of stock farming will be found, and because, in relation to their value, the transport costs of animal products such as butter, fat meat, wool and so on, are very much lower than those of grain, stock farming can here still yield a profit.

Beyond the ring of stock farming the plain turns into a deserted wilderness which cuts off all contact between the Isolated State and the world outside. But we assumed that the soil in this wilderness has the same natural properties and is potentially as fertile as that of the cultivated districts; it is thus the greater distance from the market, not the quality of the soil, which prevents the extension of cultivation to these regions.

It follows that the expansion of the ring of stock farming is limited only by the fact that the Town price for animal products barely covers the costs of transport and production incurred by the most distant producer.

With rising distance from the Town, the cost of producing animal products falls, because land rent as well as grain price declines, whereas transport costs rise. And since with growing distance from the Town production costs fall at a steeper rate than transport costs rise (Chapter 26), and since the land rent of the remotest farm in he stock-farming ring is equal to zero, we arrive at the important aw: That in all districts nearer the Town (with the exception only of the ring of free cash cropping) the land rent from stock farming must be negative (Chapter 26b).

Ultimately, the effect of a new tax is seen in the desertion of the outskirts of the plain; in the restriction of tillage to a narrower ring around the Town; and in a decline in the population (Section III).

This is but a brief summary of the course and outcome of the discussion of Part One, where we obtained our results not by reasoning alone, but deduced them from a formula on the costs and yield of agriculture, which itself was based on empirical data, one variable, the grain price, being allowed to vary.

If observed experience has been thoroughly and correctly understood and the conclusions drawn from it are consistent, this method introduces mathematical certainty into a field where mere reasoning would give rise to wholly contradictory opinions.

But the greater the achievements of this method and the more its findings lay claim to certainty, the more rigorous must be the scrutiny and criticism to which it is subjected.

III

Without abstracting from reality we can attain no scientific knowledge. This process presents, however, a twofold danger: (1) that mentally we separate what in reality is interdependent; and (2) that we base our findings on assumptions which, not being fully conscious of them, we fail to make explicit; and that we then regard as generally valid what is valid only under these assumptions.

The history of political economy offers many striking illustrations of such pitfalls.

Of such assumptions in Part One, some made explicit, some however only tacitly assumed, the following two call for more detailed scrutiny and explanation: (1) Throughout the Isolated State the soil is not merely of uniform original fertility, but, however different the grain price in the various districts, remains (with the exception only of the first ring) at the same level of fertility even after cultivation. (2) The thoroughness of tillage, of harvesting, threshing, and so on, remains the same throughout the State, no matter whether rye fetches half a thaler the bushel, or one and a half thalers. But we

8

postulated that cultivation is *rationally conducted*, making this the first and most imperative condition of our State, and subjecting to it every other consideration.

Automatically therefore the question must arise: Are these two assumptions compatible with the postulate of rational cultivation?

9 The answer must be "no"; and the reasons for this answer will be developed later on.

Since Part One does not justify this discrepancy, it should have been attacked on this point, and would have been attacked had any of its critics entered into the spirit of the work.

But if we admit this basic defect in the fundamentals, does not the entire edifice of the Isolated State collapse in ruins? In reply we will consider an analogous case.

Suppose that fertile soil may be bought and supplied at a given price, and that it is within our power to raise the fertility of the topsoil to any desired level. We would endeavour to discover what level of fertility of the topsoil will give us, after deduction of the interest on the cost of purchasing the soil, the maximum net product from the land.

In working out this problem we would first make some experiments to discover how and in what ratio the crop yield rises with the rising fertility of the topsoil. We would sow various plots with different depths of topsoil at the same seed-ratio, for unless this is done, two different problems would become confused and the experiments would fail to give a clear answer to either. Even so, the seed-ratio will be a contributory factor; for it is highly probable that if both are to produce their maximum crop yield, a 10-inch topsoil requires a different quantity of seed than a 4-inch one.

10 A second experiment is therefore necessary. In order to discover for every depth of topsoil the most appropriate seed-ratio, which will produce the maximum yield, plots with topsoils of varying depths will have to be divided into several sections and seeded at different seed-ratios.

To obtain a complete answer to the problem we must similarly isolate the influence of the other factors—variations in soil quality at the different levels of topsoil, the greater cost of ploughing the deeper layers, and so on—and make them the subject of separate experiments.

Surely the methods we accept as correct for the physical world are not out of place in the world of the intellect; and here too we must take one of two interrelated factors and study it by itself, and in turn subject the other to the same procedure?

Analogies can make this method seem probable; but they can hardly offer proof so rigorous that it is open to no refutation.

But in this everything depends on complete accuracy.

Fortunately we have proof that this method is valid in the science that allows of no deceit, in mathematics.

If in differential calculus we are trying to discover the maximum value of a function containing several powers, we consider first the one variable, holding the others constant, and when, by equating the differential with zero, we have found the value of this power, and set it in the function, we subject the second power to the same procedure, substituting for it in the function the value found for it; and we continue in this manner until every variable has been eliminated from the function.   11

If a procedure proved correct in mathematics is to justify the validity of the method we are using, we have to show that, like the mathematician, we are seeking to discover the maximum, and making this the object of our study.

In farming we have many ways of raising not only the immediate but the permanent output of a plot of land; by greater thoroughness of tillage and of harvesting, by bringing in manure, gypsum, bone-dust, guano, marl, and mould, or by adding some variety of soil that is lacking in the plot.

When such improvements are bought at a cost higher than the value of the additional product they achieve, they not only ruin the farmer who undertakes them, but reduce the total national wealth.

For the maximum net product must be the farmer's target, not the maximum gross product.

If we ask; How thorough should the farmer be in cultivation and soil improvement? the answer is this: (1) Thoroughness of labour, in gathering potatoes for example, must not go beyond the point where the last amount of labour spent on the task is still repaid by the higher output achieved. (2) Similarly, soil may only be improved to the point—but not beyond—where the interest on the cost of buying or producing the required manure is still balanced by the higher yield obtained thereby.

A higher yield is always bought at an outlay of capital and labour;   12
there must therefore be a point where the value of the extra yield

equals the value of the extra capital and labour spent on it. This is the point which represents the maximum net product.

Our method of determining the maximum net product is thus in accordance with the method which in mathematics has been proved correct for determining the maximum value of a function containing several variables; and as the mathematician, faced with several powers, considers first the one and then the other variable, holding the remainder constant, so we too may isolate the different variables which influence the net product and which are associated with the grain price, and consider first the one and then the other as the active power.

With this we have justified the relevance and accuracy of the method used in Part One.

To the question: What is the effect on cultivation of the grain price? Part One gives only a partial answer, and some aspects only of the problems are there discussed. But the influence of the grain price makes itself felt on many other factors, soil fertility for instance, or the thoroughness of cultivation; thus we see that Part One is only a step towards a full solution to our problem.

To help my readers to better understand and appreciate Part One, I shall now add a few reflections on the influence of the grain price on two variables: soil fertility and the thoroughness of cultivation. Later on these will be the subject of a separate study.[1]

13

IV

A. In the conditions of the Isolated State, where, owing to the competition of the extensive ring devoted entirely to stock farming, the price of animal products is extremely low, the fallow can only be abolished and the system of crop alternation adopted when the soil reaches a level of fertility where grain, after the bare fallow, would lodge, as I showed in Part One. But the Isolated State is founded on the postulate of a soil of the same fertility throughout the plain, with a potential yield of 8 bushel-crops (9·44 Berlin bushels per Prussian Morgen) after the bare fallow.

At this yield grain does not lodge.

Had Part One carried its argument to a logical conclusion the system of crop alternation would have found no place in the Isolated State.

[1] This was never made.

Looking now at the relation between the grain price and soil fertility in practice, we find that in densely populated countries, where the grain price is high, the soil is generally at a higher level of fertility than in sparsely populated countries, where grain is cheap. In practice therefore the question is already answered; and it is indeed remarkable that economic theory has as yet failed to expound and systematise what good sense and judgement have long since taught the ordinary farmer.

If in the absence of scientific evidence we accept as compatible with reason the lesson of experience that soil improvement attends an increase in the grain price, and if we then apply this proposition to the Isolated State, we shall see the structure of the State considerably modified thereby. Instead of soil of uniform fertility throughout the plain, we shall find, as we pass from the border towards the Town, a progressive rise in fertility; and it is possible, and even probable, that at a certain distance from the Town it will become profitable to enrich the soil beyond the point where grain begins to lodge after the fallow. At this point crop alternation would actually occupy the area which in Part One we hinted that it should have occupied had this not been fundamentally incompatible with our assumptions there.   **14**

Here then we have come upon an important deviation from the findings of Part One; and it might seem as if our method of considering one factor only at a time had led us into error.

But without the assumption of uniform fertility it would have been impossible to isolate and determine the single effect of distance from the Town (i.e. apart from the combined influence of all the factors), and the problem would not have been elucidated, but confused.

The fault lies not with our method, but with the fact that the discussion of Part One is still unfinished and has as yet given the answer to one aspect only of our problem.

In mathematics, the determination and substitution of the value of one power in a function does not tell us the value of this function: this we can only know when all the variables have been eliminated. We must follow the same procedure here.

The solution of our problem requires that when we have determined the influence of distance as such, we undertake a second inquiry, to discover the influence of distance on the most appropriate level of fertility. Only the combination of the two inquiries will produce a full result, even though it may not be the final one. Part   **15**

One contains most of the necessary data for such a calculation; for the formulae for calculating the net product are valid not merely for a given yield in bushel-crops, but for every yield up to 10 bushel-crops, and thus for the level of fertility corresponding to each of these yields. In Part One we also found a formula for the boundary between the improved and the three-field systems which is valid for every yield; only for a soil fertility corresponding to a yield of more than 10 bushel-crops are the formulae and calculations still to be found.

If we knew by what law grain price and soil fertility are associated, we could, from the existing data, work out the appropriate fertility, yield, and land rent for every distance from the Town. This would complete our picture of the Isolated State and bring it closer to reality—where all these factors are in constant interaction.

But for this the mere empirical observation that a high level of fertility is usually associated with a high grain price is not enough. Before we can study this aspect of our problem with the rigour and precision bestowed on the previous one, we have first to prove that this association is a necessary one, and to discover the law that defines the interaction between the grain price and the level of soil fertility.

16   B.   If a farm where all the work has hitherto been performed by 20 day-labourers' families hires another family, simultaneously increasing the number of draught animals accordingly, the harvest and the sowing will be finished more rapidly and consequently at the right time of year, the reaping and seeding will be more thoroughly done, the grain will be better threshed and the potatoes picked more carefully, etc.

Logically the increase in the number of labourers' families will be continued to the point where the value of the extra yield produced by the last man hired equals the wage he is paid.

The extra yield is expressed in grain, and where the farming system is the same it remains constant, no matter what the price of grain. But even where the real wage remains the same, the labourer's money wage does not vary directly with the grain price, because a portion of the money wage is independent of the grain price and must remain expressed in money, as was explained at length in Part One.

Suppose now that the annual cost of one labourer's family is 60 bushels of rye plus 30 thalers, and that the extra yield produced by the last family hired is 100 bushels of rye: here the landowner will make a profit of 40 bushels minus 30 thalers. At a rye price of:

1·5 thalers the bushel, the profit is (40 × 1·5) = 60 − 30 = 30 thalers
1 thalers the bushel, the profit is (40 × 1) = 40 − 30 = 10 thalers
¾ thalers the bushel, the profit is (40 × ¾) = 30 − 30 = 0 thalers

and at the price of half a thaler the bushel, the profit turns into a loss of 10 thalers.

It follows that at the price of 1·5 thalers more than 21 labourers may be employed to advantage, but that at half a thaler, the 20th labourer already brings a loss.

Now it is in the nature of farming—and this I must stress—that the additional yield does not rise in direct ratio to the additional number of labourers employed, but that every new labourer creates a smaller product than did his predecessor: the 22nd labourer increases output less than the 21st, the 23rd less than the 22nd, and so on.

This we see illustrated in the following progression:

The 19th labourer produces 123 bushels;
The 20th labourer produces 111 bushels;
The 21st labourer produces 100 bushels;
The 22nd labourer produces 90 bushels;
The 23rd labourer produces 81 bushels;
The 24th labourer produces 73 bushels.

It follows from this table that at the price of 1·5 thalers the bushel:

the 22nd labourer produces 90 bushels, costs 60 bushels plus 30 thalers, creates 30 additional bushels at 1·5 thalers each minus 30 thalers, which is 15 thalers;
the 23rd labourer produces 81 bushels, costs 60 bushels plus 30 thalers, produces 21 additional bushels at 1·5 thalers each minus 30, which makes 1·5 thalers;
the 24th labourer produces 73 bushels; after deducting his wage there remain 13 bushels at 1·5 thalers each minus 30, which makes minus 10·5 thalers.

At 1·5 thalers the bushel, the 22nd labourer still produces a profit; with the 23rd man profit and costs are in balance; and the 24th causes a loss.

When rye costs half a thaler the bushel, the 20th labourer produces 111 bushels, of which 51 bushels minus 30 thalers remain

18   after deduction of his wage. Since 51 bushels are worth 25·5 thalers, the 20th labourer brings a loss of 4·5 thalers. The 19th labourer produces 123 bushels, of which, after deduction of the wage, 63 bushels at half a thaler the bushel minus 30 thalers remain, or 1·5 thalers.

To maximise the net product when rye fetches 1·5 thalers the bushel the number of labourers must be increased from 20 to 23; when the price sinks to half a thaler, the 20th labourer has to be dismissed.

Let us now take two farms in the Isolated State, one near the frontier where rye fetches about half a thaler the bushel, the other near the Town, where it fetches 1·5 thalers, and let us assume that these two farms have not only soil of the same fertility, but are farmed in the same manner. Merely owing to its greater thoroughness of cultivation, the grain product of the latter farm will be larger than on the remoter farm by what the 20th, 21st, 22nd and 23rd labourers produce, and this, according to our tables, comes to 382 bushels.

What effect will this consideration have on the structure of the Isolated State as described in Part One?

Suppose now that soil of a given fertility yields 8·5 bushel-crops near the Town, but only 7·5 at the edge of the plain.

This difference in yield is the consequence of rational cultivation; and since the farmer living at the border has chosen to reap only 19   7·5 bushel-crops from soil whose normal yield is 8·5, it follows that the production costs of grain are lower at a yield of 7·5 bushel-crops than where 8 bushel-crops, the normal yield for the plain, is produced by an increased application of labour. But to what distance from the Town the plain will continue to be farmed depends on the total cost of production, and taking this into account we see that cultivation will not in fact end at the point we calculated in Part One. The boundary between the improved and three-field systems may also be not quite where we supposed it to be in Part One, although the difference will be small. But the number of miles from the Town at which tillage ceases is immaterial to the essence of our present discussion; it merely serves to illustrate our theory. The influence of the mileage is quantitative, not qualitative, and need not be considered in constructing the Isolated State. In other respects, however, this factor is of great importance, as we shall see.

At this point I should like to add a note about one finding of *The Isolated State* which, on first publication of this work, appeared grossly to conflict with conditions in the actual world.

According to calculations in Part One, conversion from the improved to the three-field system becomes profitable and raises land rent when the grain price falls to a certain point.

Between 1820 and 1826 the price of grain in northern Germany fell almost to the level where—according to *The Isolated State*— the three-field system becomes more profitable than the improved system. But the farmers of the time sought, and found, their salvation in raising the output of animal products, not in converting to the three-field system, which would have reduced the output of animal products even more than it would have reduced grain production.

In writing Part One the author was well aware of this discrepancy between his findings and conditions in reality; but he could scarcely change his findings, which followed necessarily from the entire course of his discussion.

How is this discrepancy to be explained?

1. In the Isolated State, equilibrium conditions are the basis of the whole inquiry. The cheapness of grain in Germany was an abnormal situation and could hardly be considered permanent; it was due to a series of exceptionally good harvests combined with England's ban on grain imports.

In the districts of the Isolated State where the three-field system prevails, grain as well as animal products fetch prices which are permanently low, because the consumers cannot pay a higher price than that we have assumed to be the norm.

In Germany the people continued to pay the price grain fetched before 1820; and this low price stemmed not from the poverty of the consumers but from the over-abundant supply, which was far in excess of all possible consumption. This brought about a change in the people's way of life. A considerable portion of the income formerly spent on grain was saved, and went for the most part into buying better clothes and a greater quantity of animal rather than vegetable foods. The demand for animal products, such as wool, meat and butter, rose greatly; the price of meat and butter remained nearly as high as at the time when grain was still expensive; and wool—enjoying an almost free entry into England—kept its abnormally high price. Perhaps never before has there been such a disproportion between the price of grain and that of animal products as in

those years. Whereas previously the Berlin bushel of rye had roughly
the value of 9 lb of butter or 6 lb of wool, in those years 3 to 4 lb
of butter fetched as much as 1 bushel of rye; 1 lb of fine wool cost
frequently more than 1 bushel of rye; and 1 lb of the very finest wool
cost twice as much as 1 bushel of rye.

All connexion seemed to have been severed in those years between
production costs, which in normal circumstances govern the price,
and the market price. Such abnormal conditions can, however, not
be permanent, and they have long since disappeared.

When we consider the special circumstances of the period, it
is easy to see why the fall in the grain price at a time of high prices
for animal products did not lead to the adoption of the three-field
system, but brought about an increased cultivation of feed crops.

2. In the Isolated State, the cultivated plain is surrounded by a
ring devoted entirely to stock farming, which can supply animal
products at such low prices that in the districts nearer the Town the
rent from stock farming becomes negative. But in reality the situation
is different. Most parts of Germany lie far from the primitive pastoral
countries, or are protected by high import tariffs against the competition of their products; in Germany, therefore, animal products still
fetch prices high enough to produce a rent from land used for stock
farming.

22   Nothing, however, leads more surely to the system of crop alternation than high prices for animal products; and the price-relation
between animal products and grain is a factor of prime importance
in deciding when crop alternation becomes more profitable than
improved farming.

Part One could not allow for the abnormal conditions obtaining
at the time in Germany, let alone incorporate them in its basic
framework; to do so would have turned an inquiry for laws of
general validity into a search for rules valid for one country or one
province, but useless and irrelevant for every other place. But in this
second part of our work the Isolated State will be regarded under
different assumptions,—as being surrounded by a barren desert,
not as in Part One, by a cultivable wilderness; and the results will
be closer to conditions in Germany than were the findings of
Part One.

Sensing that the proposition—that low grain prices lead to the
three-field system—did not apply to conditions in Germany, critics
have cast doubt on its accuracy; but forgetting that the discrepancy

derived from the difference in circumstance they have attacked the proposition where it is unassailable, and have brought against it arguments that cannot be maintained.

V. EXTENSION OF THE ASSUMPTION OF ABSOLUTE RATIONALITY TO ALL CONDITIONS IN THE ISOLATED STATE

In constructing the Isolated State we took an actual estate (Tellow) and imagined it at progressively greater distance from the Town (the market) and tried to answer the question: How, with increasing distance from the Town, will the farming system change on this particular estate?

Absolutely rational farm management was the prerequisite.

In this way all the conditions of this real estate were transferred to the Isolated State.

The Isolated State is founded on the actual relations obtaining at this particular place (Tellow) between the wage rate and the rate of interest; on the roads that existed in Mecklenburg; on the size of the local farms; and on many other actual conditions in this district.

Let us now extend the assumption of absolutely rational conditions to the entire Isolated State. It follows that we have to ask if this particular wage and its relation to the interest rate is natural; if it is rational to maintain roads in this condition; if farms of this particular size produce the highest land rent, etc.?

It would indeed be miraculous if in reality, where everything is still in the process of development, where every change is but a transition to a higher stage, if here the rational were already manifest in all its ultimate finality. But even had this miracle occurred, we would still have to prove that the existing state of things is rational, and show why this is so.

To obtain a full solution to our problem, we must subject to scrutiny and criticism everything taken from reality; we must discover the underlying laws, and where we have succeeded, transfer to the Isolated State these laws, and not the phenomena appearing in the real world. This, however, raises the prospect of innumerable problems, of which, together with the ones already mentioned, the following appear to be most prominent.

1. What is the wage which Nature has determined for the labourer; and what governs the interest rate?

Capital is accumulated labour product, that is, completed labour, arising out of continuous labour from one source, human activity; capital and labour are thus in essence one, differing only in the sequence of time, as past and present. Between the two there must be some relation—what is it?

This problem touches on the relation between the various classes, on the happiness and welfare of the numerous class of labourers as much as on the obligations of the rich towards the working class; our discussion therefore reaches far beyond the first conception of the Isolated State. Here, where we come to deal with man himself, the Isolated State recedes into the background; and if our discussion is still based on the concept of the Isolated State, this is because the problem seems to me to be soluable—if at all—only with the aid of the approach and the assumptions which form the basis of this hypothesis.

2. What is the relation of the land rent to the wage and interest rate?

3. What governs the land rent if the plain contains, instead of the one large Town, numerous smaller towns of equal size and equidistant from each other, and what is here the relation between the thoroughness of cultivation and the grain price?

25

4. What is the effect of the stock of capital on the interest rate?

5. The calculations on transport costs are based on the very bad roads as they existed in Mecklenburg in the first years of this century. But it is certainly not rational to maintain roads in such bad condition; and in Mecklenburg the construction of numerous highways has already much reduced the number of such roads. But since originally we endowed the Isolated State with inferior roads, determining on their basis the entire farming pattern and the extent of the cultivated area, we must, consistent with the need for rationality, ask ourselves the following: (a) In which districts and to what point of the Isolated State will highways and railroads be constructed to advantage? (b) What effect will their construction have on the size of the cultivated plain, on tillage and on national wealth?

6. From the manner in which the Isolated State was constructed, it follows that climate was assumed to be uniform throughout the plain—and it had to be so assumed for the purposes of Part One.

In any case, the Isolated State was so small that it offered no opportunity of discussing the influence of climate on agriculture.

Suppose however that this State, which is surrounded by a boundless, fertile wilderness, is endowed with a railway network which stretches to the farthest district whence grain may profitably be sent to the Town by rail. In these conditions the State will be so large that, merely owing to climatic differences, farming in the south will be completely different from farming in the north.

When we consider climatic influences on agriculture, several questions arise, of which we will mention only a few.

(*a*) How will the labourer's means of subsistence, his wage, his working capacity, and the cost of his labour change with the climate?

(*b*) How does the length of the grazing period change with latitude; what effect does this change have on the production costs of animal products in the different regions?

(*c*) Which crops are the more profitable, and thus the staple products, in the various climates?

(*d*) How does climate affect the quantity of humus which a given harvest of say 10 bushels per 100 square rods extracts from the soil, and how—assuming soil and location (in respect of distance from the market) are everywhere the same—will this quantity change with latitude?

7. In constructing the Isolated State we assumed the price of grain as given, expressing it by a specific figure. The grain price can, however, be neither arbitrary nor accidental, and now the Isolated State has taken shape, and we are removing one by one our previous assumptions and substituting for them principles of general validity, we have to ask:

Why can the Town not pay more than the given price of 1·5 thalers per bushel of rye; what determines that this is the only possible price?

Since increases in the grain price bring about continual enlargements of the cultivated area, the answer cannot lie in a scarcity of food, but must be sought rather in the conditions of the Town itself—in the difficulty or impossibility of its supplying more than a limited quantity of manufactured goods for a given quantity of food.

8. The assumption that the Isolated State has only one large Town served to simplify our discussion; but being inconsistent with observed facts it has now to be abandoned.

In practice, the origin of towns is often accidental. By the side of the first settler's hut a second settler builds another, because both stand to gain from the help they may give each other; a third and fourth settler join them, until in time a town has developed.

If they were moveable, one would like to take many towns that have arisen in this or similar ways, and plant them somewhere else.

In the rational Isolated State however, the size and distribution of the towns rests on fundamental principles; and we might state the following proposition to be the first condition of their existence:

> In regard to size and distance from each other, towns must be distributed in such a manner that their location maximises national income.

28

This will happen where trades and industries are located in the place where they produce their goods at the lowest cost, and whence they can supply the market at the cheapest price.

This leads among several others to the following questions:

(a) What determines the concentration of populations in large towns, and which industries and manufactures have their natural location in the capital?

(b) What relation is there between the size and distance from each other of the country towns and the density of the rural population?

(c) What effect does distance between farm and country town have on cultivation and on the education of the rural population?

9. What determines the price of animal products if the Isolated State is surrounded by a barren desert, not by stock farming districts?

10. The Isolated State is based on the postulate of soil not only of the same original quality, but (with the sole exception of the ring of free cash cropping) at the same level of developed fertility.

But soil fertility is a variable, depending on human enterprise, and so the question arises whether, given rational cultivation, soil of originally uniform quality will remain at the same level of fertility in the various districts of the Isolated State.

A higher level of fertility cannot be attained freely: it is bought with an outlay of capital and labour or a protective form of tillage, which are necessarily associated with a lower net product in some years. But the price of grain and of animal products determines both the size of the sacrifice and the advantage to be gained from enriching the soil; it follows that sacrifice as well as gain will differ in the various districts of the State.

It seems to follow that the optimum level of fertility is directly related to the price of agricultural products.

This approach to the subject prompts the following question:

How far must the soil in the different districts of the Isolated State be improved, assuming rational farming?

11. The entire edifice of the Isolated State originated in the question: How will the Tellow farming system change if this estate is transferred to the different districts of the Isolated State? It follows that we originally assumed all farms in the Isolated State to be of the same size as Tellow.

But to be consistent, we have to ask ourselves whether Tellow is of the optimum size to maximise the net product. This prompts three further questions:

(a) Under any given conditions, how may we determine the optimum size for farms to maximise the land rent?
(b) What is the effect of distance from the market on the optimum size of farms?
(c) What effect does a rise in the level of soil fertility have on the optimum size of farms?

12. In Part One we saw cultivation costs rise and land rent fall with rising distance between plot and farmstead; although, to avoid confusion, we assumed that all the land, from farmstead to farm boundary, was of the same fertility and farmed in the same manner.

But we are now abandoning one by one the assumptions of Part One by studying each of them apart from the rest. We have therefore to ask:

(a) Is it rational to maintain the land at one level of fertility from farmstead to farm boundary, and if it is not, what gradations of fertility will we find?

29

30

(b) If the aim is to maximise the net product of the entire enterprise, how, on large holdings, will the farming system have to change with changing distance from the farmstead?

13. The object of maximising the net product of land implies, for those farms in the Isolated State which produce wood only for their own consumption, the question: How is this wood to be produced at the least cost? This brings us to the following questions:

(a) How are the production costs of wood to be determined in any given situation?

(b) Given that the enterprises are of the same size, how do production costs of building timber and firewood change with increasing distance from the Town?

(c) Given a change in the value of wood, what changes in forest management have to be adopted in the different districts of the Isolated State (particularly with regard to the optimum growth cycle and the optimum time of felling the timber) if the wood is to be produced at the lowest possible cost?

31   14. In the Isolated State as originally constructed, farm buildings were assumed to be uniform in all the different districts. Is this rational?

Farm buildings require a four-fold annual outlay:

(a) Interest on the capital invested in their construction;

(b) Repair and maintenance;

(c) Depreciation, or the annual decline in value;

(d) Insurance against fire.

The more substantial the construction of the buildings, the less will be the costs listed under (b) and (c) and the greater those listed under (a) and (d).

It follows that there must be a way of constructing farm buildings which minimises the total costs.

Rational farm management calls for the maximisation of land rent. This maximum can only be attained where, though the buildings fully meet their purpose, their costs consume the smallest possible portion of the farm product. Part of the answer to our problem lies therefore in the question: What building methods will minimise the recurrent costs debited to the annual product?

This brings us to the following points:

(*a*) How may we determine the incidence of the building costs for any given year, and how are these costs distributed among the various branches of the enterprise?

(*b*) Since the production costs of timber decline in inverse ratio to increasing distance from the Town (if only because land rent—an element in the price of timber—falls so rapidly), and since in consequence the price-relation between the various building materials—oak, pinewood, bricks, tiles, straw, etc.,—changes continually with distance, it follows that one construction method cannot be the best for every district of the Isolated State. Therefore we must ask how building methods will vary with increasing distance from the Town —will walls be made of brick, of clay, of panelling, or planks—so as to reduce to their minimum the average annual incidence of building costs.

32

15. In discussing taxation in Part One we regarded as constant the wage rate, the rate of interest, the thoroughness of cultivation, and soil fertility. In the present extension of the whole discussion, where all these factors are considered variable, the question arises: What is the effect of taxation on all these factors?

16. In our previous discussions we considered only an average yield of soil. But in the actual world oscillations in soil productivity from year to year introduce manifold disturbances into the economy, causing frequent misery and destitution among the people. This brings us to the following questions:

(*a*) What changes have to be introduced into the normal routine of a farm in years of abnormal productivity? Is the effect of such years the same in all the districts of the Isolated State?

(*b*) In years of exceptionally good or bad harvests the cost of production ceases to govern the grain price. What determines the price in such years?

33

A satisfactory answer to the last question would serve the speculations of the grain dealers.

17. The phenomena we observe around us are transitions to a state still unattained and distant.

In the Isolated State, however, we have concentrated on the ultimate condition, the object realised. Once this goal has been attained the steady state sets in and there is no more change; and we shall find regularity and order where in the period of transition so much seemed unintelligible chaos. But in the real world the steady state cannot exist, for the following reasons:

(1) A human being changes at the various stages of his life—how much more so will the succeeding generations be different from their predecessors! Mankind is still groping for a distant goal, which it cannot yet discern clearly, indeed can scarcely even guess at.

(2) Even where one generation has recognised something as its goal, the time required to attain it will often far exceed the life span of any human being.

(3) Nature possesses properties and forces whose discovery and right use appears to be among man's highest tasks, because they have the power to make his labour more fruitful and rewarding, and to promote human welfare to a high degree. But Nature reveals her secrets only slowly; and since every great discovery brings changes, perhaps even total change, to the life of society, it follows that in the process of reaching the goal, industrial activity is itself subject to change. Nevertheless, despite this constant change the single, isolated factor which is the object of our study contains the seed of a development which is certain, neither fortuitous nor arbitrary. Just as we know what tree will grow one day from the acorn planted in the ground, so we may recognise and contemplate the final goal, provided that no outside influences intervene. This, then, is the justification of our method of focussing on the steady state and making it the basis of our argument; because the insight such a method gives us will shed light on the obscure occurrences of periods of transition and development.

When we apply this mode of reasoning to the Isolated State, we find that we have to compare the initial with the subsequent effects on the welfare of society of industrial inventions, improved communications and so forth. Thus we shall be looking into the mysterious process of development.

When we consider the manifold and complex nature of the problems we have raised, when we recall that in everything transferred from experience to the Isolated State the condition of rational behaviour must be met, we realise that not only the points we have referred to, but virtually every aspect of society must be made the subject of a separate inquiry, so that what is rational may be distinguished from what exists; and it becomes obvious that the solution to our problem will not be the work of one man, or even of one generation. It is the work of history itself, which over many generations accumulates what man achieves. Only some day in the future will an investigator, who is possessed of all the facts, gain insight into the end and purpose of past development and from the fragments reconstruct the whole.

This realisation might well discourage any man from venturing on the task. But here we see the supreme importance of the proof we have given: that the result obtained by studying one factor only at a time, holding all others constant, is not a false result, but merely incomplete, and that it will remain so until every other factor has been subjected to a similar inquiry. Thus every research, into any aspect of the problem, however small, contributes to the building of the great edifice.

I think that I need scarcely apologise to readers who accept my approach and understand the vastness of the task if in this work I offer only fragments; if in the different chapters the exposition is uneven in that the author lingers longest over points that occupied much of his time, whereas others he only touches on; and if, finally, some of the chapters raise new problems without attempting a solution. If he can but inspire others to further study, the author is content.

II. AN OUTLINE OF THE ISOLATED STATE, PART TWO, SECTION ONE[1]

1. The central question Thünen tries to answer here is: Is the current low level of wages the natural one, or does it arise through exploitation, which the labourer cannot prevent? What in fact is the natural *share of the product which the labourer should receive? He finds that economists up to his time had not answered this question. They were concerned to describe things as they were, rather than to ask whether this was the natural state of things.*

2. Thünen starts his own inquiry by going to the frontier of the Isolated State, where land rent is zero. Here an attempt to put up wages would make land rent negative, forcing a contraction in the radius of the cultivated area; labourers would crowd into this contracted ring, forcing everyone's wages—theirs and those of the workers already there—down below what they were before.

But this situation is based on the prevailing rate of interest. Once this is allowed to vary, the wage can rise without these unfortunate consequences, and the question now becomes, can the rate of interest be lowered so as to give the worker a larger part of the product of labour, and so increase his wage? Thünen argues that conventional explanations of the nature of interest do not explain the basic causes of the rate of interest at all.

3. Thünen then goes on to study the nature of capital. His basic assumption is that all capital is past labour, stored up. To study the origin of capital, he transfers the Isolated State momentarily to the Tropics, to show how man, forced to create capital anew, will do it. A man may work for 10 years and produce in each of those years a surplus of 10 per cent over his needs. At the end of the ten years he can take a year off from production to serve his needs, and use that year to make capital. After that, with the aid of the capital, he can produce every year 50 per cent over his needs. In effect then his capital produces 50 − 10, or 40 per cent above his needs. He can lend his capital out to someone, and that person will find it worthwhile to

[1] A full translation exists in B. DEMPSEY, *The Frontier Wage* (Chicago 1960), 187–367.

pay for the use of the capital 40 per cent, the value of the surplus it produces. Thus it is seen that the rate of interest, which is (100 plus 10, or 110)/40, or 36.4 per cent, represents the wages of current labour divided by the revenue from past labour. *The interest rate is subject to the rule that application of capital yields diminishing returns. Therefore the more capital is created, the lower the interest rate and the more is available for wages. The question now narrows itself down to: What payment to workers and capital-producers would yield the greatest benefit to both? This central question Thünen answers by considering as a model the frontier of the Isolated State.*

4. Consider this frontier. Here there is no land rent. All produce of the soil will be shared between those who create capital and those who till the soil, producing a surplus necessary to create more capital. All capital can be reduced to terms of grain, which must be stored to feed the people who produce the capital. All workers here are free agents, that is, free to transfer their labour to another sort of work. Tillers can become capital-creators at will; and capital-creators, tillers.

5. Consider the Isolated State as in a static condition, with a static number of workers. Imagine then the addition of a new farm. (Thünen argues that this does not conflict with the assumption of a static condition, for two reasons. (1) the State may be regarded as infinitely large, so that an addition of one farm equals zero. (2) in any case the new farm need not be formed in actuality. The possibility *of its being formed is enough to produce the same result.)*

6. Two groups of workers produce the new farms. (1) Directly, those who clear the land: they are the "capital producers". (2) Indirectly, those who tilled the existing farms, and then produced the surplus to feed the capital producers. That surplus, the capital producers must have borrowed at interest. Now, the capital producers require workers to till the new farm. What part of the produce of the farm will they pay out as wages to the new tillers? What part will they keep for themselves, as a return to investment? It must be remembered that the capital producers are themselves workers. They are free at any time to become tillers. And tillers are free at any time to start another farm, i.e. to become capital producers.

7. The central question now is to determine the rate of wages in such a way that it does not depend on the rate of interest—otherwise we would learn nothing. Earlier Thünen has shown algebraically that the interest rate itself is related to the size of the surplus produced over current consumption.[1] *He therefore seeks to devise an expression relating wage to surplus, without introducing interest rate.*

8. *Thünen assumes that the new farm is tilled by* n *workers, and each works with the capital embodied in the new farm.*

We can reduce this to the total number of years of work embodied in each tiller's share of the capital. This we call q.

The total amount of capital is therefore nq. *It is expressed as labour-years, but can be conveniently thought of in another way, as the number of workers needed to produce the same sum in* one *year. That is, each tiller uses capital that required the full-time work of* q *men for one year. All tillers work with the labour of* nq *men, embodied in capital.*[2] *Any worker needs a certain amount of subsistence to support him and his family every year. This we call* a.

We imagined a theoretical number of nq *workers whose labour was needed to create the capital of the farm; the total subsistence they consumed was* anq.

This means of subsistence had to be produced from the soil by another group: those who tilled the soil of the existing farms while the new farm was being cleared. Let us assume that the surplus produced by each was y. *Therefore the number of tillers on existing farms, whose labour was (in effect) exclusively devoted to providing a surplus for the capital-producers, is equal to* anq/y.

We have now calculated the total labour needed to set up the new farm, in terms of the number of workers completely employed in the course of a year. It consists of:

the capital producers, nq, *plus*

the surplus-producers, anq/y

Adding[3], $nq + anq/y = nq(a+y)/y$

Let us return to the tillers of the new farm. Every year, let us assume, the product of each tiller is p. *As there are* n *tillers, the total product of the farm is* np.

---

[1] His formula for the rate of interest, using the symbols described below, is
$$\{p-(a+y)\}/q(a+y)$$
(Chapter 13).

[2] Thünen's translation of q from years of labour into equivalent men working for *one* year has provided a rich source of confusion. Critics have argued that q itself depends on the rate of interest z. But if this is known, y is known: i.e. Thünen assumes as known what he is trying to discover. Cf. DEMPSEY, *op. cit.*, 99–100. Braeuer's presentation of the formula simply avoids this difficulty by making new symbols (n_c and n_s) for the numbers of capital producers and capital savers, and finding an equation between n_c and n_s.

[3] Braeuer's formula here is $n_c (a+y)/y$, where n_c is the number of capital producers, q does not occur.

The tillers of the new farm will receive wages, which will contain two elements. One is the amount of a worker's subsistence, which we have called a. *The other is the surplus necessary for the production of new capital,* y. *Both these elements are the same as for the workers on the old farms. If each tiller receives a wage of* a+y, *then the total wages of the tillers of the new farm are* n(a+y).

We can deduct this sum from the total revenue produced by this farm:

$$np - n(a+y)$$

This is the amount left to the capital producers.

We saw above that the number or capital producers was nq(a+y)/y, *so that the revenue for each of them is* n(p−(a+y)) ÷ nq(a+y)/y,[1] *or* {(p−(a+y))} y/q(a+y).

This is convenient, because n *has disappeared; henceforth we can simply talk about one worker.*

This then is a formula for the return to capital. We wish now to know at what value of y *will it reach a maximum, or in other words at what level will the capital producers maximise their income? A precise and generally-valid answer is possible only by using differential calculus. We differentiate the function above in relation to* y, *setting the differential at 0.*

Then $d\left(\dfrac{(p-(a+y)y}{q(a+y)}\right) = d\,\dfrac{(py-ay-y^2)}{q(a+y)}$

$= q(a+y)(p-a-2y)\,dy - (py-ay-y^2)\,q\,dy = 0$

$\therefore\ (a+y)(p-a-2y) = py-ay-y^2$

$ap - a^2 - 2ay + py - ay - 2y^2 = py - ay - y^2$

$ap - a^2 - 2ay - 2y^2 = -y^2$

$y^2 + 2ay = ap - a^2$

$+a^2 = +a^2$

$(a+y)^2 = ap$

$\therefore\ a+y = \sqrt{(ap)}$

---

[1] It is to be noted that the three *y*s in this expression refer back to two different things That in the main numerator refers to the surplus which *will* be produced by the new tillers; those in the main denominator refer to the surplus *already* produced by the old tillers. Yet the two *y*s must be assumed to represent the same quantity. That is, *y* already exists; and therefore (since *a* exists) the natural wage is already established. Thünen is then interested only to determine the *level* of that wage through a mathematical formula. Cf. DEMPSEY, *op. cit.*, 109–12.

*This then is a formula for the wage which maximises the revenue
of the capital-producers. It is in effect a function of* y, *or the surplus
produced by the tillers, because* a *is known. It is a wage which does not
originate in the relation between supply and demand, nor from the
needs of the worker, but from the free self-determination of the worker.
Thünen calls it the* natural wage. *Expressed in words, it is the geomet-
rical mean of the essential subsistence needs of the worker* (*measured
in grain or money*) *and his product. The wage is greater than the
worker's needs in precisely the same degree that the product is above
the wage.*

9. *This is the wage which maximises the capital-producer's income.
But in chapters 16–23 Thünen goes on to show that the natural wage
simultaneously achieves these further objectives:*

(a) *it gives the wage-earning tiller the highest interest for the surplus*
(y) *which he produces* (*Chapter 16*).

(b) *it defines the level to which it is advantageous to apply capital
to a given area of land, in order to save labour* (*i.e. an existing
farm, rather than applying the capital to new land*) (*Chapters
17–18*).

(c) *it produces revenue from capital with the least expenditure of
labour* (*Chapter 20*).

(d) *it achieves equilibrium between the reward for the labour contained in the capital and the reward for labour in wages* (*the
surplus of which, above subsistence needs, can be lent at interest*)
(*Chapter 21*).

(e) *from all these, it follows that it maximises national revenue.*

10. *Thünen has sought to investigate the relation between wages and
the rate of interest from several different points of view. Through all
of them, the expression, "the wage* $= \sqrt{(ap)}$", *has proved correct.
Thünen therefore asserts that this is the natural wage, that is the wage
that corresponds to the organisation of men and of the physical world.*

11. *But this natural wage is based on conditions at the frontier of the
Isolated State. Under European conditions, there is no land to be
found without a landlord; and so the worker has no freedom to reject
the low wage offered by the employer in favour of the cultivation of a
new, previously uncultivated piece of land. Here the wage* $= a+y$;
but y *constantly tends to decrease while* z, *the rate of interest, increases. It is here to the advantage of entrepreneurs to push wages
down. National income may rise, but nothing passes to the workers;*

Thünen quotes an empirical example from Mecklenburg. Workers cannot escape from this vicious circle, because (1) their bare subsistence wage does not allow them to accumulate a surplus, so that all new capital formation is in the hands of a capitalist class; (2) they cannot educate their children. Yet in North America, where there is unlimited fertile soil at virtually no cost, as in the Isolated State, and where (also as in the Isolated State) the improvement of transport constantly pushes the agricultural area out to cover a wider area, the wage $\sqrt{(ap)}$ has been attained.

CHAPTER 19

174 # THE WAGE IS EQUAL TO THE EXTRA PRODUCT OF THE LAST LABOURER WHO IS EMPLOYED IN A LARGE ENTERPRISE

Editor's Note: A lengthy extract is given from this chapter because it deals with the concept of marginal productivity which is relevant to Part I.

IMAGINE an estate employing more than one hundred labourers. The amount of labour required to cultivate this estate is not a fixed quantity, for the land may be tilled more or less carefully, and the grain threshed, or the potatoes gleaned with greater or less thoroughness.

Take potato picking for example.

175   If only those potatoes are gathered that have been lifted to the surface with the hoe or the spade one labourer can collect more than thirty Berlin bushels a day. But if a hand-hoe has to be used to dig up the potatoes still left in the soil, the labour product per person will fall immediately, and very sharply. The more the farmer insists on thorough gleaning, the smaller will be the labour product; and if he means to harvest the last bushel contained in a plot of one hundred square rods, so much additional labour will be required, that the labourer hired for this purpose cannot feed himself from what he produces, let alone satisfy his other needs.

Suppose that the total quantity of potatoes grown on a plot of one hundred square rods is a hundred Berlin bushels.

176   How thoroughly will a rational farmer have the potatoes gathered? So thoroughly, without doubt, that the value of the extra output is in balance with the labour cost of its production.

For example, if the value of potatoes used for sheep-feed is 5 shillings the bushel, and the daily wage is 8 shillings a worker, the

When the number of people engaged to gather them is	The harvest is	The last person hired therefore produces an increment of
4	80 bushels	
5	86·6 bushels	6·6 bushels
6	91 bushels	4·4 bushels
7	94 bushels	3·0 bushels
8	96 bushels	2·0 bushels
9	97·3 bushels	1·3 bushels
10	98·2 bushels	0·9 bushel
11	98·8 bushels	0·6 bushel
12	99·2 bushels	0·4 bushel

employment of a ninth person will bring an additional product of 6·5 shillings (1·3 bushels multiplied by 5 shillings) but will cost 8 shillings, resulting therefore in a loss of 1·5 shillings. But the eighth person employed costs 8 shillings and produces an additional output of 10 shillings (2 bushels multiplied by 5 shillings); he therefore produces a profit of 2 shillings. It follows that the farmer who wishes to obtain the maximum net product will employ about 8·6 days' labour per labourer in picking potatoes, and content himself with a product of about 96·8 bushels.

If the daily wage is as high as 15 shillings, which is easily possible in large-scale potato production, where labourers have to be attracted from a distance, the additional product obtained by employing a seventh labourer will only just cover the wage. In this case (assuming rational management) only 94 out of the 100 bushels contained in the plot can profitably be harvested.

But if the potatoes are worth 16 shillings the bushel—as horse-feed for instance, or used in distilling or other industries—it would, at the daily wage of 8 shillings, be profitable to employ 11 days' labour per labourer, and 98·8 bushels could then be harvested out of the 100.

At a daily wage of 15 shillings and a potato price of 16 shillings the bushel, the eleventh labourer will not fully cover his costs.

The thoroughness with which the grain is threshed from the straw is subject to rules very like those of potato picking.

Where more labourers are employed, the often very appreciable amount of grain lost in harvesting may be greatly reduced; the crop may be cut, bound and brought in at the optimum time; the harvest finished more rapidly; and the grain, instead of being mown with the

177

scythe, may be cut with the sickle or chopped off with the short-handled scythe. Here again the number of workers will be raised until the value of the economies derived from their labour covers, or slightly outweighs, the cost of their daily wage.

It follows:

1. That where the value of the product remains constant, a wage rise reduces the number of workers that may be employed, and the yield of the crop to be harvested and threshed.
2. That where the wage remains constant, the effect of a rise in the value of the product is precisely the opposite. More labourers may be profitably employed; the crop harvested with greater care and threshed more thoroughly; and yield will rise in consequence.
3. That as long as he continues to derive a profit it is in the entrepreneur's interest—be he manufacturer or farmer—to go on raising the number of his labourers; and the point at which the wage paid to the last labourer absorbs the extra output he produces is the margin[1] which sets the limit to this increase. Conversely the wage equals the additional product created by the last man hired.

178

Because the number of labourers cannot be raised or reduced by fractions, it is impossible, in small concerns, to establish the precise point where cost and product are in balance; but any given enterprise will employ now more, now less labourers than the maximum net product would warrant, so that the error in the detail evens out when we regard the total picture.

Small concerns suffer from this disadvantage not merely with respect to the number of their workmen, but with respect to the number of draught animals, tools and machines they use. This, incidentally, is one of the factors operating in favour of large-scale undertakings.

Our last example referred only to the more efficient harvesting of the products of the soil; but our conclusions remain valid for labour spent on raising the soil yield and obtaining larger harvests. An increase in the labour force makes it possible to till, drain and clear the land more thoroughly and to seed at the optimum time: to ensure, in short, a more uniform crop yield, and appreciably raise

[1] *Grenze,*

the mean product; and the addition of marl and mould, and of soils lacking in the plot, will in normal circumstances greatly raise the productivity of soil. All these improvements have this in common: the effect of their quantitative increase does not rise proportionally but at a diminishing rate, eventually becoming equal to zero.

179

Suppose, for example, that the addition to any given plot of half an inch of mould raises yield by half a bushel-crop (half a Berlin bushel per hundred square rods), but that another half-inch will raise the yield by only roughly three-eights of a bushel-crop; a third half-inch by about a quarter of a bushel-crop; and so forth, until eventually we reach the point where further increments of mould will not merely fail to increase output but will have adverse results.

Since labour costs are directly related to the amount of mould that is added, whereas their effect diminishes and ultimately becomes equal to zero, there must be a point—as with all the farming operations we have mentioned—where labour costs are in balance with the value of the improvements. This is the point to which the rational farmer will carry his improving.

The relation between the cost and the value of labour determines, not only each specific operation, but the choice between higher and lower farming systems: is it worth buying a larger product at a greater outlay of labour?; is it worth cultivating inferior soil which rewards labour with a smaller product?

Indeed, we may say that the entire problem of rational farming consists in discovering, for every branch of agriculture, the corresponding term in the two rising series—increased labour costs and higher yield—so that we may be able to discover the precise point where the cost and the value of labour are in balance: for it is at this point that the net product is maximised.

180

The practical farmer's success depends largely on his ability to find approximate solutions to this problem. The farmer with a predominantly theoretical grounding in his subject tends to lack this ability entirely. This should not astonish us, for in this respect our science is still in its primitive beginnings; and as yet our textbooks barely touch the problem which ought to permeate the subject and form the basis of a full synthesis.

A comparison between Germany and North America is here of interest.

In Germany, cultivation is feasible and land may be farmed at the daily wage of 12 shillings and a rye price of 1 thaler 12 shillings the bushel, though the reward of a man's day's labour will here be a product of only one-fifth of a bushel of rye.

But in North America, from the most moderate accounts, a man's day's labour costs at least 32 shillings and rye, in the interior of the country, is worth barely 1 thaler the Berlin bushel. Every operation where a man's day's labour fails to bring an additional product of two-thirds of a bushel of rye is here associated with loss.

181   What a vast difference in the farming of these two countries is due to this one factor!

An article from a North American newspaper, discussing which type of immigrant is most likely to do well, comments:

"The least successful are those who have studied economics, for in our country the problem is not to squeeze a several per cent higher output from the soil but to reduce expensive labour."

This is an apt comment on our science as at present taught. The discipline of a true science should teach the student to assess the relevance of all the data, and should protect him from the very errors the trained economists are today making in America. If it fails in this—as our science so obviously is doing at the moment—it is proof of the subject's immaturity.

An ancient myth pervades our agricultural writings: that whatever the stage of social development, there is one valid farming system only—as though every system that is more simple, every enterprise that adopts extensive methods to economise on labour, were proof of the practising farmer's ignorance.

The Isolated State in its Relation to Agriculture and National Economy

PART TWO

THE NATURAL WAGE AND ITS RELATION TO THE RATE OF INTEREST AND TO LAND RENT

SECTION TWO

FRAGMENTS FROM THE INQUIRIES AND FROM THE PLAN OF THIS WORK

(Extracts)

1. THE SOURCES OF LAND RENT
(Chapter 4, Sections 1–3)

Thünen postulates three sources of land rent: situation rent (which he expresses by a new formula using labour costs), intensity rent, and rent arising from the permanent improvement of the soil.

First source, Formulae for the size of Land Rent

If, to simplify the argument, we assume that the capital which the labourer requires for his work and which is contained in his tools, livestock, and so forth, belongs to the landowner, who draws interest on this capital from the workers, the land rent springing from the labour of one family may be represented as follows:

The labour product is p
of this the labourer receives $\sqrt{(ap)}$
The interest which the capitalist receives for
the capital of q years' labour, or $q\sqrt{(ap)}$
bushels, at an interest rate of $\{\sqrt{(ap)}-a\}/aq$, is: $\{\sqrt{ap}(\sqrt{(ap)}-a)\}/a$

The land rent therefore comes to:

$$p-\sqrt{(ap)}\left(1+\left(\frac{\sqrt{(ap)}-a}{a}\right)\right)$$

$$= p-(ap/a) = 0$$

This means that if the farm lies in the district where the natural wage is determined,[1] land rent = 0.

---

[1] i.e. at the margin of settlement.

Let the wage for the district which serves as the regulator for the wage and the interest rate be $A = \sqrt{(ap)} = af$, then the interest rate,

$$z = \frac{\sqrt{(ap)} - a}{aq} = \frac{f-1}{q}$$

66 Here the rent is $z(qA) = qaf(f-1)/q = af^2 - af$.
But land rent is $p - A - R = p - af - (af^2 - af) = p - af^2$, when R = capital utilisation.

If we substitute these values, the land rent is

$$= p - af - qaf(f-1)/q$$
$$= p - af - af^2 + af = p - af^2$$

According to Chapter 2,[1] with rye at $\frac{1}{2}$ thaler the bushel, the wage at Tellow which is the standard for the whole State when this estate lies at the frontier of the Isolated State where land rent = 0, is:

$$\sqrt{(ap)} = 173 \text{ Berlin bushels of rye}$$
$$a = 123 \text{ Berlin bushels of rye}$$
therefore $\quad f = 173/123 = 1\cdot406$
$$p = af^2 \quad = 123 \times 1\cdot406^2$$
$$= 123 \times 1\cdot976$$
$$= 243 \text{ Berlin bushels of rye.}$$

From the estimates made for Tellow (Chapter 2), the annual labour-product of each worker is 243 Berlin bushels of rye (242·9 bushels).*

It is important to note that wage and capital utilisation have together produced the simple formula af^2.

The wage A is $\qquad\qquad\qquad af$
Capital utilisation R therefore $= af^2 - af = af(f-1)$
$$= A(f-1)$$
Together $= Af$

---

* Editor's note to the edition of 1863: To demonstrate the exact correspondence, we have at this point substituted the values found for Tellow in Chapter 2,[2] although in the rest of the fragment we have retained the figures Thünen himself used in the manuscript.

[1] Not reproduced here.　　　[2] Of II. 2, not translated here.

Here capital utilisation has been traced back to labour, and as one year's labour is the measure of capital, so A is shown to be the measure of capital utilisation also.

If we use L to denote land rent, then:

$$L = p - af^2$$

and the annual labour product of one man has three constituents:

1. Wage A $= af$
2. Capital utilisation $R = af(f-1)$
3. Land rent L $= p - af^2$

$$A + R + L = p$$

When $a = b$ thalers $+ c$ bushels of rye, the general formula for the land rent for the district where the bushel of rye costs x thalers is:

$$p - f^2\{(b/x) + c\} \quad \text{bushels of rye}$$

The land rent of the farm is proportional in this case to the number of labourers employed.

This explains why the wealth of the great Russian landowners is counted not by the land they possess, but by the number of peasants living on it.

This measure, however, may be applied only where soil is of the same quality and farmed in the same manner throughout.

Second source

Suppose that at the border of the Isolated State a farm, as large as Tellow, is cultivated by 10 labourers' families.

Let one man's labour product be 240 bushels, then
  P, the total product, equals   2400 bushels
Let the wage be 150 bushels. For 10 labourers this
  is   1500 bushels

The estate rent is therefore   900 bushels

Let the capital invested in the buildings and equipment be equal to 12 years' labour at 150 bushels, or 18,000 bushels. This yields a return on capital of 900 bushels, or 5 per cent.

With more intensive cultivation more labourers may be put to work on a given area of land, although the output of each additional labourer hired will be less than that of his predecessor. But the wage equals the value of labour.[1] (Cf. Part Two, Section One, Chapters 16–19.)[2]

We shall discover the value of labour if from the labour product we subtract the interest on the capital with which the labourer works.

Let the increment in the total capital which becomes necessary with the employment of an additional labourer be t years' labour, i.e. At bushels. It follows that the value of labour is $(p - Atz)$ bushels. But the value of labour is equal to the wage, therefore to A. A therefore equals $p - Atz$, and consequently $p/(1 + tz)$.*

69   Given that the wage and the value of the work done by the

$$
\begin{aligned}
\text{11th labourer} &= 135 \text{ bushels of rye} \\
\text{12th labourer} &= 122 \text{ bushels of rye} \\
\text{13th labourer} &= 110 \text{ bushels of rye} \\
\text{14th labourer} &= 99 \text{ bushels of rye} \\
\text{15th labourer} &= 89 \text{ bushels of rye} \\
\text{16th labourer} &= 80 \text{ bushels of rye} \\
\hline
&= 635 \text{ bushels of rye}
\end{aligned}
$$

it follows that the hire of these 6 labourers will raise the product of the enterprise from 2400 to 2400 plus 635, or 3055 bushels.

But the value of the work of the last man hired determines the wage of all the other labourers.

The total product	= 3035 bushels
The wage of 16 labourers at 80 bushels of rye	= 1280 bushels
The difference	= 1755 bushels

* (t years' labour includes:
1. The capital contained in the equipment used by this additional labourer.
2. The capital required to enlarge the barns for storing the product of the last man hired.

It does not include:

The capital contained in the house, furnishings and clothing necessary to make the labourer fit for his work; because the interest on this form of capital is contained in the means of subsistence, and is paid out of the wage.)

[1] i.e. the marginal value.
[2] The reader is referred to Dempsey's translation, *op. cit.*, p. 294-318.

On the capital t, which varies with the number of labourers, the interest has already been brought into account, since the calculation does not include the whole increment in the labour product but only the portion left after deduction of the interest.

The interest on the capital originally invested (above called rent) comes to	900 bushels
When this is subtracted from 1755, a surplus remains of	855 bushels

This surplus is the basis of a land rent accruing to the owner.

In all our previous discussions land rent sprang from the advantage enjoyed by a better quality soil, favourably located, over land of poorer quality or farther from the market. We have now come to the second source of land rent: the rise in intensive cultivation.   70

But this intensified cultivation is associated with a progressively declining wage and is, apparently, achieved at the labourer's expense.

This, however, is not absolutely necessary.

If for the entire Isolated State the labourer's means of subsistence may be represented by 50 bushels of rye plus 25 thalers, then at the border, where rye is worth half a thaler the bushel, the means of subsistence expressed in rye come to 50 plus 50, or 100, bushels; near the Town, where 1·5 thalers is worth only as much as 1 bushel of rye, they are 50 plus $16\frac{2}{3}$, or $66\frac{2}{3}$, bushels.

If the wage is one and a half times the means of subsistence, the real wage, 100 bushels ($66\frac{2}{3}$ multiplied by 1·5), has the same value as have 150 bushels at the border, and the labourer will live as well on it.

Given that all farms are equal in size, it follows that if farms near the border can give profitable employment to only 10 labourers, the ones nearer the Town will be able to hire an 11th, 12th, 13th, and, very near the Town, a 14th labourer, the value of whose work is still 99 bushels; and these labourers need not be worse off than those living near the border.

The owner of land near the Town enjoys therefore a twofold advantage:

1. Adopting the very simplest form of cultivation, the three-field system, he obtains a surplus which forms the source of a land rent; because the worker's labour product expressed in rye remains constant, whereas the wage expressed in rye falls (the real wage remaining constant).

11

71   2. A lower wage[1] makes possible more intensive farming and
               greater thoroughness of cultivation, producing consequently a
               surplus over and above the wage that is paid.

Neither point affects the real wage,[2] which remains $1.5a$ throughout.

But if, as a result of the great increase in their number, the labourers
agree to work for a lower wage, the farmer will be able to hire more
and more of them, and land rent will continue rising to find a limit
only in the fact that the wage cannot sink below a (see Part Two,
Section One, Chapter 14 III).

Third source

If the wage falls from 0·39 to 0·28 bushels of rye, soil improvements become profitable which before would not have paid: marling;
the construction of sewage farms; the addition of humus; the improvement of the physical quality of the soil by the addition of
constituents its lacks; deepening the top layer; and so forth.

Some of these, like the improvement of defective soils by the
addition of deficient mineral constituents, are indestructible and
become part of the land; others, like the construction of sewage
farms, require only annual repair and maintenance permanently to
raise the soil yield; and others yet, such as the addition of marl and
mould, are again consumed by the harvest (in so far as they are not
associated with a simultaneous improvement in soil quality). How-
72   ever, where the rotation is directed primarily to the production of
feed, the addition of marl and mould will permanently raise soil
fertility—for the larger the feed crop, the larger the amount of
manure that is replaced.

We need include in our calculations only the interest on the capital
invested in improvements which permanently upgrade soil. But
capital that is well spent produces besides interest an annual profit.
However, interest and profit are not distinguishable in the long run,
and both become part of the land rent, of which they form the third
constituent.

The second constituent of land rent differs essentially from the
third; in the one the capital associated with a greater use of labour

---

[1] Here Thünen evidently means "lower real wage expressed in bushels of rye";
in the previous paragraph he was writing about real wages expressed as a ratio to the
means of subsistence, i.e., partly in money and partly in rye.

[2] i.e. expressed as a ratio to means of subsistence.

is repaid annually at a profit, whereas in the other, the capital that raises land rent remains fixed in the soil.

It is extremely important to distinguish between the three constituents of land rent, especially (as I shall show at greater length) in considering taxes on farming.

It may seem inconsistent that in Part One we attributed land rent to the relative savings on freights made by the farm nearer the Town as compared with the one at the border of the State, whereas we now ascribe it to the difference in the wage when this is expressed in rye. Upon closer examination, however, we find that both explanations derive from the same source.

In Part One costs, and therefore wages, are given one-quarter in money and three-quarters in grain; and when thus expressed costs remain constant throughout the Isolated State. But the value of grain on the farm varies with the cost of sending it to the Town. At the border of the State land rent equals zero. As the Town is approached the value of grain rises—and this increment in value is the source of land rent.   73

But in the present context the wage expressed in rye is variable, because the labourer, in buying his basic necessities, does not spend the same amount of rye in the different districts of the Isolated State. Yet the product of labour, expressed in rye, remains constant. With approach to the Town, the constant labour product, p, and changing wage (both measured in rye) create therefore a surplus, which is the source of a land rent.

The two methods have this in common: that the production costs of grain do not rise directly with the value of grain, and that when the value of grain passes a certain point a surplus is created which forms a land rent.

What here we call p is that which remains of the gross labour product after deduction of the value of the fodder and seed, the repair and maintenance of the barns and stables, the costs of management, and of all the other costs associated with farming, with the exception only of the wage and the interest on the invested capital.

On soil of uniform fertility, farmed in the same way, the gross labour product will be the same in all parts of the Isolated State. But at the frontier of the State the amount of grain required to maintain and repair the equipment, buildings and so on, and to pay for the purchase of such articles as iron tools, is larger than near the Town. It follows that the portion of a man's gross labour product that is   74 left is smaller at the border than near the Town and that p, expressed in bushels of rye, rises with proximity to the Town.

Thus our method of considering p expressed in bushels of rye constant does not tell us the total amount of land rent. But we are not concerned here with the abolute amount of land rent, expressed in figures, only with the reasons for its origin. On the other hand in Part One, where we endeavoured to determine the amount of land rent, the method there used was the more appropriate.

Our present method is however more comprehensive and complete than that of Part One.

2. THE RELATION BETWEEN PROFIT AND LAND RENT
(Chapter 4, Section 5)

Thünen considers the effect of industrial plants upon the land rent of farms producing raw materials for them, and is led to stress the importance of a complete analysis of the effects which any change in a part of the economy may have on the other parts.

92   We know that the establishment of a small town raises land rent in the district where this town buys its provisions; in other words, in the region of this town land will now yield a higher rent than it did before the town existed.

93   If this is the effect on land rent of towns with a population of 2000, will towns with only 1000 or 500 inhabitants have a similar, if smaller, effect? The answer is "yes", for the factors operating to raise land rent are the same, whatever the size of the towns.

But because we are incapable of establishing the limits of this,[1] we are prompted to ask a further question, namely: How will the establishment of a factory or large distillery on a farm affect the local land rent?

Suppose the distillery is set up by an entrepreneur who owns a complex of estates which can supply the potatoes, wood and peat required for his distillery. The owner will, when estimating the product of the distillery, take into account (1) only the normal rental of the land on which the potatoes are produced; (2) only the existing market price of the wood used; and (3) if he owns peat bogs which were valueless before, he will debit only the wage he pays his labourers.

i.e. to the influence of any small town on rents in the surrounding area.

The entire surplus of the distillery will then be regarded as business profit.

Now suppose that the owner of another, single, estate, producing neither potatoes, wood nor peat, also sets up a distillery. What effect will this have on the value of wood and potatoes and on the land rent of the farms and estates in the neighbourhood?

First Case. B, the farm closest to A, has now the choice of selling its surplus wood to one of the near-by towns or of selling it to A. The town price still governs the value of the wood on farm B, and if its owner does not want to take advantage of A's predicament, he can let its owner have the wood at the usual price (i.e. the ruling price at B plus the cost of transport to A). But if B cannot supply all the wood required for the distillery, and A has to buy some from C, a farm half a mile farther on, the value of wood at farm B will undergo a change. For if the price of wood, which is determined by the market price in the town, is the same at B and at C, say, 4 thalers per cord, and transport from C to A costs 1 thaler the cord, A will have to pay 5 thalers the cord, and at B, whence transport to A costs only half a thaler the cord, the value of wood will rise from 4 to 4·5 thalers. There will be a similar change in the value of potatoes; thus the establishment of a distillery at farm A raises land rent at B.

94

Second Case. B is able to supply all the potatoes and firewood required by A. If several other farms lie at the same distance from A as does B, B cannot force A to pay more than the "natural" price, and it seems that there will be no change at B in the value of the wood or the total amount of land rent.

With this we are back at a previous position, and again we are unable to give the explanation for a law which, on a larger scale, is at work in the formation[1] of towns.

These findings overlook, however, the following significant point:

When B sells its wood to A, the town—the market—loses the wood it used to buy from B, and to obtain what it needs it will have to buy wood from farther afield. This raises the price of wood in the town, which in turn raises its value at farm B. As a result, A will no longer be able to buy its wood from B at the previous price; in this way the establishment of a distillery at A raises the land rent at B. For the same reason, the price of potatoes in the town will also rise,

95

---

[1] *Entstehung.* Evidently Thünen means "influence", though later he implies that the effect of factories, towns, etc. on the surrounding countryside provides part of the reason for their existence.

though to a lesser degree, since potatoes are brought from a greater distance than is firewood and thus from a wider ring.

Let us now return to the owner of the complex of estates which itself produces the potatoes and fuel used in his distillery. Once the distillery is set up, the wood these estates used to sell to the town is consumed inside the complex. This, as I have shown, raises the price of wood in the town. Once the price has risen, the owner of the complex will no longer be able to charge his distillery account with wood at the former price, but must assess this according to the present price, which is higher. This raises the rent of his forest, although the profit of his distillery will fall by the same amount. In the town there will be a slight, but only a very slight, fall in the price of spirits.

In these conditions we see a land rent springing directly from an industrial enterprise, and vanishing when this is abandoned.

96

It may be that when the price of wood has risen, the distillery will no longer be able to carry return to capital or wages at the full current rate; but as long as estates and distillery together yield a higher product than the estates formerly did alone, the owner would be foolish to abandon his new undertaking.

If we take instead of a distillery a glass-works, this process is illustrated even more strikingly, and on a larger scale.

Suppose a small town buys most of its wood from a near-by forest. If in the forest the wood costs 3 thalers the cord, and transport to the town costs 1 thaler the cord, the town price per cord will be 4 thalers. Now suppose that the owner of the forest sets up a glass-works which consumes the total annual increment of his forest, 1000 cords. When all the costs have been deducted, the glass-works utilises wood at 3·5 thalers the cord;[1] thus the newly-established factory permanently raises ground rent by 500 thalers per annum. But the town, which can no longer buy wood from the local forest, has now to go farther afield for this commodity, and the greater expense of the transport will raise the market price to 5 thalers in the town; thus the value of the wood in the forest belonging to the local landowner rises to 4 thalers the cord. But the glass-works utilises wood at 3·5 thalers only; so that the man who owns the forest and the complex of estates will lose 500 thalers per annum. Does this mean that he should abandon the glass-works? By no means, for if the glass-works

[1] Thünen implies that the existence of the extra demand drives the price up by 0·5 thalers a cord.

disappeared, the price of wood would sink to 4 thalers in the town and to 3 in his forest. His best policy is to restrict the size of his glass-works in order to limit its consumption of wood, selling the surplus to the town to the extent that in the forest it remains worth at least 3·5 thalers the cord.[1]

What we have been saying about distilleries and glass-works applies even more to large factories, salt and coal mines, and so on.

97

A simple estimate telling us whether a given factory can supply its products as cheaply as can foreign industry, or at a slightly higher price, will not tell us whether the establishment or extinction of this factory adds to, or diminishes, national wealth. For this, we have to know and consider the effect this factory has on cultivation, on the return to capital, on the wage, and on the revenue raised by taxation.

If the salt-works at Sülz were to be abandoned, the price of fire-wood, and with it land rent, would drop very considerably; the peat bogs, which today yield an appreciable rent, would lose their value; and many people would become unemployed.

The indirect influence exerted by industry on land rent has received scant recognition from economists. As a result, mistakes are readily made in practice—yet one more explanation of the unscientific behaviour common among statesmen.

It is worth noting that the effect of industries on land rent is normally apparent only in the cultivation and production of commodities which, in relation to their value, are costly to transport. The effect of a new town on the London market, depriving it of 100 or even 1000 loads of grain, is so minute that the resulting increase in the grain price can scarcely be expressed in figures.

Every new town, and every new factory, raises the return to capital and wages as well as land rent. As a result, capital and labourers increase so rapidly that within a short period return to capital and wages will have reverted to their former level. The rise in land rent, on the other hand, is lasting, because land is fixed in amount and cannot be increased.

98

The proposition that the establishment of a new town causes only an imperceptible rise in the price of grain, refers only to the price obtaining throughout the country as a whole; for we have already

---

[1] The argument here is far from clear. In fact there would be nothing wrong if the owner did not restrict size but charged himself 4 thalers for his own wood for use in his glass-works, so long as the total return were increased thereby. That would depend on the relative return from glass and from wood for fuel, about which Thünen says nothing.

seen that in the district where the town buys its grain the price will rise appreciably.

Conclusion: The extra product has either to be brought from farther afield—at higher transport costs—or is obtained by means of more intensive tillage—at higher production costs. Either course will raise land rent, as we have shown.

It follows that even where, as in Mecklenburg, the landowners' interest is regarded as the only true interest, the national interest, it will pay this class to look kindly on the success of industrial undertakings; and, even though the landowner may have to pay a slightly higher price for domestic manufactures than for those imported from abroad, the resulting increment in the value of his own products will amply compensate him for the small sacrifice he has to make.

A comparison of the Prussian grain price with that in the Rhineland, taken on a 14-year average, offers a striking illustration of the way in which a higher density of population raises the price of grain—and with it land values. The ratio is as 32 Silver Groschen to 51.[1]

3. THE ROLE OF TAXATION AND GOVERNMENT SPENDING: PRIVATE AND SOCIAL BENEFIT

(From Chapter 4, Sections 4 and 6)

Thünen considers the social benefits created by government investment in education and roads. He stresses the revolutionary economic effects of railways, and suggests criteria for railway investment.

* * *

76-
77
It is both the duty and the interest of a ruler to regard as one the total income of all his subjects; and in choosing between different taxes designed to yield a given revenue, he must choose the one that will do least to reduce the total national income.

If an inquiry were to show that the national income is highest at the wage $\sqrt{(ap)}$,[2] it would become the ruler's interest and his duty to improve the education of the working class by the use of state

---

[1] 30 Silver Groschen (*Silbergroschen*) equalled 1 Prussian current thaler; 12 new thalers equalled 14 Prussian current thalers.

[2] Thünen has already sought to show this in Part II Section 1.

funds, thus hastening the day when the natural wage will be the ruling one.

Hitherto, the promotion of material prosperity has often seemed to conflict with the other ends of state; and it is generally accepted that prosperity—the possession of material goods—must be subordinate to moral welfare.

But if our conjecture that national income attains its maximum when $A = \sqrt{(ap)}$ is correct, then these two objects, moral and material welfare, are no longer incompatible: for we have proved that this particular wage is possible only where the people have attained a high level of intellectual and moral education.[1]

If we regard the capital spent on working-class education as part of national wealth, because it is repaid, at ample interest, by the workers' higher labour product, the factory employment of children, which is detrimental to their schooling, is not merely reprehensible from the moral but also from the economic point of view. Thus again, apparently divergent interests are reconciled.

*   *   *

If a highway is built, and a tax is levied on all the farms that use   81
it, these farms, despire the new imposition, may still attain a higher value than they had previously. *Every single tax should have to justify its existence in the same manner.*

A highway yields no interest; railways produce high returns on the invested capital. Given that rail freights are as 1 to 2 compared with road freights, highway construction is nevertheless justified, because the benefit these bestow on the entire nation outweighs the interest on the invested capital, and because the prosperity of the country as a whole will gain—even though the citizens will have to pay the interest on their building by some tax or other. Why cannot   82
this principle be applied to railways?

And should this be done one day, then the effects of this great invention will be incalculable, and what has happened hitherto will pale compared with what is yet to come. If the interest on the capital invested in railways is renounced, freight charges may at least be halved.

---

[1] Thünen suggested this when writing of North America in Part Two, Section 1, Chapter 22, though he did not prove it. Cf. DEMPSEY's translation, *op. cit.*, p. 328.

In the Isolated State endowed with the Mecklenburg roads of thirty years ago, the State (according to Part One) extends for 31·5 miles; with modern highways it would have an extension of 52·5 miles; with railways, of 77 miles.

This vividly illustrates the vast effect railways will have on the welfare of the nations, an effect which will be all the greater if the interest on the capital invested in their construction be foregone, so that freight charges (by weight and mileage) may be halved. The cultivated plain would then stretch up to 154 miles from the Town; and the Isolated State would occupy an area nearly twenty-five times as large as with bad roads. So marvellous is the effect of improvements in transport and of cheaper freights!

But however beneficial cheaper freights may be, the thought of cheaper passenger fares must arouse some misgiving. Not everyone who travels by rail travels on business; many people do so merely for pleasure. This unproductive travelling, like the consumption of every luxury, deserves to be more highly taxed, not rendered easier.

The value of the shares of many railway lines have today reached heights which were undreamt of once. If the state controlled these lines, freights might immediately be halved, without any change in passenger fares, and the interest on the invested capital would still be repaid. In view of this, the governments would be well advised to take over the construction of the railways, instead of leaving this, as now, to private citizens.

83

104

Not even the most benevolent ruler of a great empire like Russia can give his subjects cheaper consumer goods by fostering industrial development inside his realm; much less can he present his people by command with southern fruit, wine or colonial products not native to his realm.

But an invention of our day, which will for ever redound to the honour of the human spirit, has made possible the impossible, at any rate brought us nearer to the day when it will be so: I mean the steam engine, and its application to railways.

Products of no value in the interior of Russia, which therefore could not stimulate the local population to achieve higher output, may now be sent by rail to distant regions to be exchanged for foreign products and for manufactured goods that can give pleasure to the Russian people.

A railway from St. Petersburg, via Kalinin, Moscow, Kaluga, Tula, Orel and Kharkov, to the Crimea, would connect the largest cities of this empire, its most densely populated regions, and the Black Sea with the Bay of Finland. A second line, from Riga via Vilnyus to Odessa, would cut across the fertile plains of eastern Poland which today, having no markets, are scarcely more than wilderness; it would convert these vast stretches into highly cultivated farming land and would create a trade route for the exchange of products between north and south.

105

These two lines would extend for nearly 500 miles; and since normally it is impossible to construct one mile of railway track for less than one-quarter million thalers, the building of these lines would seem to surpass even the powers of an empire as great as Russia.

Measured in thalers the outlay seems astronomical: it becomes rather less so when we take another unit as our standard. It is scarcely possible to conduct a military campaign of 200,000 to 300,000 men for less than sixty million thalers; the proposed lines would therefore cost as much as two campaigns. But two campaigns are nothing when we look at history; and to attain some political objective or avenge some insult Russia would not hesitate to engage in a two- or three-year war, and would certainly find the means of doing so.

Why not for railways?

War not only consumes what is spent on the army, but it destroys the prosperity of the defeated nation—and often, in the hazards of the struggle, the wealth and happiness of both the warring parties.

What a difference between this and the money spent on railways! Money thus spent yields interest; and the attendant rise in population and prosperity augments the national wealth, the state revenue, and the international standing of the country that builds railways.

If Riga and Odessa were connected by rail, Poland's eastern regions would grow immeasurably richer, and a new population would arise in them. Riga and Odessa, the termini of such a line, lie outside Poland's frontiers before the division,[1] which means that the separation of Poland from Russia and the reconstruction of her old frontiers would become associated with a decline in the prosperity of the millions of Poles who live in eastern Poland.

106

---

[1] i.e. before the First Partition of Poland in 1772, when the tract through which this railway would pass went to Russia. The whole kingdom of Poland was part of the Russian Empire when Thünen wrote.

If there is any way by which the Polish people may learn to accept Russian sovereignty, it is by linking their material prosperity to Russia.

But politics must not enter my work.

Railways will have another great and beneficial effect: the princes, correctly guided by the feeling that the wealth, power and international standing of their states will in future come to depend on railways, will have little time for warring. If they mean to survive and prosper, they will devote all their power to constructing railway networks.

In the future, when railways will have spun between the different countries a web of economic interdependence and mutual prosperity, the nations themselves will cease to tolerate war.

4.   THE INFLUENCE OF CLIMATE ON AGRICULTURE
(Chapter 4, Section 7)

Thünen considers the effect of relaxing the assumption of uniform climate in the Isolated State, and suggests how an inquiry into the effect of climate should be carried out.

106   In discussing the Isolated State in Part One, we had to consider climate a constant factor; and as the plain was there no more than 63 miles in diameter, the minor variations in climate occurring over so small an area would have anyway offered little subject for omment.

107   But suppose now that the Isolated State is covered by a railway network, the interest of whose construction costs is the responsibility of the state and is not provided out of the receipts of the railway lines: the cultivated plain will here attain a diameter of 308 miles, or roughly the distance from the most southerly tip of Calabria to the far north of Jut and.

Suppose, furthermore, that the capital of this huge State lies centrally between these two points, roughly at latitude 48° north; that it is surrounded by a boundless, and completely level, plain of uniform fertility, which has a railway network but no waterways. This is the canvas on which one day the picture may be painted.

As yet there is no one, least of all the author, capable of undertaking the task (of analysing the effect of climate), for we possess hardly any of the necessary data. I can do no more at present than set down a few opinions and reflections, and express some hopes. But a rich man with the necessary background knowledge, who made this study his life-task, could live in the satisfaction that he was an important benefactor of mankind, that his life was devoted to a noble purpose.

Even the very best of our agricultural textbooks are right and valid only for a given set of circumstances; that they fail to make this explicit, and so convey an air of general validity, is a most grievous defect.

The effect of the relation between the wage and the value of the labour product is scarcely ever recognised in agricultural theory, and the influence of climate is generally ignored: two important explanations of the fact that farmers with a scientific training in their subject tend so readily to make mistakes, sometimes losing all their property in consequence.

108

Such failures imply, not that scientific knowledge is useless, or indeed harmful, to the farmer, but that our science is at present still in its primitive beginnings.

The picture we have indicated would help to fill this gap in our science.

But a mere journey from Calabria to Jutland would not in itself qualify the investigator to paint the picture. This would require:

1. That he picks a place—roughly every fifteen miles or at every parallel of latitude—where he stays until he has discovered all that there is to know about the average local crop yield and the labour costs of its production; i.e. until he knows everything about the gross and net product of the soil in this district. This will take him at least a month in each place.
2. Ability and knowledge to discern what part in his findings for any place is accounted for by distance from the sea, altitude, irrational farming, and variations in the soil type, so that he may apply his findings to the Isolated State.

But this so considerably complicates the problem that it will probably be insoluable without the co-operation and encouragement of governments; though I believe that when the man capable of undertaking the task is found, duty and self-interest will challenge the governments to co-operate with him.

109   When the man is found, and has done the work, he will likewise know the answer to the following questions:

1. How does the soil yield change with latitude, assuming that soil is everywhere of the same quality, with the same humus content?

2. The farther south we go, the less man needs fires to warm his dwelling places, heavy warm clothes, or houses built against wind and frost. In the south man's basic needs are therefore less than in the north. What effect does this have on the wage?

3. The farther south we come, the greater is the heat of summer and the more enervating labour; the smaller, therefore, the amount of work a labourer can perform. What in practice is the relation between climate and work?

4. With the increasing heat southwards, the soil progressively loses its moisture, and the production of a good wheat crop requires a soil with far more clay than in the north. By how much must the soil content of clay rise with progress southwards, if the land is to be suitable for wheat production in all parts of the Isolated State?

5. In northern Russia, even in northern Poland, the autumns are so cold that winter grain is sown in August or in the first days of September; and here the tillage for winter grain coincides with the harvesting of the summer crop. In these regions no previous crop
110   leaves the soil sufficiently early in the year to prepare it adequately for winter grain: the cold climate consequently makes the fallow a prerequisite of cultivation. In Italy on the other hand, the interval between the harvesting of the preceding crop and the seeding of the winter grain is so great that the fallow, as a precursor of winter grain, becomes entirely unnecessary. Indeed, it becomes positively harmful in the south, since soil that is tilled in the intense heat of the summer months loses a great deal of its humus content; so that here the soil ought to be shaded during summer. How, then, can we generalise about the benefits or drawbacks of the fallow, if we fail to consider climate?

Thus, even when the value of the product and labour costs are everywhere the same, the farming system of the south will differ from that of the north.

6. In the far north of the Isolated State (as we are at present imagining it) the pastures feed the livestock for barely five months out of the twelve, and winter feed has to be produced to keep the animals for at least seven months. But at the southern tip of our State vegetation scarcely ever ceases growth, and the cost of producing winter feed sinks to a trifle: animal products will therefore be much cheaper to produce than in the north.

How will the grazing period change with latitude?

7. In the most northerly latitudes all the field work has to be completed in a space of five or six months; at the other extremity of our State it is interrupted for barely two or three months.

To cultivate a given area of land and reap a given harvest, the north has to employ, keep and feed many more men and draught horses than has the south. In winter these labourers will be short of work, because the days are short, and because frost puts a stop to all field work. But despite the shorter annual work-time, and quite apart from the fact that the rougher northern climate creates greater basic needs, the Swedish worker, like the Italian one, must earn enough to keep himself. This must create enormous differences in the labour and production costs of grain.

8. A further fundamental distinction between farming in the northern and southern halves of our circular State springs from the fact that there are products in the south, such as olives, oranges, rice, maize, silk and wine, which nature has denied the north, where they are cultivated artificially and at no profit. But rice and maize yield a far larger quantity of nutriment from a given area of land than do our own varieties of grain; and in the north, only the potato yields an equivalent amount from a given area of land. Different crops will be the staple products under the various climates, depending in each district on which yields the largest net product. Did we but have precise data on the production costs of each crop, and a scale showing the progressive decline in their yield with progress northwards, we would be able to establish the boundaries of the different staple crops in the same way as we established the boundary between the improved and three-field systems in Part One, and to draw up a map of the Isolated State, shading the regions where the different crops predominate.

Arthur Young, in his *Travels in France*, produced a map of that country showing the boundaries of the zones of the olive and the vine respectively, so providing us with an illustration of the effects of climate on the production of two of France's staple crops.

For the Isolated State as we are now imagining it—endowed with railways—we can, even without detailed knowledge of the influence of climate, know the following facts:

1. In the south, the higher productivity of the soil, the smaller needs of the labourers, the more regular employment the whole year round of the men and draught animals and the longer grazing period all combine to make the production of basic necessities far cheaper than in the north.

It necessarily follows that cultivation will stretch farther to the south than the north (taking the Town as our central point), and that the cultivated plain will not remain circular, but will assume another, probably oval, shape.

113   2. Southwards from the Town the fallow becomes progressively less useful; in the opposite direction, more and more important. And as the fallow loses its function, the advantage it bestowed on the three-field and the improved systems over the crop alternation system (that irrespective of the product of a given area they reward labour with a larger product) diminishes, and may altogether vanish.

It follows that the various farming systems will not form concentric rings around the Town; and the ring of crop alternation in particular will stretch farther in a southerly than in a northerly direction.

3. Suppose that the cultivated plain is surrounded by a grass-covered wilderness on which there are few trees: in these conditions the ring of stock farming will take on a very different appearance.

The two chief costs in stock farming are caused by the production of winter feed and the construction and maintenance of winter shelter for the animals.

Neither of these costs is incurred by nomadic tribes. Without a settled residence, these people spend the winter in the south, where vegetation never ceases growth entirely, and in summer, when sun and drought dry out the pastures of the south, they drive their herds north. The districts surrounding a state that extends from the 38th to the 58th parallel embraces every climate necessary for nomadic life; the wandering shepherds will provide the Isolated State with

114 livestock, hides, butter and wool, and in exchange, they will obtain the little they require in clothes, weapons, and so forth. Reciprocal

barter will tie the nomads to the Isolated State, and in the course of the year they will travel round the State as the earth circles round the sun.

There is perhaps no other occupation where the returns are as great as in nomadism. The settled farmer, who is tied to one particular place, cannot compete with the roving shepherd; and in the Isolated State the construction of railways will extinguish the ring of stock farming.

Nomadism is, in these conditions, a way of life which corresponds to, and is justified by, the principles of political economy.

Again we see rational processes at work in history. And for primitive peoples the roving life has great attraction. The wanderer escapes the extremes of climate—intense heat and bitter cold alike— the settled farmer has to bear; his work causes him little strain; the daily change of scene affords continual diversion; no laws restrict his freedom. It is thus easy to see why, as long as its pastures are not threated by other tribes, a nomad people will never settle down to till the soil without a struggle.

But by farming and industry about a hundred settled families can live off the area required by a single nomad; so that this carefree mode of life will cease once the world's population has increased and every strip of land throughout the Globe has become valuable.

---

5.   CHANGES IN OUR ASSUMPTIONS   115
(Chapter 4, Section 8)

Thünen considers the effect of relaxing the assumption that there is a single Town. He shows that the pattern of population distribution will have important effects on rents and agricultural patterns.

1. Let the State depicted in Part One (which we will call A) be surrounded by a barren desert instead of a fertile wilderness.

2. Let the plain contain, instead of only one large town, many smaller ones of uniform size and three miles distant from each other.

3. Let the price of grain and agricultural products be the same for all the towns: 1·5 thalers. Let each town have its own mines and salt works.

4. Let the soil of the plain be not merely of uniform fertility, but farmed in the same manner throughout. Will there be any land rent in these circumstances, and if so, what will be its source?

For the State described in Part One we found:

> that land rent springs from the advantages enjoyed by farms nearer the Town over those at the border whose output is still required to meet the demand; and that at any given place the size of the land rent corresponds precisely to the relative savings made on the cost of sending the product to the Town when measured against the cost of transport from the remotest farm.

When we apply this explanation of the source of land rent to state B, where no farm needs to send its grain farther than two miles,[1] we find that the advantage of one farm over another disappears almost entirely, and that land rent becomes so negligible in amount that we may regard it as virtually equal to zero.

116

Thus it would seem that the congregation of people in large towns is the source of land rent, and that where the population is distributed among smaller towns the land rent, as a significant element of national income, disappears, becoming return to capital and wages.

On the other hand the labour spent in hauling agricultural products over long distances is unproductive, and savings made on such labour can only augment national income.

In densely-populated, actual, countries, where small and medium-sized towns abound and grain need be taken only a few miles to market, land rent as well as grain price is high.

The *Prussian State Journal*, No. 153, 1842, contains a striking illustration of the effect of density of population on the grain price, and consequently on land rent. Over an average of 14 years (1828–1841 inclusive) the rye price per Berlin bushel was:

Province	Silver Groschen and Pfennige
East and West Prussia	32.6
Posen	34.6
Brandenburg and Pomerania	37.9
Silesia	36.11
Saxony	41.1
Westphalia	47.4
Rhineland	51.1

[1] Assuming that the towns are all 3 miles apart on a square grid, the figure is actually 2·122 miles, being $\frac{1}{2}\sqrt{(3^2+3^2)}$.

117

A dense population, and the presence of numerous small towns, has thus the same effect on the grain price as in state *A* the proximity of the large town. This would be readily understandable if the densely populated provinces had to import grain from afar. But Saxony and Rhineland as well as Belgium grow normally as much grain as they can use and have no need of regular grain imports.

Whereas, in theory, the distribution of the population among many small towns should depress grain price and land rent in state *B* to their minimum, in practice the exact opposite happens.

How is this contradition resolved? By undertaking cultivation which is more intensive the higher the price of grain: for this forms the second source of land rent.[1]

We have seen that an increase in the rye price from 0·5 to 1·29 thalers the bushel is associated with a fall in the wage from 0·39 to 0·28 bushels; and that the thoroughness with which the work is done, together with the superior—though more expensive—mode of cultivation, are here raised to the point where the product created by the last man hired just manages to cover the wage he is paid.

The reverse is also true: the rye that is produced by the last man costs the landowner not less than 1·29 thalers the bushel.

Should the average grain price fall once intensive cultivation has reached this point, the last man hired has to be dismissed, because his labour product will no longer cover his wage; and the grain he produced over and above his own consumption will be withdrawn from the market. If, as we must assume, the number of consumers and their demand has not altered, the fall in output will promptly create a shortage, which will again raise the grain price. The upshot is that in the given situation a price of less than 1·29 thalers is impossible; and this price is entirely independent of the distance between farm and market.

118

The landowner gains nothing from the grain produced by the last man hired (nor from the last day's labour spent on doing the work more thoroughly), but since the grain produced by every labourer engaged before the last one costs him less, and all of it sells at one price, he obtains a surplus—which forms the second source of land rent.

Suppose there is another, smaller, town in state *A*, about ten miles from the large one, which has in the past enjoyed unrestricted trade with the large town and has drawn all its food from the surrounding district, which we will call its supply region.

[1] See pp. 263–6.

What will happen to land rent in this region if the large town puts an embargo on the local grain?

The near-by farms have now no choice but to sell their grain to the small local town. This is precisely what they have always done; but in the past, when they had the constant choice of selling the grain in either town, the market price in the small town was invariably governed by the price obtaining in the larger one. But the distance of the small town to the edge of its region is so trifling that, according to the principles developed in Part One, the price of grain must fall (where there are no potential sales to the large town) until the land rent is nearly zero. Such a fall in the grain price reduces intensive farming and grain production alike.

Here there are two possible situations.

1. The small town uses as much grain as before the embargo.

In these circumstances the needs of this town can be met only if there is no change in intensive farming and if grain price and land rent remain what they were before; so that here the law that the size of the land rent depends on the distance between farm and market would not come into operation.

2. The small town uses far less grain than before the embargo.

Here intensive cultivation will decline. The improved will give way to the three-field system, and the thoroughness of cultivation will be reduced to the point where labour yields the maximum net product.

Once cultivation has fallen to this point, the distance from the market becomes the sole determinant of land rent, which, owing to the smallness of the supply region, will be entirely negligible in amount.

The question: What is the land rent in the Isolated State B? thus reduces itself to another: How much grain do the smaller towns use, and what can their inhabitants pay for it?

Here the critical factor is not the absolute price of grain, but its relative price, that is, the relation between the grain price and the cost of the goods the landowner buys for his grain.

And this is determined, on the one hand by the relative distance and productivity of the mines and salt works, and on the other by the relative efficiency of the factories and workshops.

Thus we see that industrial progress is vital to agriculture, and it would be foolish to argue about their relative precedence.

Because the inventions and improvements that have been made in industry outweigh by far those made in farming, the price of grain has risen continuously for several centuries.

6. THE ORDER AND DISTRIBUTION OF TOWNS
IN THE ISOLATED STATE
(Chapter 4, Section 9)

Thünen inquires into the reasons for the location and distribution of towns and is led to an analysis of the factors of industrial location. Considering the concentration of industries in large cities, he anticipates Weber's account of industrial agglomeration.

Two assumptions have formed the basis of our inquiry:

1. That the Isolated State contains only one large Town.   120
2. That it contains very many smaller towns, of the same size and equi-distant from each other.

These are inconsistent; and if we abandon them we have to ask the following questions:

What determines the relative position of the towns in the Isolated State in respect of size and distance from each other?

This divides itself into four separate inquiries:

1. What is the effect on the price of products and on the size of the   121 land rent of the small towns and the industries that are found in the rural districts?
2. Towns of one size, distributed regularly throughout the country, would be accompanied by a rise in population and land rent. What then prevents this even distribution of towns?
3. An increase in the rye price would be accompanied by an expansion of the cultivated area, a growth of capital, and consequently by a nation's rise in wealth and population. Why, then, is the rye price exactly 1·5 thalers the bushel and not higher?
4. What effect do railways have on the size of towns?

I shall add a few reflections on points (2) and (4), although I cannot enter into detail.

At the edge of the cultivated plain in the Isolated State *A*, the land rent equals zero and the population is sparse.

The construction of railways would give this district the cultivation pattern, the land values and the population now obtaining in the district 6·5 miles from the Town.

However, if the population of the Town were distributed over numerous small towns, and spread evenly throughout the country, cultivation would everywhere be as intensive as it is near the Town—which would be far more profitable than a railway network.

122   Why then is the population of the large Town not divided among many smaller ones? The reasons are as follows:

1. In practice, deposits of ore, salt and coal are most unevenly distributed. The metal has to be extracted from the ore where this is found; and factories working in metals will naturally locate near the mines and ore deposits, which we assume to exist only near the Town.

2. The focal centre of a country is the natural residence of the head of the government; the seat of the highest offices of justice and administration, of army headquarters, the higher institutes of learning, art collections, etc.

3. The presence in the capital of the court, the concourse of scholars, men of science and state officials, the theatres, museums, etc., afford many more social attractions and amenities than the provinces could ever offer. This explains why many rich citizens, living off interest or the revenue from their estates, will spend at least the winter in the capital.

4. To cater for the needs and pleasures of all the citizens assembled in the capital for any of these reasons, a great many people of the artisan and service class are required—merchants, artists, craftsmen, domestic servants, labourers, and so on; and because they are certain to find employment there will be no shortage of such people.

123   The reasons for the concentration of population in the capital are too obvious and simple to offer material for further study.

Of far greater importance and difficulty is the question: whether industries which draw their raw materials from, and sell most of their products to, the provinces, are also better located in the capital?

The following are the reasons against the location of industries in the capital:

1. Raw materials are more expensive than in the country towns on account of the higher cost of transport.

2. Manufactured articles incur the cost of haulage to the provincial towns whence they are distributed to the rural consumers.
3. All necessities, especially firewood, are much more expensive in the large town. So is rent for flats and houses, for two reasons: (1) construction costs are higher because raw materials have to be brought from a distance and are consequently more expensive, and (2) sites that may be bought for a few thalers in a small town are very dear.

Since food, as well as fuel and housing, cost so much more in the large town, the wage, expressed in money, must be much higher than in the small one. This adds appreciably to production costs.

Another circumstance adding considerably to living expenses in the large town is the fact that potatoes, measured by relative nutritive value, are here hardly any cheaper than bread: in smaller towns, the same nutritive quantity of potatoes costs barely half as much as grain. | 124

The following factors, on the other hand, favour the location of industries in large towns:

1. Only in large-scale industrial plants is it profitable to instal labour-saving machinery and equipment, which economise on manual labour and make for cheaper and more efficient production.
2. The scale of an industrial plant depends on the demand for its products.
3. The number of buyers depends, in provincial towns, on the number of countrymen coming in to sell their products, or passing through on their way to the capital.

For instance, a countryman may visit the capital to sell his products, and decide to buy some liquor. It will be cheaper for him to buy this in the capital, even if it costs him half a thaler more than he would pay in the provincial town two miles from his farm, because he would have to make a special journey to fetch the local alcohol.

And the wealthy landowner, for whom money is no object, will not buy more alcohol than he immediately needs, because the time spent in storing and protecting it would be for him sheer waste of time.

This explains why it may happen than an entrepreneur who has set | 125
up a large distillery in a provincial town or on a farm will sell his

alcohol in the capital, whence it will be distributed to the rural districts.

4. For all these reasons, large-scale plants are viable only in the capital in many branches of industry. But the division of labour (and Adam Smith has shown the immense influence this has on the size of the labour product and on economies of production) is closely connected with the scale of an industrial plant. This explains why, quite regardless of economies of machine-production, the labour product per head is far higher in large than in small factories.

5. People aware of possessing an exceptional skill or talent will not wish to waste their time on other work, where they can achieve nothing outstanding, but will move to the capital, to devote all their energy to their particular skill; in return they will reap ample reward.

Thus the capital attracts outstanding talents—among business men, artisans and labourers as well as among scholars and civil servants—and in this way is able to obtain a significant advantage over the provinces.

6. The large town offers buyers and sellers far more guarantee of being able to buy and sell at current prices.

The great merchant has not the time to consider the special situation of his customer and fix the price of the article he wants to sell according to the buyer's needs or knowledge. He has an established price; which protects the customer from sharp practice. Besides, in the presence of so many competitors the attempt to cheat the customer would be scarcely worth the trouble.

The advantage the large has over the small town is strikingly illustrated in the sale of agricultural products. In a town with only two grain dealers, one may happen to be ill, or in some kind of financial difficulty and short of orders. Only one buyer remains, and if he behaves according to the principles of business, he will frequently offer the farmer less for his product than the ruling price. For the farmer, eager to sell his product, the value of the grain he has brought to the market-town is no longer what it was back at his farm. If he cannot sell his grain in the town, he has to take it somewhere else; for him its actual value therefore equals the price grain will fetch in the next market-town, minus the cost of its transport from one place to the other. In practice, therefore, the monopolising merchant may often buy grain far below the actual price. But even worse—and far more frequent—is the likelihood of the two local merchants agreeing on a price to offer farmers for their product, and sharing the profit made on this monopoly. The ultimate result of such selfish behaviour will of course be (a) to drive the grain business to another town, or (b) to lure other grain merchants to the town in the hope of easy gains, which will bring down the local dealers' profits, or (c) to convince the farmers that their best policy is to bring to the town only grain whose sale they have negotiated in advance.

127

The last expedient however causes the farmer much loss of time and money; and he would rather sell his grain in the large town, where he may be certain of obtaining the correct, even if a sometimes slightly lower, price for it.

The large town will therefore buy more cheaply than the small one in this respect.

There is even less security in selling grain or other produce in small towns without a local dealer; for the inhabitants will normally only buy what they can use at once. If less grain than is required at the moment is brought to market, the price will rise; if more, the farmer will scarcely be able to sell his surplus grain, butter and so on, at any price.

This insecurity, and the inconvenience it causes the farmer, explains why, taking annual averages, small towns pay far more for grain, butter and so on than would follow from their location in relation to the capital (which governs the grain price).

7. Where factories and workshops employ machinery and equipment that has been produced in the large town and is incapable of being locally repaired, each repair will cost much in transport, and will give rise to considerable and harmful delays in production.

Since it takes machines to produce machines, and these are themselves the product of many different factories and workshops, machinery is produced efficiently only in a place where factories and workshops are close enough together to help each other work in unison,[1] i.e. in large towns.

128

1 "*die sich einer dem andern die Hand bieten und gemeinschaftlich an einem Werke arbeiten*".

Economic theory has failed to adequately appreciate this factor. Yet it is this which explains why factories are generally found communally,[1] why, even when in all other respects conditions appear suitable, those set up by themselves, in isolated places, so often come to grief.

Technical innovations are continually increasing the complexity of machinery; and the more complicated the machines, the more the factor of association will enter into operation.

In agriculture, also, we see the importance of association. If a colony of farmers settles in the region of the Missouri river (not the state of Missouri), then this community, though the soil be inexhaustibly fertile and the climate perfect, is bound to perish, because the labour spent on taking its produce to markets to be exchanged for the tools, clothes and materials required by the settlement will be too costly and time-consuming.

But if the settlers associate themselves with artisans of every kind—with manufacturers, craftsmen, miners, and so forth—in such a ratio that every member of the community is fully occupied at his particular calling, then this community will not merely survive, but all its members will fare far better than they would have done had they remained in Europe.

129 To obtain the right ratio of occupations the community will have to be large. In industry, likewise, there are a great many undertakings that can supply their products at reasonable prices only when conducted on a large scale: mining for instance, where the cost of penetrating the over-burden and many other costs are the same, no matter whether the shaft produces much or little ore.

Mineral and salt deposits, a numerous body of settlers, and the association of many different occupations, are the conditions under which, soil and climate being favourable, a community will prosper even if it has little or no communication with the outside world. If any of these conditions be absent, the wilderness will be tamed only gradually, by one cultivator settling near another and working at his side.

When we weigh the arguments for the location of factories and trades in country towns against those in favour of their concentration in the capital, we find the nature of the industry determines its location.

[1] *gesellschaftlich.*

Factories and workshops processing raw materials of little value in relation to their bulk and weight, which need no complicated machinery, no extensive division of labour, and which therefore can supply their products almost as cheaply on a small as on a large scale, belong properly to the provincial towns or even to the countryside itself.

These, as I showed in Part One, include distilling and linen weaving.

All other industries, where opposite conditions obtain, have their rightful place in the capital.

7. THE ROLE OF POPULATION DENSITY   134
(Chapter 4, Section 11)

Thünen considers the social costs which have to be borne in rural areas with sparse populations.

The question: How, in the Isolated State, does the denser or sparser population of the various districts affect the distribution of the country towns as regards their size and distance from each other?, brings me to the following problems, which have not yet been discussed.

1. What is the effect on land rent of the distance of a farm from the small country town whence it buys its recurrent needs?
2. What is the effect of population density on farming costs?

Suppose now:

1. that the advantages of association in trades and industries allow of no town with a population of less than 2000 souls;
2. that 1500 people per square mile are employed in agriculture in   135
   the section of the ring of the improved system nearest to the Town, but only 500 per square mile at the edge of the cultivated plain;
3. that a town of 2000 people is required for every 10,000 employed on the land;
4. that the supply region of each town, that is, the district buying its necessities from the town, forms a square. Hence the region of a town in district *A* is equal to 10,000/1800, or 5·55 square miles, and in *B*, the remoter district, it is 10,000/600, or 16·66

square miles.[1] In district A, the distance between the towns comes to $\sqrt{(5\cdot55)}$, or 2·36 miles; in district B to $\sqrt{(16\cdot66)}$, or 4·08 miles.

A farm lying halfway between two towns is distant from either town,

in district A 2·36/2 = 1·18 miles
in district B 4·08/2 = 2·04 miles

Difference   0·86 miles

There are two possibilities in this situation.

1. All agricultural work is performed with the same thoroughness in both regions, and in both the people employed in farming enjoy the same comforts and conveniences.
2. In both regions the same amount of money is spent on the maintenance of the buildings and equipment, the labourers' keep, the children's education, and medical care.

136   In B, the following, amongst other services, will be more expensive than in A.

1. If the farm has to send a messenger to the town twice a week to fetch the recurrent requirements, the farm lying centrally between two towns in district B will have to pay its messenger a wage which is higher by the extra distance of 1·72 miles (2 × 0·86) than the wage the farm in district A need pay its messenger.
2. The craftsmen from the towns who work on the farms have to make a longer journey, for which they must be remunerated.
3. Higher fees have to remunerate the doctor who is called out to attend the sick for the greater expense of his journey and the additional time loss.

In B, the buildings and equipment will be in a worse state of repair, the workers will live less comfortably, and in particular the doctor will be summoned to attend only the more serious cases.

---

[1] This is evidently a slip. Thünen must have thought that he had written 1800 and 600 two paragraphs above, instead of 1500 and 500.

*The effect of sparse population on the rural areas in region B as
compared with region A*

This is particularly well illustrated in religious instruction and in
the schooling of the children. If 150 people live on a farm one-tenth
of a square mile in district *A*, but only 50 on one of equivalent size
in district *B*, and in both the schooling is equally good, then education on the farm in *B* will be three times as expensive per head as in
A. The same applies to the preacher's salary, and so on.

If the costs per head of religious and school instruction are to be
the same in both regions, three farms must in *B* combine to maintain
one school; in the bad road and weather conditions of winter the
children will have to walk across the fields to go to school, which is
liable to affect their health, and certain to reduce attendance. 137

If the densely populated district has one church and one preacher
to the square mile, and the costs per head are to be the same in the
densely and the sparsely populated district, the latter will be able to
afford only one church and preacher to every three square miles. This
makes it much more inconvenient to go to church and reduces
attendance; it means, moreover, that the minister has a far more
difficult task and will not be able to perform his duties, particularly
the supervision of the schools, as efficiently as a minister in district *A*.

What happens in practice?

Neither tendency will probably be fully realised, and their conflict
will give rise to a compromise situation.

It would be interesting to discover what principles—if rational
choices may be assumed—decide this process in reality; though the
matter contains far too many difficulties for me to undertake the task.

I can state, though, that here too, immediate material interest is
likely to be the guiding principle. People will put up with a broken
window pane if the repair seems comparatively too expensive; and
in a situation resembling that of region *B* they will probably accept a
less comfortable mode of life, inferior dress and education than are
enjoyed by people in a situation akin to that of *A*; but if the day
labourer's wage expressed in rye is everywhere the same, they will
probably eat rather better food, in particular a greater quantity of
meat.[1] 138

---

[1] Because they will be able to buy meat at net farm price, without added transport
costs. They are worse off in relation to town-produced products but better off in rela-
ion to other farm products.

Human nature will be torn between different appetites, and people will weigh up and compare the various pleasures they may purchase.

If one particular non-essential article becomes too costly, we make do with less of it and spend the money saved on something that seems to bring us relatively greater satisfaction. But the pleasure and enjoyment of life as a whole is the object and control of human action. Different peoples, at different stages of prosperity and development, will necessarily have differing valuations for the goods of life: for in this already every individual human being acts according to the wildest whim.

But it is impossible to deny that education and learning belong to a class of goods or pleasures the consumption of which is restricted or ceases when they become too costly and conflict with other pleasures, such as for instance the possession of decent clothes. And since we have seen that the education of the common man becomes progressively more difficult and costly the sparser is the population, we arrive at the painful conclusion that even within the restricted confines of the Isolated State, the level of education and intelligence will differ in the different districts. How much more so must this be true then of the vast spaces of our globe!

This explains why the natives of thinly peopled regions so often are primitive and savage.

North America is here an honourable exception. But it is a country inhabited by immigrants, who bring with them a respect for knowledge and education impossible for a people that is working itself out of a state of barbarism. Besides, the ease with which the settler may make a living in America does much to preserve and spread this attitude to learning.

139

Let us see now whether the provincial towns will all be of the same size in the Isolated State. It seems likely that in this matter also, diverging tendencies will yield a compromise; for the advantages of association grow with the increasing size of towns, whereas the increasing distance between the towns, a corollary of their growth in size, is a drawback for the country. In all probability the provincial towns near the capital will not be at a regular distance of 4·08 miles from each other, and their population will not be limited to 2000; they will be closer to each other, and also larger.

Nearer the capital, their larger size, together with the increasingly busy traffic along the roads, will make the provincial towns progressively more suitable as industrial centres; and the industries will in turn contribute to the growth of these towns.

It is worth noting that railway construction will rob of all their force the arguments against the development of the capital, and will strengthen those in favour of such growth.

Thus we may say with certainty that railways will make an important contribution to the development of the large towns, and that, *but for the fact that railways will promote also the prosperity of the rural districts surrounding the provincial towns*, the latter would decay in consequence.

140

8. THE DYNAMICS OF THE ISOLATED STATE: ARE THERE OBSTACLES TO ITS EXPANSION? (Chapter 4, Section 10)

130

Thünen relaxes the assumption that the Isolated State is in a steady state. He allows it, theoretically, to expand in population, and considers the results.

Hitherto we have regarded the Isolated State as existing in an equilibrium condition. For the moment let us relax this assumption and regard the State as dynamic.

When cultivation extends to the district where rye fetches 1.29 thalers the bushel, the following conditions will obtain as regards the wage and the interest rate:

On the farm five miles from the Town:

a is equal to	78·4 bushels
the wage $\sqrt{(ap)}$	$132 = 1.685a$
the worker's surplus $y = \sqrt{(ap)} - a = 53.6$	
the rate of interest z	$= 5.8$ per cent

The year's labour of one family, which in cultivating the wilderness is engaged in the production of capital, is rewarded with a rent of $yz = 53.6 \times 5.8/100 = 3.1$ bushels of rye $= 0.04a$.

The combination of a high wage and a high interest rate is a powerful stimulus to population growth and the production of capital; population and capital will therefore increase rapidly.

This is what happened at the beginning of this century in the eastern states of North America, and is still happening farther west, where highly fertile land, on navigable rivers, may still be had for little or no money.

131   It is common knowledge that the population of North America has doubled these last 25 years; without immigration it would have doubled in perhaps 30 years. The growth of capital and population will continue as long as fertile land, conveniently located for the market, may be had cheaply. But one day, when the banks of the navigable rivers have been taken into possession, new settlers will have to move deeper into the interior, where, even though the soil be just as fertile as near the rivers, the wage and the return to capital are nevertheless bound to be lower, because the greater cost of taking the labour product to the (more distant) market means that its value is much lower than near the rivers. In other words, the settler in the interior of the country has to exchange a larger portion of his labour product for his needs.

The same holds true of the Isolated State in the process of development. Every cultivator arriving later has to settle farther than did his predecessor from the Town, which is the market for his produce; so that for him wages and return to capital are lower than for the settler who preceded him.

If we use Tellow as our model, conditions at the edge of the cultivated plain of the Isolated State (31·5 miles from the Town according to Part One) are as follows:

a is equal to	109 bushels of rye
the wage	156 bushels of rye $= 1 \cdot 43a$
the surplus	47 bushels of rye $= 0 \cdot 43a$
the interest rate	3·65 per cent.

For his year's labour, the labourer who is producing capital obtains a rent of $yz = 47 \times 3 \cdot 65/100 = 1 \cdot 72$ bushels,

$$= 0 \cdot 43a \times 3 \cdot 65/100 = 0 \cdot 016a$$

132   When cultivation extends only as far as the district where rye costs 1·29 gold thalers the bushel, i.e. about 5 miles from the Town, the rent of the capital-producing labourer is 3·1 bushels of rye, or

$= 0\cdot04a$. When the area of cultivation is extended from 5 to $31\cdot5$ miles from the Town, the rent for one year's labour falls by:

1. expressed in rye at the ratio of $3\cdot1$ to $1\cdot72 = 100:55$, i.e. 45 per cent.
2. expressed in basic necessities at the ratio of $0\cdot04a:0\cdot016a$ $= 100:40$, i.e. 60 per cent.

The fall in rent is thus significantly less when rent is expressed in rye than when it is expressed in basic necessities. But since the value of rye varies with the district, basic necessities provide the only reliable measure.

The production of capital by labour costs:

1. the strain and effort of the work;
2. abstinence from the articles of pleasure which the worker might buy from his surplus.

A free man will accept such strain and abstinence only if he thinks the compensation worth the trouble. This compensation consists of the rent on the accumulated capital on which, without having to work, he will be able to subsist in future. The prospect of an old age without toil, the desire to secure an easier existence for his children, are powerful motives to induce a man to undergo strain and privation for the best years of his life. But the reward must be worth the sacrifice. Where it is so small that men no longer think the compensation adequate, the production of capital will cease.

133

Human nature prevents the rent accruing to labour from falling below a certain level; and in the Isolated State, where this rent becomes progressively smaller with increasing distance from the Town, a limit is set to the expansion of the State.

We saw that where the soil is cultivated only as far as five miles from the Town, one year's labour, spent on the production of capital, is rewarded with a rent of $0\cdot04a$, or $1/25a$, but that, where cultivation stretches up to $31\cdot5$ miles, the rent for one year's labour is only $0\cdot016a$, or $1/63a$. In the first instance a family may, without having to work, live on the rent of 25 years' labour; in the second this would require 63 years' labour.

Our calculations show that the Isolated State will expand up to $31\cdot5$ miles from the Town, beyond which point it cannot grow; and that at the border, labour is rewarded with a rent of $1/63a$ for one year's labour. At such a low rent, it is probable that the desire to accumulate capital will be outweighed by the inclination to spend the wage surplus, though this will depend largely on the disposition of the people.

If for his year's labour the labourer obtains a rent of only $1/63a$, this does not mean that he need work for 63 consecutive years to draw a rent of a bushels. If he invests his annual surplus, the interest will bring nearer the day when he is able to draw a rent of a bushels.

134

On this our calculations (compound interest) show that 47,[1] annually invested at the interest rate of 3·65 per cent, will, after 33 years, produce a capital of 3000, which at the given interest rate yields a rent of 109—which equals a.

Our estimates on the wage and the interest rate show that it takes 33·6 years of a labourer's work and frugality to obtain for him a rent on which, without having to work, he may exist—albeit meagrely[2] —in his old age.

This coincides fairly closely with the duration of a man's health and capacity for work.

---

[1] Thünen gives no units here.   [2] *nothdürftig leben kann.*

INDEX

Agglomeration, industrial xl, 285
Alcohol production, in stock farming
  zone 175-6
Animal products 149-56
  high price of, in Germany 237-8
  price of, in relation to grain price
  161-4
  See also Sheep farming

BACKE, H. xli-xlii
Belgian system
  compared with Mecklenburg (improved) system 84-95
  fertility and yield of 84, 86, 88-93
  labour costs in 93-4
  land rent of 85, 87, 89
  population density under 87-8
  potatoes in 135-7
  See also Crop alternation system
BRINKMANN, T. xxxi, xlii
Butter
  location of xxxvii
  price of 150-2, 161-2
  transport costs of 149-50

Capital 248-52
Catch crop, advantages and disadvantages of, in improved system
  80-1
Cattle, dairy, profitability of, compared with fine-wool sheep 178-179
  See also Animal products, Butter,
  Milk, Stock farming
Chicory 184
CLARK, J. B. xl
Climate
  effects on northern and southern
  Europe of 278-80
  influence on agriculture of 240-1,
  276-81
  suggested inquiry into 277-9

Clover
  in Belgian system 91-3
  seeds 184-5
Corn Laws, in England 180, 186-7
Costs xxiv-xxvii, 24-32
  See also Cultivation costs, Labour
  costs, Timber
Crop alternation system xiv, (glossary) xlix
  characteristics of, compared with
  three-field and improved systems
  101
  fertility degree of 53-4
  higher fertility of 82-3
  modified form of, in mountain
  districts 104-5
  non-profitability of, in Isolated
  State 140-1
  See also Belgian system
Cultivation costs, of grain 24
  in relation to distance from farmyard 58-60
  See also Labour costs

Dairy cattle *see* Cattle
DEMPSEY, B. xix, xl, 248, 250, 251,
  273
Displacement rent xxxiv-xxxvi, 109,
  116
Distance
  between plot and farmstead 56-61,
  68-9
  fall in net product with 164-70
  from market, influence of on farming system and crops xxiii-xxiv,
  8-17, 106-90, 227-8
Distilling, in stock farming zone 175-
  176

Education
  costs of, in areas of sparse population 293-4

299

302 INDEX